STE

"Jim Stengel occu_____ _____que place in the business world. Using the wisdom and insights gained from his successful business c___ __ powerfully demonstrates in *Grow* that busine __ tha___ a higher purpose their north star far outperform the__ c___ _tition. In page after page, he argues convincingly that in t_day's world, im___ _ng people's lives and having a positive social impact are the best prescriptions for long-term success. By combining a scientist's rigor with a storyteller's gifts, he has produced a brilliant, must-read book supremely suited to our times."

—**Arianna Huffington, president and editor in chief, *The Huffington Post***

"When you start reading *Grow,* you may well feel a little skeptical about the ideal and its bottom-line value. But you'll soon become intrigued—and then utterly convinced. Jim Stengel shares his beliefs and his experience with a generosity bordering on the reckless; and he has the hard, clean numbers to bear his teachings out."

—**Sir Martin Sorrell, CEO, WPP**

"People search for meaning in their lives. Leaders who can infuse meaning into business strategies, work plans, and even organizational structures can inspire dramatically higher levels of performance. Jim Stengel's book *Grow* is a tool kit for turning the power of ideals—or what we at P&G think of as purpose—into competitive advantage and sustainable growth."

—**Robert A. McDonald, chairman, president, and CEO, Procter & Gamble**

"Some say brands are dying in the age of social media and the like. Jim Stengel says, in effect, that's nonsense; and he has the track record times ten to prove it. Sustainable differentiation has never been more essential, and effective branding is the only winning game in town. But branding done right is no less than a way of life—encompassing culture, connection, intimacy, and ideals lived with unrelenting passion; so much more than merely following the whims of the latest market research. A landmark book tailor-made for the times! Read it, absorb it, live it!"

—Tom Peters, co-author of *In Search of Excellence*

"In *Grow,* Jim Stengel presents a new powerful model for business. An innovator and a marketing veteran, Stengel shows how companies can leverage social networks to spark and sustain the conversations that are taking place about their brands every day. This is a must-read, not just for marketers, but for all business leaders."

—Sheryl Sandberg, COO, Facebook

"Every executive understands the value proposition—the economic attributes around which you sell. Jim Stengel explains the power and urgency of the values proposition—the principles for which you stand. This breakthrough book, filled with original ideas and engaging stories, will inspire you to rethink what truly matters to your company and career. Pick it up, then put it to work!"

—William C. Taylor, founding editor, Fast Company, and bestselling author of *Practically Radical*

"*Grow* doesn't just give insight into Jim Stengel's brilliant career with P&G, it provides evidence and inspiration for any leader to be in touch with and pursue their ideals."

—John Wren, president and CEO of Omnicon

"We all seek growth! And one of the best ways to achieve it is certainly to learn the lessons from Jim Stengel's *Grow*. In this fascinating book in which proven and new recipes are mixed to create a successful path toward growth, I personally discovered ideas that are exactly what we need in today's business environment."

—Maurice Lévy, chairman and CEO, Publicis Groupe

"Jim Stengel is a pioneer. Not only has he cracked the code on growth, unlocking the mysteries of what drives supercharged performance, he gives us something more profound. When you truly and measurably improve other people's lives, your life and the life of your business and brand improve exponentially. Mystery solved. Truth unleashed."

—Roy Spence, chairman and co-founder, GSD&M; CEO and co-founder, The Purpose Institute; and author of *It's Not What You Sell, It's What You Stand For*

"This is an important book for our time. Jim Stengel proves that business growth accelerates with an inspiring ideal at the center of a company. He then takes you on a journey that will forever change how you approach business. Read it and apply its lessons, and reap the benefits of faster growth."

—Andrea Guerra, CEO, Luxottica Group

"What does your business stand for in the eyes of the people most important to your future? What should it stand for? The right answer is what will make your best customers tell their friends you are indispensable. And for that, Stengel is the indispensable read. He has written the bible on how to transform your company culture into the strategic weapon that slays rivals and pays dividends. I've seen it work in Jim's leadership at P&G and in our work at Intuit. It is not a cosmetic tint; it goes to the core of your firm's reason for being, your role as a leader, and what will drive your most important customers to trust what you do."

—Scott Cook, co-founder and chairman of the Executive Committee, Intuit Inc.

GROW

HOW IDEALS POWER GROWTH AND PROFIT AT THE WORLD'S 50 GREATEST COMPANIES

JIM STENGEL

2 4 6 8 10 9 7 5 3 1

First published in the United States in 2011 by Crown Business, an imprint of the Crown
Publishing Group, a division of Random House, Inc., New York

First published in the UK in 2012 by Virgin Books,
an imprint of Ebury Publishing
A Random House Group Company

Copyright © Jim Stengel 2011

Jim Stengel has asserted his right under the Copyright, Designs and
Patents Act 1988 to be identified as the author of this work.

Every reasonable effort has been made to contact copyright holders of material reproduced in
this book. If any have inadvertently been overlooked, the publishers would be glad to hear from
them and make good in future editions any errors or omissions brought to their attention.

All rights reserved. No part of this publication may be reproduced, stored in a retrieval system,
or transmitted in any form or by any means, electronic, mechanical, photocopying, recording or
otherwise, without the prior permission of the copyright owner.

www.randomhouse.co.uk

Addresses for companies within The Random House Group Limited can be found at:
www.randomhouse.co.uk/offices.htm

The Random House Group Limited Reg. No. 954009

A CIP catalogue record for this book is available from the British Library

The Random House Group Limited supports The Forest Stewardship Council
(FSC®), the leading international forest certification organisation. Our books
carrying the FSC label are printed on FSC® certified paper. FSC is the only forest
certification scheme endorsed by the leading environmental organisations,
including Greenpeace. Our paper procurement policy can be found at:
www.randomhouse.co.uk/environment

ISBN: 9780753540664

Book design by Leonard W. Henderson

Printed and bound in England by Clays Ltd, St Ives plc

To buy books by your favourite authors and register for offers, visit www.randomhouse.co.uk

For my brother Bob (1959–2010),

who lived a life of higher ideals.

CONTENTS

CONTENTS

PART II
The Five Must-Dos

Contents

GROW

Introduction

The Ultimate Growth Driver

Maximum growth and high ideals are not incompatible. They're inseparable.

The data from a ten-year-growth study of more than 50,000 brands around the world show that companies with ideals of improving people's lives at the center of all they do outperform the market by a huge margin. The chart below captures this fact.

An investment in the Stengel 50, the top 50 businesses in my ten-year-growth study, would have been 400 percent more profitable than an investment in the Standard & Poor's (S&P) 500. The counterintuitive fact is that doing the right thing *in*

*S&P 500® is an index of five hundred stocks chosen for market size, liquidity, and industry grouping. *Source*: Millward Brown Optimor.

1

your business is doing the right thing *for* your business. Those that embrace that fact are the ones that dominate their categories, create new categories, and maximize profit in the long term.

How can ideals be the ultimate growth driver? How can ideals drive extraordinary growth in your own business and career?

Let me show you.

Ideal

A Definition

IDEAL (ī'dē(ə)'al), *n.* **1.** The key to unlock the code for twenty-first-century business success. **2.** The only sustainable way to recruit, unite, and motivate all the people a business touches, from employees to customers. **3.** The most powerful lever a business leader can use to achieve competitive advantage. **4.** A business's essential reason for being, the higher-order benefit it brings to the world. **5.** The factor connecting the core beliefs of the people inside a business with the fundamental human values of the people they serve. **6.** Not social responsibility or altruism, but a program for profit and growth based on improving people's lives.

PART I

The Big Picture

The Ideal Factor

Great Businesses Have Great Ideals

W hat makes a business grow beyond the competition? What powers an enterprise to the top and keeps it there?

I've been fascinated by these questions throughout my business career, from my first job after college to my seven years as global marketing officer of Procter & Gamble (P&G) to my current work as a senior management consultant, an adjunct professor at the UCLA Anderson Graduate School of Management, and a board member of Motorola Mobility and AOL.

I believe I've found the answer. It is a new framework for business, based on improving the lives of the people a business serves, that is rooted in the timeless fundamentals of business and human nature. The latest research, including a ten-year-growth study I conducted of more than 50,000 brands around the world, has inspired and validated this new framework. By operating according to the principles in this framework, the world's best businesses achieve growth three times or more that of the competition in their categories.

The central principle of the new framework is the importance of having a *brand ideal,* a shared goal of improving people's lives. A brand ideal is a business's essential reason for being, the higher-order benefit it brings to the world. A brand ideal of improving people's lives is the only sustainable way to recruit, unite, and inspire all the people a business touches, from employees to customers. It is the only thing that enduringly connects the core beliefs of the people inside a business with the fundamental human values of the people the business serves. Without that connection, without a brand ideal, no business can truly excel.

You will hear a lot about brands in what follows, but a word of explanation first. I use the words *brand* and *business* interchangeably. A brand is what a business is all about in the hearts and minds of the people most important to its future. In any competitive market, what drives margin and growth and separates one business from another—for employees, customers, partners, and investors—is the brand. And what increasingly separates great companies and businesses from good, bad, or indifferent ones is brand ideals.

I first saw the full potential of brand ideals in several line management roles at Procter & Gamble, and then as the company's global marketing officer. The evidence I'm going to present shows that an ability to leverage brand ideals is also what increasingly separates great business leaders from good, bad, or indifferent ones.

Think about what and how you buy in your business and personal life. Whether it's household products or enterprise data services, what ultimately determines why you buy from one company rather than another? It's their brands' images and reputations and the relationships you have with them. A brand is simply the collective intent of the people behind it; a brand defines who you are and what you stand for as a business to everyone the business touches, from employees to end consumers. If you want great business results, you and your brand have to stand for something compelling. And that's where brand ideals enter the equation.

Great business leaders of the past have always understood and acted on this, explicitly or implicitly. When William Hewlett and David Packard founded Hewlett-Packard (HP) in 1939, and in the process kick-started all of Silicon Valley, they explicitly focused their business on making a contribution to society through technology. They didn't call this a brand ideal, but that's what it was. As Dave Packard said, the reason people join together in a business is to "make a contribution to society, a phrase which sounds trite but is fundamental." And as Bill Hewlett said, "We operated on the assumption that if we made a contribution to society, rewards would follow."

Indeed they did. The ideal of improving people's lives with ever-advancing technology has kept HP going—and growing—through thick and thin ever since. The company lost momentum in 2011, as most tech companies do at some point due to the rapidly evolving sector. Still, HP's record of growth in the decade of the 2000s was impressive; according to global research firm Millward Brown Optimor, HP grew their brand value from $5 billion in 2001 to $35.4 billion in 2011.

In my research visit to HP, in several long interviews, I felt HP people—even with the dramatic and unsettling change in their management and board—had internalized the power and potential of a brand ideal, and how it inspires growth. HP director of market research Deepak Sainanee told me, "In terms of growth and margin, brand is really what it comes down to in the end." It's no coincidence, as we'll see, that HP, one of the world's largest technology companies, is beginning to leverage a powerful new evolution of its brand ideal, in spite of the turmoil in senior management.

Today's most successful business leaders are also leveraging brand ideals. Brand ideals, my research associates and I have found, are what enable today's greatest companies to set the pace in their categories and leave their competition far behind.

THE 400 PERCENT ADVANTAGE

Recall that chart we just looked at in the introduction. Over the 2000s the Stengel 50, the top businesses in my ten-year-growth study, have generated a return on investment 400 percent better than the Standard & Poor's 500. As we will see, the Stengel 50 are achieving this remarkable success thanks to operating in harmony with their brand ideals. In so doing, the Stengel 50 are riding the crest of a building wave that is reshaping all of business, a dramatic, inexorable rise in the contribution of intangible brand value to total business value.

Brand research and consulting firm Millward Brown Optimor—I partnered with them in my research for this book, and I'll be referring to them often—has a well-established proprietary methodology for calculating brand value. Millward Brown Optimor determines intangible earnings by examining a business's financial results and calculating the percentage of demand for its offerings that is attributable to brand alone. When Millward Brown Optimor recently looked at the contribution that brand equity has made to the market capitalization of the Standard & Poor's 500 from 1980 to 2011, it tracked the birth and development of an ongoing trend.

In 1980 virtually the entire market capitalization of the S&P 500 companies consisted of tangible assets (cash, offices, plants, equipment, inventories, etc.). In 2010 tangible assets accounted for only 40 to 45 percent of the S&P 500 companies' market capitalization. The rest of their capitalization consisted of intangible assets, and about half of that—more than 30 percent of total market capitalization—came from brand.

The growth in the importance of brand value over the last thirty years is unmistakable. Brand value is now most companies' single biggest asset, and the consequence is that business leadership and brand leadership are converging in every industry and every sector of the economy. The world's best companies have responded to this by ensuring that they bring together business leadership and brand leadership in the C-suite and throughout their organizations.

In short, businesses are now only as strong as their brands, and nothing else offers business leaders so much potential leverage. That is why I believe every business leader—whether you are selling cars, chemicals, or cosmetics—needs to think and act like a brand leader.

The business case for brand ideals is not about altruism or corporate social responsibility. It's about expressing a business's fundamental reason for being and powering its growth. It's about linking and leveraging the behaviors of all the people important to a business's future, because nothing unites and motivates people's actions as strongly as ideals. They make it possible to connect what happens inside a business with what happens outside it, especially in the "black box" of people's minds and how they make decisions. Ideals are the ultimate driver, my research has found, of category-leading growth.

One way or another, I've been homing in on the business value of ideals since I was an eleven-year-old kid in Lancaster, Pennsylvania, with a neighborhood paper route and a lawn-cutting and snow-shoveling business. In hindsight all three jobs showed me that understanding what my customers valued and trying to improve their lives produced a big payoff. These weren't things I thought about consciously, of course; rather, I did them intuitively.

Knowing that the arrival of the paper punctuated the day for the retirees on my route, I knocked on the door, handed them the paper, and took a moment to chat. This brought me lots of freshly baked cookies and other treats and little tips through the year, and over-the-top tips at Christmas.

In snow shoveling and lawn cutting, I always looked for more that I could do for each customer. I was upselling before I ever heard the word. Could I shovel the sidewalk and the driveway as well as the front walk? Could I trim the hedge as well as cut the lawn? When customers went away for the summer or on a long vacation, I said, "I want to keep the yard looking nice for you, so why don't I mow your lawn every five to seven days?" That made each mowing easier because I wasn't hacking through deep grass, and I got paid more for cutting the lawn more often. All in all it was a nice portfolio of work until I graduated to more serious jobs, such as a summer on a road crew.

My first grown-up job, after graduating from Franklin and Marshall College in Lancaster, provided a complementary lesson on understanding customers' fundamental values. Time-Life Books was then moving from New York City to Alexandria, Virginia, and I joined its editorial department there. I enjoyed helping assemble and market multivolume book sets on a wide range of subjects, but the longer I was there, the more I felt that the organization was going to hit a wall.

Again, this is all in hindsight, but the leaders of the business failed to question the continuing viability of their business model. They had an organization with great equity in packaging and presenting infotainment, nonfiction subject matter with targeted demographic appeal. But they never asked, "What's special about this organization? What do we stand for in our customers' minds? What can we do if they stop buying book series on World War II and the Old West?"

In the years after I left to pursue an MBA at Pennsylvania State University's Smeal College of Business and then joined Procter & Gamble, the leadership of Time-Life Books kept ignoring that question even as it grew more urgent. Scattered successes kept Time-Life Books alive until 2003. Its decline through the 1980s and 1990s paralleled the birth and growth of niche cable television, which met the same infotainment needs in the form of channels such as the Learning Channel, the Weather Channel, the Food Network, the History Channel, and the Discovery Channel.

Can you imagine Time-Life entering that mix as a channel of its own or as a producer of programming for the new channels? Certainly a business with Time-Life's value in the public's mind had a genuine chance to do so in the early-to-mid 1980s. As the 1980s drew to a close and the 1990s wore on, however, it became harder and harder to conceive of Time-Life pulling off such a move.

Perhaps those who know the Time-Life culture intimately will say it was never possible, or that the business never had sufficient resources of its own or enough of a draw on the resources of its parent company, first Time, Inc., and then Time Warner. Well, compare how the National Geographic Society built on the brand value of *National Geographic* magazine to create the National Geographic Channel, extending their brand from magazine into new channels and offerings.

Remain stuck inside your current business model, and your business's days are numbered. Make a brand ideal your North Star, and the sky's the limit. That's because a brand ideal powerfully inspires continuous innovation toward a higher-order benefit. In what follows, I'll share many examples of how today's most successful business leaders orient their innovation programs around their brand ideals. You'll hear about this directly from the leaders themselves, as they shared their insights, principles, and practices with me during my research visits to their category-dominating businesses.

Because Time-Life's leadership never asked what the organization's reason for being was besides selling multivolume book series, they were never able to rally the organization around a higher-order ideal of improving the lives of the people they served. If Time-Life had seized the ideal of satisfying people's endless curiosity about the world's wonders, as the Discovery Channel soon did (as we'll see, ideals cannot be proprietary, but distinctive ways of fulfilling them can be), it could have envisioned a transition to other media before its existing business model became obsolete. If not a cable television channel or content producer, Time-Life might have become a dot-com that attracted growing communities of interest in different subject areas, as AOL did and continues to do. And as Facebook, Zynga, LinkedIn, and China's RenRen are doing so effectively, as they too attract communities of people around common interests.

WHY CHOOSY MOTHERS REALLY CHOSE JIF

Going to work at P&G brought me into one of the world's great companies with extraordinary people and capabilities. The pivotal assignment of the early part of my career there was working on Jif peanut butter, a $250 million business in P&G's food and beverage division. From assistant brand manager to brand manager to associate marketing director, I was involved with the Jif business for six years, an unusually long time compared to P&G's traditional career path, in which managers on the rise usually moved to a different business every two years.

Over the course of those six years I did a number of things that P&G didn't do then, beginning with putting together a small but diverse team. We had a Korean American woman, an African American woman, a white woman from Oregon who had previously been in the sales organization, and a white male engineer who had moved into marketing from manufacturing. The diversity of this group was remarkable not just for P&G but for a mid-1980s management team in general.

I brought this team and our ad agency team, from Grey Advertising in New York, to meet the farmers who grew the peanuts for Jif on a contract basis. When we had a new ad campaign, I took the video or visuals to the factory in Lexington, Kentucky, and stayed there for twenty-four hours so that I could show them to all three shifts and get their feedback and input. And before it became the vogue, we did an unusual number of in-home visits and shop-alongs with moms.

These in-home visits and shop-alongs sharpened our sense of Jif's core customers from simply women between the ages of eighteen and thirty-four to highly engaged moms with children from toddler to early elementary school age. My guiding thought was that Jif should become the most loved peanut butter by exemplifying and supporting what these moms valued. So we had to have the highest quality and make sure there were no traces of carcinogenic aflatoxins, a toxin produced by mold, in the peanuts we used. We had to address moms' concerns about healthfulness and nutrition in general. We had to have great taste that young kids loved.

Jif had abandoned its famous "Choosy mothers choose Jif" slogan for "Taste the 'Jifference' in Jif." I thought the older slogan really expressed what we stood for, and I brought it back, an unheard-of move at P&G.

When the folks from Grey met the peanut farmers and our workforce in Lexington, and saw millions of peanuts being sorted for the slightest imperfection with laser scanning, they were blown away by such insistence on quality control. This deeper understanding of our superiority led to a full-page newspaper ad campaign headlined "The Answer Is No." The ad featured a photo of a jar of Jif with little paragraphs explaining that our peanut butter had no cholesterol, no preservatives, no artificial colors or flavors, and so on. It was based on the top ten questions that moms asked us about Jif.

In tune with our overall effort to support moms' values, we did national promotions where we donated 10¢ a jar to local PTAs. Even in the mid-1980s, without the databases that are now available, we were able to apportion the donations very accurately by retail store and school district.

The creative energy these efforts brought to the Jif team at P&G, not just in marketing but in manufacturing and other functions, transformed the business from a sleepy one to an explosive growth story. We achieved record market share, gaining two full share points in a market where fractions of a share point had been all but impossible to win without eroding margin. We also attained record profitability, with increases in total profit and profit margin of 143 percent and 110 percent respectively in the first year of our efforts. We did even better the following year. These results became a highlight of my career and the careers of the key members of my small management team.

Looking back on my largely intuitive decisions about the business, I can see how they exemplify the power of ideals. By explicitly aligning the business with moms' values, we implicitly—and subconsciously—aligned it with a fundamental ideal of human growth. We became more than a peanut butter maker. We became a partner with moms in their young children's development. It presaged the creation of Pampers' subsequent, more profound partnership with moms in their babies' development, which I'll discuss in detail later.

If you're willing to embrace the same concept and align your business with a fundamental human ideal, you can achieve extraordinary growth in your own business and your own career. My research shows that your growth rate can triple. Imagine the possibilities that creates for you, your people, and your community.

The Ideal Factor—a shared intent by everyone in the business to improve people's lives—keeps renewing and strengthening great businesses through good times and bad. It's what links businesses as different as buttoned-down consulting firm Accenture and revved-up Red Bull, the lifestyle drink of Gen Xers and Millennials. The commitment of these businesses and their leaders to ideals of improving people's lives emerged in my global ten-year-growth study of long-term performance in more than 50,000 brands, which I will detail in the following chapter.

Does a shared goal of improving people's lives sound, well, too idealistic for the rough-and-tumble of business? What about practical, hard-nosed goals such as making the quarterly numbers, increasing market share, and cutting costs?

All are crucial, but the best businesses aim higher. When many business leaders articulate mission and vision statements, they typically talk about having the best-performing, most profitable, most customer-satisfying, most sustainable, and most ethical organization. Strip away the platitudes, and these statements all aim too low. And when they mention the customer, it's the customer as seen from the company's point of view and in terms of the company's agenda.

Even when it's a start-up talking about new markets, a mission statement in this form boils down to: "We want our current business model to make or keep us the leader of our current pack of competitors in current and immediately foreseeable market conditions." This is a formula for mediocrity, locking an enterprise into a business model based on the agenda of the business, not that of the customer. But business models have to change with market conditions, and the only sure basis for creating viable business models over the long term is when a business and its customers have a shared agenda. For example, as we'll see in the next chapter, a central impetus for the high growth of Brazil-based energy giant Petrobras has been the agenda of sustainable development it shares with the Brazilian people.

By linking a business's core beliefs with fundamental human values, an ideal of improving people's lives clarifies the business's true reason for being. And this in turn supports open-ended processes that can drive many different business models in succession.

Don't get me wrong. It's necessary to want to be the best-performing enterprise around, with the highest standards, the best people, and the most-satisfied customers. Again, however, this simply doesn't aim high enough and look far enough ahead. To hit higher targets and get and stay in front of the competition requires an ideal.

THE FOUNDATION FOR GROWTH AND PROFIT

Procter & Gamble had a remarkable run in the first decade of the twenty-first century. But in 2000, it was in big trouble, having recently lost $85 billion in market capitalization in only six months. Its core businesses were stagnating, and its people were demoralized.

A. G. Lafley, then the CEO, asked me to take on the role of global marketing officer to help transform the culture of the company to one in which "the consumer is boss." I jumped at the challenge, and proposed building the best marketing organization in the world, attracting the best talent—with focus on growing the market share of the majority of our businesses—and making our marketing known, recognized, and admired by all the people important to P&G's future. This included current and prospective employees, all our agencies, the business media, investors, and of course our retail customers and end consumers.

To hit these big targets we needed an even bigger goal: identifying and activating a distinctive ideal (or purpose, as P&G dubbed it) of improving people's lives inside every business in the P&G portfolio. We could then establish each business's true reason for being as the basis for new growth, and we could link them all into a strong foundation for P&G's recovery by building each business's culture around its ideal.

Every P&G business had to communica\
nally and externally. Most important, A. G. Lafl\
rest of the senior management team expected \
leader to articulate how each brand's individual ide\
P&G's overarching mantra of improving people's lives, ⎯d
to model that; and we had to measure all our activities and
people in terms of the ideals of our brands and the company as
a whole. The success of that effort brought P&G extraordinary
growth from 2001 on, as I'll describe.

Ideals unlock the code for twenty-first-century business success because they leverage timeless truths about human behavior and values in business and in life. They enable life to influence business and business to influence life.

Pampers' brand ideal, for example, its true reason for being, is not selling the most disposable diapers in the world. Pampers exists to help mothers care for their babies' and toddlers' healthy, happy development. In looking beyond transactions, an ideal opens up endless possibilities, including endless possibilities for growth and profit.

A viable brand ideal cuts through the clutter and clarifies what you and your people stand for and believe. It transforms the enterprise into a customer-understanding machine, personalizing who your best customers are and what values you share with them. It helps crystallize your business's existing and potential points of parity and points of difference with the competition. It illuminates your organizational culture's strengths and weaknesses, so that you can see what needs to change and what doesn't, what's negotiable and what's not, what can be outsourced and what is core.

Highly adaptive and flexible, a brand ideal is not tied to a particular business model and has no expiration date. It generates effective new business models, strategies, and tactics before the current ones have lost their freshness and begun to

..oduce diminishing returns. On the other hand, the surest route to business obsolescence is ignoring or misunderstanding the significance of ideals.

Most important, a brand ideal enables leaders to drive results by being absolutely clear and compelling about what they value. Few leaders articulate that well. It can't just be numbers and money. Numbers and money alone will not motivate and drive great performance and bring or keep valuable people on board. The higher your position as a leader, the simpler and more robust your message must be to translate across varied individuals, teams, groups, divisions, and business units. Ideals do that because they speak to universal human instincts, hopes, and values.

P&G's growth in the 2000s was a life-changing journey of discovery for me into the drivers of sustained business growth, and I'll be sharing lessons from that experience throughout this book. I'll also be sharing lessons from my research, teaching, and consulting since I left P&G in 2008, especially the ten-year-growth study I mentioned, the Stengel Study of Business Growth.

I'll recount the full story of the Stengel Study in the next chapter. But the title of this chapter sums up its central finding: great businesses have great ideals. That is what emerged most prominently when I mined the data and conducted additional quantitative and qualitative research on the top 50 businesses in the Stengel Study with teams at Millward Brown Optimor and the UCLA Anderson Graduate School of Management, reverse-engineering how these companies work to see what they have in common. We saw that great businesses have great ideals.

Equally important, we found that the leaders of these businesses follow common practices, each in their unique style. We found today's most effective business leaders:

- Discover a brand ideal of improving people's ɩ. one of five fields of fundamental human values.
- Build their organizational culture around the brand ideal.
- Communicate the brand ideal to engage employees and customers.
- Deliver a near-ideal customer experience.
- Evaluate their progress and people against the brand ideal.

I'll open up these activities—the crucial imperatives for twenty-first-century business success—in detail in subsequent chapters. As part of the research for this book, I conducted "deep dive" observational visits and interviews with senior executives at a variety of category-leading businesses—Method, Discovery Communications, Pampers, Innocent, Jack Daniel's, Zappos, Visa, HP, Motorola Solutions, Lindt, and IBM, among others—and you'll hear directly from these executives about the role that ideals play in their long-term strategies, their business models, and their daily leadership practices.

In what follows I'm going to show you how to unleash the hidden power of ideals in every part of your business. You'll see how you can track the benefits quantitatively to top- and bottom-line growth, and qualitatively to increased employee morale and productivity and increased customer satisfaction, loyalty, and advocacy for your business.

Ready?

Let's start with a close look at the Stengel Study of Business Growth, its methodology and findings, and its implications for your business and career.

2

The Stengel Study of Business Growth

The seed of the Stengel Study of Business Growth was planted in the last part of my tenure, from 2001 to 2008, as P&G's global marketing officer. In 2006 my senior management colleagues and I occupied an enviable but dangerous position. Under A. G. Lafley's superb leadership, we had righted, repaired, and modernized a 169-year-old ship, which at the start of the decade was listing badly and in danger of sinking. Since *Advertising Age* had asked in a September 25, 2000, cover story, "Does P&G Still Matter?," the company had piled up a series of record-breaking years. We had built substantial organic growth in the longtime P&G portfolio, we were making an absolute win of our $53.4 billion acquisition of Gillette in 2005, and we were handily beating our competition. We were without question the envy of our peers, and P&G was once again a darling of Wall Street.

Be careful what you wish for, as the saying goes. Extraordinary success is one of the most dangerous situations in business. Sticking with a winning model too long has sent countless businesses down the tubes. No longer threatened by a burning platform, P&G now faced an insidious, no less lethal threat: complacency.

Building on success, sustaining growth over the long term, is the ultimate challenge in business. Meeting that challenge always requires both continuity and change. Human nature being what it is, however, the people in an organization will always prefer status quo continuity to change.

It is relatively easy to lead change when there is a burning platform and a business is under severe survival pressure. For example, I began consulting with Toyota after they lost significant consumer trust because of product safety recalls in 2010, and they were eager for ideas about how to strengthen their organization and their brand. In addition to recovering lost consumer trust, their burning platform included how to win against global competitors such as Ford, GM, Hyundai, and VW, and how to build loyalty with Gen Xers and Millennials, the next generations of car and truck buyers after aging baby boomers.

It is far more difficult to lead change when things are going well, or even just okay. People do not change—in fact, they actively resist changing—if they do not see, think, and feel the need for it. Everyone in business today is extremely stretched, working nearly 24/7 on the tasks at hand. To accept and join in change, which always includes new kinds of work and different behaviors, people need to feel it is absolutely necessary for them individually and for their company. P&G in 2006 did not feel the need to change.

If you stop leading change, however, you stop leading. And if an organization stops changing and growing, it becomes vulnerable to competition.

My challenge in 2006 as global marketing officer was to keep P&G marketing—and with A. G. Lafley and the rest of his senior management team to keep P&G at large—restless. How could we avoid complacency, keep the fire burning, and accelerate growth when we were already winning?

I always learned a tremendous amount when visiting fast-growing companies with different business models and different cultures. As P&G's GMO, I did this frequently, with a few members of my team when I could, visiting Nike, Nestlé, Google, Hearst, GE, Target, and Toyota, to name a few.

Benchmarking against the best performers resets your standards and challenges your growth assumptions—it makes you restless. I wanted all of our employees to have a similar experience, so they too could feel restless and reset their standards, and P&G could grow even faster and further.

I began challenging my corporate marketing team to benchmark the world's fastest-growing businesses and brands, no matter what category they were in. I asked, "Who is growing faster than we are on key financial measures, and what can we learn from them?" I asked this question so often, the team sometimes piped the question back at me before I finished saying "Who—?" But it never seemed to make the top of the priority list; it was a nice-to-do versus a must-do. It almost became a joke: "There Jim goes again, pestering us about who's growing faster and how they're doing it."

In the middle of 2006 I put myself and my team on the hook to make it a must-do to find the answer. I went to A. G. Lafley and urged that we commission a study to identify and learn from businesses that were growing even faster than we were, in whatever industry. A.G. heartily endorsed the idea.

I then told my team that we had to come up with significant insights on growth for P&G by the annual senior leadership meeting in 2007, and we set the near-term goal of studying the fastest-growing brands over the previous five years as the basis for that. Rich DelCore, my director of finance for the marketing function, led the effort with an internal team representing many P&G functions: finance, marketing, research, purchasing, and HR. We selected Millward Brown Optimor as our outside partner, based on its global BrandZ database and the interpretative savvy of its people, who deeply understand the role of brand equity in growing businesses.

No brand database is perfect. None covers every possible brand or even every possible business category. BrandZ, for example, does not include footwear and motorcycles in many markets. This excludes superb businesses such as Nike and Harley-Davidson from consideration.

Other databases have at least equally significant gaps, however, and BrandZ is indisputably the world's largest brand equity database, covering more than 50,000 brands in thirty-one countries and within 380 categories around the world from 1998 to the present. The data are based on more than 2 million consumer surveys and professional interviews around the world.

Millward Brown Optimor's proprietary brand valuation methodology is the basis for the BrandZ Top 100 Most Valuable Global Brands, which the *Financial Times* publishes every spring. The study is prepared with data from Bloomberg and from consumer research firm Kantar Worldpanel. Both Millward Brown Optimor's parent company, Millward Brown, a global research organization with seventy-eight offices in fifty-four countries, and Kantar Worldpanel are subsidiaries of WPP, the world's largest marketing services, communications, and research agency holding company, with revenues of $15 billion. The result is that Millward Brown Optimor can deploy global resources in brand data mining, analytics, and related consulting services that are second to none.

Rich DelCore and the internal P&G team spent countless hours with the team from Millward Brown Optimor, including Mario Simon, Benoit Garbe, Joanna Seddon, and Dan Lewen, probing the fastest-growing brands and what we could learn from them. I joined the combined teams at key points, and saw their energy increase as the study progressed. They were like detectives intent on solving the biggest and toughest case they had ever faced, assembling clues that put them on the verge of a breakthrough.

By the summer of 2007 the combined P&G and Millward

Brown Optimor project teams had assembled five-year financial trends on twenty-five businesses that had grown even faster than P&G over that period. The teams then dug behind the numbers with additional research, including interviewing business executives, agency leaders, brand experts, and academics at Harvard, Duke, and Columbia.

My expectation was that we would learn good tactical stuff about how the fastest-growing businesses were allocating resources to digital media, balancing innovation with their core products and services, streamlining global operations, handling HR issues, and so on. We did indeed get these kinds of insights.

The unexpected thing that leapt out was much bigger, however. The study did not set out to highlight or test the business value of ideals. We went in looking strictly for superior financial growth, and only after that for whatever the top-ranked businesses were doing differently from the competition in their category. When we probed to that level, however, we again and again found that the world's fastest-growing enterprises were organized around ideals of improving people's lives and activated these ideals throughout their business ecosystems.

The team and I were totally unprepared for this, and for its consistency across very different businesses in different geographies, in both B2B and B2C categories. The central finding—that businesses driven by a higher ideal, a higher purpose, outperform their competition by a wide margin, and frequently create both new businesses and entire new business sectors—corroborated what I had implicitly believed and acted on throughout my career. Ideal-driven businesses grow fast and sustain that growth. And while P&G was already learning this through its focus on a deeper meaning, a deeper purpose behind its brands, the best performers in the group of twenty-five—companies such as Apple, Google, Red Bull, Starbucks, and Target—had even greater clarity, consistency, commitment, and creativity in the way they leveraged the power of ideals.

When we shared this study and our recommendations in November 2007 at the annual three-day meeting for senior executives from headquarters and around the world, the impact was profound. During and immediately after the presentation, the room was eerily silent.

To cite one of its many implications, the study challenged P&G's paradigm of moving people around frequently. The companies that were growing the fastest had a different paradigm. In recruiting and hiring they looked for people whose values fit with their brands, and they tended to keep people working in the same areas for much longer. In so doing they developed executives who were visionaries for their brands. This in turn enabled these businesses to operate at a faster clip than we did, to act—very effectively—on intuition more than we did, and to create imaginative brand experiences that went well beyond the basic functionality of their products and services.

The study made everyone think, and become restless again. Like all great enterprises, P&G is full of people who hate to lose and love to win. Learning that, successful as we were, we still trailed a lot of other companies, both B2B and B2C, got everybody's competitive juices flowing. Matching and surpassing this new standard became a rallying cry and catalyzed a major new growth initiative at P&G.

After helping to launch this growth initiative, I left P&G in November 2008. I had completed the job I set out to do as GMO, helping to turn the company around and position it for future growth. I was also restless to explore, and better understand, the brand-ideal–driven growth that the study revealed. I felt in my gut that there was a good deal more to the puzzle than I had learned so far. If I remained at P&G, the daily pressures of corporate management would always take precedence over solving that puzzle. I wanted to partner with like-minded people to accelerate this nascent movement in business, show other companies its potential, and teach emerging young business leaders about it.

It was therefore as a consultant and as an adjunct professor at UCLA Anderson that I decided to reach out to Millward Brown Optimor again. I called Benoit Garbe and said I wanted to partner with them. What I had in mind was an even larger study of growth over a longer period of time—ten years if possible, compared to the five years we'd looked at before—and against a more comprehensive performance metric. I was determined to identify and understand sustained growth over a significant span of years, not just take a snapshot of brand and business value at a passing moment. And I wanted to measure not just growth in financial value but also growth in consumer commitment to brands, and probe the connection between the two. I wanted to get to the bottom of what drove long-term growth, and develop a framework to bring it to life in any business, for any leader.

So Millward Brown Optimor and I designed the Stengel Study of Business Growth. Our objective was to develop a validated framework that leaders could apply to accelerate growth in their businesses over a sustained period of time. To produce a breakthrough list of best companies, Millward Brown Optimor and I had to define the what, when, and how of the study. We needed to figure out what to measure companies against, the period of time when these measures would apply, and how we would implement them.

Every research study or scientific experiment is a test of a central premise, a burning question. Millward Brown Optimor and I both believed that great brands grow as they do because they connect deeply with people. That was the central premise the Stengel Study had to probe. Our burning question was threefold: Are the bonds that people form with brands the ultimate growth driver? If so, what kind of bond generates the most growth? And how can businesses leverage it?

With this in mind, we set out to identify the B2B and B2C brands that grew and created deeper relationships with people over the past decade. Then we examined whether these relationships translated into stronger financial performance.

The BrandZ database was our starting point. But in using this rich resource, the Stengel Study went well beyond both single-moment-in-time rankings, such as Millward Brown Optimor's own BrandZ Top 100 Most Valuable Global Brands, and the 2006–7 study at P&G, and did so in three ways.

First, rankings of brand value at a single point in time do not track growth, and they are naturally biased toward the largest brands at the time of the study. Such rankings inevitably include large brands that are faltering for one reason or another, perhaps seriously, and thus not necessarily models of best practices. By focusing on the rate of growth over time, the Stengel Study could identify exemplary growth stories among small, medium, and large businesses.

The 2006–7 study at P&G had tracked growth over time, but I felt its five-year span was not long enough to identify the cohort of highest sustained growth and excellence. So the second key difference in the Stengel Study is a full ten-year span, 2001 to 2011, including periods of both boom and bust in the wider economy.

The third key difference is something I just mentioned. The Stengel Study of Business Growth thoroughly examines the interrelationships of people's bonding with brands and the growth in those brands' financial value.

With the what and the when confirmed, we needed to move

on to the how. We began by screening the BrandZ data on more than 50,000 brands around the world to identify the ones with the highest loyalty, or consumer bonding, score. Millward Brown's bonding score is a composite metric that captures the highest level of engagement and commitment that brands create with people. It is not only a good proxy to define the strength of the relationship between a brand and the customer; it is also highly correlated with share of wallet.

Our first pass at ranking the brands accordingly considered the overall bonding scores of the brands at the global and country level, their bonding scores relative to category, and their growth over time. This provided us with a first list of the brands that people loved and valued the most around the world, including brands ranging in size from $100 million in revenues to well over $100 billion.

The second part of the analysis was confirming that these highly bonded brands with strong consumer momentum had generated faster, greater business value growth. We conducted a financial valuation of the brands on top of our list at two points in time. To track brand value growth we took a weighted average of the absolute growth in a brand's financial value over the ten-year period, its rate of growth, and its growth relative to its category. When we looked at multibrand companies such as P&G, LVMH, or the Coca-Cola Company, we analyzed each brand in the portfolio on its own.

THE STENGEL 50

The Stengel Study of Business Growth ultimately identified 50 brands with extraordinary growth over the 2000s relative to their competition. These top 50 brands across all categories have created more meaningful relationships with people. They have far outpaced their competition in brand value. And they have contributed to faster and greater business value growth. In pure financial terms, the Stengel 50 as a whole grew three times faster over the 2000s than their competitors and the overall universe of brands we analyzed. Individually, some of the fastest-growing of the Stengel 50, such as Apple and Google, grew as much as ten times faster than their competition from 2001 to 2011.

The Stengel 50 includes businesses in twenty-eight categories. There are B2B companies, retailers, luxury brands, and high-technology enterprises. The list includes brands that have been around for over a century and others launched in the past decade. There are many European and U.S. brands, but there are also great brands from the rest of the world, including Brazil, Russia, the United Arab Emirates, India, and China. While the fifty brands span a wide range of price points, most are premium priced in their categories, another indication of their strong customer relationships.

Here are the Stengel 50 and their main lines of business:

Accenture, management and enterprise consulting services
Airtel, mobile communications
Amazon.com, e-commerce
Apple, personal computing technology and mobile devices
Aquarel, bottled water
BlackBerry, mobile communications
Calvin Klein, luxury apparel and accessories
Chipotle, fast food
Coca-Cola, soft drinks
Diesel, youth-targeted fashion apparel and accessories
Discovery Communications, media
Dove, personal care
Emirates, air travel
FedEx, delivery services
Google, Internet information

Heineken, beer

Hennessy, spirits

Hermès, luxury apparel and leather goods

HP, information technology products and services

Hugo Boss, luxury apparel and accessories

IBM, information technology products and services

Innocent, food and beverages

Jack Daniel's, spirits

Johnnie Walker, spirits

Lindt, chocolate

L'Occitane, personal care

Louis Vuitton, luxury apparel and leather goods

MasterCard, electronic payments

Mercedes-Benz, automobiles

Method, household cleaners and personal care

Moët & Chandon, champagne

Natura, personal care

Pampers, baby care

Petrobras, energy

Rakuten Ichiba, e-commerce

Red Bull, energy drinks

Royal Canin, pet food

Samsung, electronics

Sedmoy Kontinent ("Seventh Continent"), retail grocery

Sensodyne, oral care

Seventh Generation, household cleaners and personal care

Snow, beer

Starbucks, coffee and fast-food retailer

Stonyfield Farm, organic dairy products

Tsingtao, beer

Vente-Privee.com, e-commerce

Visa, electronic payments

Wegmans, retail grocery

Zappos, e-commerce
Zara, affordable apparel

These businesses are in alphabetical order rather than the numerical order usual in brand or company rankings, because it is much less important how they stand in relation to one another than how they stand in relation to their categories and to all brands in general. We ran the analysis in 2009, 2010, and once more in 2011—at the latest possible date before this book went into production—to check for consistency and ensure that we were taking the worst of the Great Recession into account. My conviction was that to maximize the study's usefulness, it had to include both the general economic boom of most of the 2000s and the general economic bust of the decade's closing years.

As you can see, the list includes a few businesses, such as BlackBerry and HP (whose growth in the 2000s I already mentioned), that were encountering rough weather of some kind as the 2010s began. Yet over the ten-year period examined by the study, these businesses delivered extraordinary financial returns. BlackBerry, for example, achieved a 116 percent compound annual growth rate in brand value from 2001 to 2010. In 2011 they lost 20 percent of that, but their ten-year return was still stellar.

All businesses go through tough times, and the most important step to surviving them and coming out stronger is often renewing brand ideals. In chapter 11, I'll take you inside two companies in the midst of evolving their brand ideals, Motorola Solutions and HP, one of the Stengel 50, and show you the extraordinary positive impact this is having on their respective employees and customers.

While Millward Brown Optimor was rerunning the Stengel Study metrics to encompass a full decade, I engaged teams of graduate student researchers in testing and interpreting the incoming data through a second-year MBA marketing course at the UCLA Anderson Graduate School of Management, which I co-teach with Professor Sanjay Sood. Sanjay and I have made the entire course a research lab for the Stengel Study. Our research objective: investigate whether and how ideals contribute to the category-leading growth of the Stengel 50 brands and others, and whether the framework in this book is valid and repeatable.

Every class provides an opportunity to test ideas and share observations with sixty of the world's brightest young MBA students. During the first offering of the course, a team of four students—Jessica Kellett, a native Californian with a keen interest in sustainability and a passion for community and customer engagement; Michal Zeituni, also from California, with a primary professional interest in strategic marketing and consumer insight; Eliot Wadsworth, a guitar-playing Bostonian with deep knowledge of the entertainment media industry; and Juan Pablo Villegas-Karpf, from Bogotá, Colombia, with marketing experience across several industries—made the Stengel Study the subject of their required second-year applied-management research thesis.

In consultation with Sanjay and me at UCLA and Benoit at Millward Brown Optimor, this team crawled all over the Stengel 50 to test the role of ideals. In addition to extensive desk research, they conducted face-to-face and phone interviews with roughly thirty executives, academic researchers, and business consultants. At the end of the project, they presented their findings not only to Sanjay and me but also to a separate review board of other UCLA Anderson faculty. The faculty reviewers grilled Jessica, Michal, Eliot, and Juan for two hours. Afterward the student team was shell-shocked, but they had come through with flying colors. Equally important for me, I must admit, so had the Stengel Study.

The rest of the 120 students who took the course the first time Sanjay and I offered it (we taught two sections of 60 students each) divided up in teams of two or three for ideal-related case studies of a business of their choosing, inside or outside the Stengel 50. We have continued to have the students do these case studies of Stengel 50 and other businesses in subsequent offerings of the course.

As I mentioned earlier and as I'll describe in detail in later chapters, I also tested the Stengel Study findings in my "deep-dive" observational visits and interviews with leading executives at several Stengel 50 businesses and in consulting work that involved dozens of brands.

These combined research efforts were soon producing rich information and insight on ideal-driven growth behaviors inside businesses. I felt we had cracked the code on something transformational for understanding and achieving business growth. But although we were reading the code inside the Stengel 50 businesses, I couldn't feel satisfied until we were able to read it in the attitudes and behaviors of people outside those businesses, buyers and consumers of these brands.

The team's analysis of the extended success of the Stengel 50, compared to the competition in their categories, provided strong evidence that ideals positively influence people's purchasing behavior and advocacy. But it didn't tell us directly and precisely about the nature of this influence and its importance relative to other motivations.

The question nagged at me: how could we prove whether or not brand ideals decisively influence the attitudes and behavior of people outside a business, the brand's consumers?

I knew this wasn't going to be an easy task. Talk to people

about why they buy certain brands rather than others, and ideals are not at the top of their list. The language of these brand conversations tends to be generic ("it's good") or functional ("it works well," "it's cheap," "it's good quality"). In part, this is because deeper motivations and higher-level concepts tend to be complex and hard to express, and we often revert to what is easy to articulate. But it's also because human beings like to believe that we are more objective and dispassionate in our choices than we really are. In reality, as academic research in cognitive neuroscience has now established, our decisions and choices are decisively influenced by emotional and instinctive reactions that we often aren't consciously aware of. This is "the power of thinking without thinking," as Malcolm Gladwell describes subconscious mental processes in his bestseller *Blink*. Within the market research world, a race is on to acquire the knowledge and tools to go inside "the black box" of customers' minds at this subconscious level.

Millward Brown launched its neuroscience practice in 2010, and I asked Benoit if they could participate in extending the Stengel Study to include people's subconscious attitudes to Stengel 50 brands versus their competition. The team at Millward Brown designed research that allowed us to look at what associations selected Stengel 50 brands and their competitors "activate" in people—thoughts and feelings they may be unable to articulate. The resulting research gave us a fascinating look at the associations that these brands activate in the minds of consumers. I will share more on this fascinating learning in a few pages.

Now, what exactly did the Stengel Study find? And what implications does it have for you and your business?

THE RESULTS OF THE STENGEL STUDY OF BUSINESS GROWTH

There are four profound findings from the Stengel Study that are the foundation of this book:

1. Brand ideals drive the performance of the highest growth businesses.
2. The brand ideals of the highest growth businesses center in one of five areas, or fields, of fundamental human values.
3. The highest growth businesses are run by business artists, leaders whose primary medium is brand ideals.
4. Business artists excel in similar practices that constitute an operating system for generating and sustaining high growth.

STENGEL STUDY FINDING 1.
BRAND IDEALS DRIVE THE PERFORMANCE OF THE HIGHEST GROWTH BUSINESSES.

The first and central finding of the Stengel Study, validating the 2006 P&G study across a longer-term sample and more comprehensive performance metric (consumer bonding and financial growth), is that leveraging ideals of improving people's lives is driving the performance of the world's fastest-growing businesses.

The Stengel Study team and I analyzed each business in the top 50 to identify its ideal, and we found all brands had an ideal of improving life in some way appropriate for their category. Some brands, like Google and IBM, have obvious life-improving ideals. Google exists to immediately satisfy every curiosity, IBM to help build a smarter planet. Other brands, like Moët & Chandon and Diesel, bring an extra dimension to life, providing their consumers with a special experience that enhances life. Moët & Chandon's ideal is to transform occasions into celebrations, and Diesel's ideal is to inspire imagination and endless possibilities in style.

So when I use the phrase "improving life" when I discuss brand ideals, there is, of course, a continuum in how deeply these fifty brands impact life. But they all do impact life in their own ways. The appendix contains a complete list of the Stengel 50 with their ideal statements, as my team and I see them.

STENGEL STUDY FINDING 2. THE BRAND IDEALS OF THE HIGHEST GROWTH BUSINESSES CENTER IN ONE OF FIVE FIELDS OF FUNDAMENTAL HUMAN VALUES.

As my team and I analyzed the ideal statements, we also looked for patterns among them. Do the individual ideals fall into any similar fields? Or are the ideals unique in fifty different ways? We actually found they grouped into five very rich and interesting fields. That gave us the second critical finding of the study: the ideals driving category-leading growth at the Stengel 50 cluster into five fields of fundamental human values that improve people's lives by:

- **Eliciting Joy**: Activating experiences of happiness, wonder, and limitless possibility.
- **Enabling Connection**: Enhancing the ability of people to connect with one another and the world in meaningful ways.
- **Inspiring Exploration**: Helping people explore new horizons and new experiences.
- **Evoking Pride**: Giving people increased confidence, strength, security, and vitality.
- **Impacting Society**: Affecting society broadly, includ-

38

ing by challenging the status quo and redefining categories.

Arriving at and defining these five fields of fundamental human values took some time, as we experimented with grouping the top 50 businesses from different perspectives. We sought advice from market research experts, peers, and people in complementary fields like psychology. No matter what angle we approached the problem from, however, we kept homing in on the same five human values.

It was at this point that I turned to Millward Brown's neuroscience team and asked them, "Can we test how the ideal statements of individual brands and the five ideals fields resonate with people subconsciously?"

Graham Page, who heads Millward Brown's neuroscience practice, and his colleagues Dr. Barbara O'Connell and Dr. Sarah Walker, devised a test to measure the implicit associations, the unconscious network of ideas and feelings, that people have with selected Stengel 50 businesses compared with some of their competition. A technical term for what Graham, Barbara, and Sarah did to measure these unconscious ideas and feelings is *neural pathway activation and decay.* They "activated" people's associations by showing them different brands (in this case, brand name and logo) and then asking them to quickly but accurately decide if a string of letters was a word (one of the ideals) or not (a nonsense word). The faster a person identifies one or more of the ideals-field words as real words after seeing a brand tells us which ideals the brand has activated and the strength of that association.

The experiment didn't ask people directly whether they consciously associated attributes or fields with certain brands. Instead, it relied on the fact that every time a person sees or thinks about something, including any word or image, a network of associations is activated in the neural pathways of the brain. The firing of neural pathways leaves a chemical trace that decays slowly, so that the pathway remains active, with decreasing intensity, for a period of time. This makes it easier and quicker to trigger pathways which have been recently activated than those which have not been recently activated. So if a person identifies a word such as *explore* faster after seeing one brand's name rather than another's, it indicates that the person associates the quality of exploration more strongly with one brand than another.

Using both these new implicit measures that modern neuroscience makes possible and traditional explicit measures of people's conscious associations, Millward Brown found that people experienced the Stengel 50 brands as being deeply ideal-based and as being more ideal-based than their competition.

The associations between the ideals fields and the select Stengel 50 brands were even stronger in the implicit measures than in the explicit ones, showing that the ideals and ideals fields influence people at the most fundamental level of their gut reactions. These neuroscience-based measures of subconscious attitudes, thoughts, and feelings demonstrate the essential nature of the brand ideal and its power to maximize business growth. This evidence shows that ideals indeed move markets individual by individual.

I was enormously excited by these findings and their implications for maximizing business growth. Many leaders intuitively understand that their businesses and brands need a higher purpose in order to have a more important place in people's lives than the competition. They just don't know how to judge whether they have positioned their businesses and brands in the right space.

The five ideals fields, five areas of fundamental human values, provide a way to make those judgments. They give you an acid test for gauging the validity and growth potential of an ideal, and show whether you are aiming high enough and have a chance of engaging people at the level of their most profound concerns, needs, beliefs, and values.

You might find it useful, as I do, to think of the fields as different types of soil that are advantageous for different types of ideals. There's no hierarchy among the ideals fields. Equally valuable things take root and grow in all of them. And these fields are not mutually exclusive; they can overlap.

The possible overlap of two or more of the five areas represents a powerful strategic tool. Just keep in mind though that no brand or business can be all things to all people. Across the Stengel 50 every business primarily grows in one of the five fields, but may also find growth in one or, at most, two of the other fields. For example, as a spirits brand, Jack Daniel's is very much in the business of connecting people in social occasions. But within that context, which applies to all brands in the wine, beer, and spirits categories, Jack Daniel's represents an attitude to life—call it maverick independence—which goes back to its founder, Jack Daniel himself, and which the business has profitably cultivated ever since. Later we'll see how they've done this.

Likewise, a luxury car brand such as Mercedes-Benz may appeal to customers' needs for joy as well as evoke pride through automotive power and refinement. And Lindt's chocolates elicit joy while also helping to impact society positively through sustainable cocoa harvesting.

Here is how I sort the Stengel 50 in relation to the five fields:

The Stengel 50 Brands in the Five Fields of Fundamental Human Values

Eliciting Joy	Enabling Connection	Inspiring Exploration	Evoking Pride	Impacting Society
Coca-Cola	Airtel	Amazon.com	Calvin Klein	Accenture
Emirates	BlackBerry	Apple	Heineken	Aquarel
Lindt	FedEx	Diesel	Hennessy	Chipotle
MasterCard	Natura	Discovery Communications	Hermès	Dove
Moët & Chandon	Rakuten Ichiba	Google	Hugo Boss	IBM
Tsingtao	Starbucks	HP	Jack Daniel's	Innocent
Vente-Privee.com		Johnnie Walker	L'Occitane	Method
Wegmans		Louis Vuitton	Mercedes-Benz	Petrobras
Zappos		Pampers	Snow Beer	Royal Canin
Zara		Red Bull		Sedmoy Kontinent
		Samsung		Sensodyne
		Visa		Seventh Generation
				Stonyfield Farm

Note how brands in the same industry may be centered in different fields, and how brands in disparate industries may be centered in the same field. All the wine, beer, and spirits brands have business models that depend on people coming together in social occasions, as I noted in relation to Jack Daniel's, but furthering social connection may or may not be a particular brand's essential brand ideal. Likewise, not all luxury brands are primarily about evoking pride, whereas fashion brands at more affordable price points, such as Zara and Diesel, centered in the ideals fields of joy and exploration, respectively, also evoke pride for consumers. And a desire to improve the

world links businesses as differen.
Petrobras.

The bottom line is that if your busi.
ing an ideal in one of these five fields c
values, you're likely not positioned for sig..

The most powerful questions I ask client
them are, "Is your business, or is each of your   ../-
ing in one of these fields? If not, why not? And in   .e you
articulating it in a way that is inspirational to employees and
customers?"

The discussions that ensue are so deep, powerful, and
transformational that it's worth looking more closely at each of
the five ideals fields.

Eliciting Joy

Businesses with ideals of activating experiences of happiness,
wonder, and limitless possibility create moments of happiness
that engage our thoughts and emotions as well as our physical
senses. A signature example of a P&G business rediscovering
its ideal in this field, and then revealing it in a powerful new
way, is Downy fabric softener (called Lenor outside America).
Downy's historical positioning focused on its functional benefits. Add Downy to the wash, and make the towels softer
and fluffier. A team spending time with consumers in their
daily lives gradually discovered the potential for Downy to do
something much more interesting: satisfy people's need and
desire to stimulate and renew the senses of touch, smell, and
sight. This became the basis of a new brand ideal for Downy,
far more inspirational than anything in its fifty-one-year history.

It's interesting to note that Downy's ideal was directly inspired by consumer interactions, versus Red Bull, for example,
where the ideal flows more from the vision and personality of

ideals are born in many different ways, which we experience in the deep dives later in the book.

This Downy ideal led to a "feel more" positioning that centered Downy in the ideals field of eliciting joy, which in turn sparked innovative new product formulations, scents, packaging, and consumer communication. One of the most dramatic illustrations took place in Latin America, where the Downy team was working with P&G's regional and country teams on cues for fragrances, messaging, and packaging with special appeal in those markets. Joining low-income mothers to spend a day with them as they shopped, took care of their children, and did household chores, including hand-washing clothes, the team saw how access to water was one of the biggest problems for these women.

Obvious? Neither P&G nor any of the competition had addressed the problem, despite the huge amount of money that the millions of low-income households in developing countries spend on laundry products.

Inspired by their brand ideal, the Downy team wondered if they could make low-income Latin American women's lives easier while delivering on the potential to provide a more re-creative, senses-renewing experience. They asked P&G scientists if they could invent a formulation for Downy that required less rinsing. The resulting low-rinse version of Downy—simply called Downy Single Rinse—became a breakthrough product not only in Latin American countries but in low-income markets around the world. It evoked moving testimonials from low-income women in developing countries about the positive difference it made in their lives. It added extra impetus to the Downy team's efforts, as well as helped to motivate P&G employees in general.

The sum total of all this went straight to the bottom line.

In market share performance, Downy became P&G's fastest-growing brand worldwide for three years in a row.

Enabling Connection

Forging connections—between a brand's customers, between customers and their community, and even between different communities around the world—is important. Just look at the value Facebook has created by focusing 100 percent of its business model on connecting people. Some key concepts among businesses with brand ideals in this field are "connect," "listen," "reach," and "community."

One of the best examples of enabling connection is Natura, the fast-growing Brazilian cosmetics and personal care products company. Founded in 1969 in São Paulo, Natura is approaching $3 billion in sales, mostly in Brazil. It has a direct-to-customer sales force of more than a million people, using an Avon-type business model in the service of an ideal of helping people to live in greater harmony with themselves, others, and the world.

Natura has always been about well-being and strengthening relationships. The company itself articulates its brand ideal as "well-being and being well" (*"bem estar bem"* in Portuguese). Just five years after starting the business in 1969, founder Antônio Luiz da Cunha Seabra abandoned going through retailers so he could build consumer relationships one-on-one through his largely female sales associates. Rodolfo Guttilla, an executive director at Natura, sums up his company's ideal rather philosophically: "Well-being is about a harmonious relationship with oneself. But it is also about having empathetic, successful, and gratifying relationships with others and nature."

"Well-being, being well" is not just Natura's philosophy, it is their business strategy. In 2007, they launched a new label with environmental information, to help inform people about their consumption. Also that year they switched to organic alcohol in their perfumes, and in 2009 all soaps were "greened"—no more synthetic or animal ingredients.

Here, let me offer an observation that applies to making a brand ideal in any field the basis of competitive advantage. After companies like Stengel 50 brands Natura, Seventh Generation, and Method showed the appeal of "green" products, larger established players launched competing brands and set out to gain market share. They had some initial success as the category attracted broader groups of consumers. But when the Great Recession hit, consumers abandoned the established players' new green lines, which were all priced at a premium, for cheaper traditional products. The growth of the "green" household products category suffered a big hit.

Here's the kicker. The businesses that consumers saw as authentically in tune with "green" brand ideals—Natura, Seventh Generation, and Method—kept growing. They kept gaining profitable market share, even as Clorox, for example, lost more than a third of its market share and distribution from 2009 to 2011 on its Greenworks brand. Meanwhile, Seventh Generation and Method grew their revenue in double digits; we'll see how Method drives continuous growth in the next chapter. The point is brand ideals enable the fastest-growing businesses to keep innovating through good and bad economic conditions.

Bringing a brand ideal authentically to life for customers is a big challenge. But the payoff is also big, as we'll often see throughout this book.

Inspiring Exploration

A brand ideal of inspiring people to explore and experience the world around them helps customers learn, gives them powerful tools, and invites them to reinvent themselves and their world. Apple produces tools for creative exploration and self-expression. Google exists to provide safe and easy access to information by helping users navigate the Web, sample and acquire books and other media, or just get directions, to name only a few of its steadily increasing number of services. Amazon.com has become the signature exploratory shopping medium of our time.

In chapter 5, we'll take a deep dive at Discovery Channel and the other cable channels in the Discovery Communications portfolio. In different ways, they are all about satisfying curiosity about the mysteries of the world.

French luxury goods maker Louis Vuitton is another classic example of a brand that embodies exploration. For more than 150 years, Louis Vuitton has existed to accentuate people's journey through life. Back in 1812 in Jura, France, Louis Vuitton lived this ideal early in his life, well before he began selling his trianon canvas trunks. When Louis was old enough to travel, he made a 400-kilometer journey to Paris by foot to begin his career as an apprentice luggage maker. Now, 200 years later, the brand begun by a young apprentice still inspires exploration as an $8 billion brand. Its famous stores are travel destinations of their own: tourists represent the dominant share of sales in the flagship store on Paris's Champs-Élysées. And beyond its stores, everything the brand does is about accentuating, celebrating, and romancing journeys. One of my favorite advertising campaigns is Louis Vuitton's appropriately named "Core Values" campaign, which vividly brings to life Louis Vuitton's ideal. The campaign features amazing people—like Bono, Mikhail Gorbachev, and Catherine Deneuve—on their journeys through life, photographed by Annie Leibovitz. One recent ad featured Angelina Jolie in Cambodia, with the caption "A single journey can change the course of a life. Cambodia, May 2011." Angelina Jolie has traveled to Cambodia numerous times for humanitarian reasons and has an adopted son from the country.

Evoking Pride

Building confidence, supporting self-expression, and inspiring passion are hallmarks of brands helping to develop a personal or communal sense of pride. Target, a consistently excellent company that dropped just below the top 50 in the Stengel Study because of the impact of the recession, provides a good example. Target's brand ideal is "to help customers express themselves for less," and the key is self-expression. What makes Target's "Expect more, pay less" value proposition powerful isn't simply the appeal of spending less money—it's that Target's combination of beautifully designed, high-quality products and discount prices allows shoppers to express themselves by buying goods that reflect who they are and not just what they can afford. The ability to express oneself leads to a strengthened sense of identity, and pride in that identity.

Within the Stengel 50, Hermès, L'Occitane, Mercedes-Benz, Snow Beer, Calvin Klein, and Hennessy all evoke pride in a sense of personal accomplishment, security, and confidence across the whole spectrum of price points.

Few brands are stronger at evoking pride than Jack Daniel's, and the clear understanding of this from successive generations of leadership at Jack Daniel's has guided it to a dominant leadership position. We'll learn more about Jack Daniel's in chapter 4.

Impacting Society

Brands that impact society address people's desire to live, work, and play in more effective, efficient, harmonious, and sustainable ways. They generally emphasize a broad societal impact in their appeals to customers and end consumers. These brands overcome challenges, redefine approaches, or are revolutionary in their categories. They are about making systems function better, whether it's the system of the individual human body with fresh, natural food (Stonyfield Farm, Innocent, and Chipotle), business and technology systems (Accenture and IBM), or our interface with the environment (Method, Seventh Generation, and Petrobras).

I don't want to leave Petrobras, the Brazilian energy giant that is the Southern Hemisphere's biggest company, stuck in those parentheses. Think an oil and gas company can't really operate according to an environmentally conscious brand ideal? BP notoriously marketed itself as going "beyond petroleum," only to see investigative reporters raise troubling questions about its safety and environmental practices after lethal, costly disasters at its Texas refinery, ongoing problems on its Alaska pipeline, and the huge 2010 oil spill at one of its exploratory wells in the Gulf of Mexico. Many of these news media accounts looked beyond BP to the poor safety and environmental record of the energy industry as a whole.

But Petrobras's brand ideal, "To support the sustainable development of Brazil and every country it operates in," is not an empty promise. The Global Reporting Initiative, the Reputation Institute, and the Dow Jones Sustainability Index, among other third-party measures, consistently rank Petrobras at the top of the energy industry for walking the walk, as well as talking the talk, on environmental impact and sustainability.

Dove's brand ideal is "to celebrate every woman's unique beauty." Dove aims to go beyond individual consumers and to help bring about an evolution in how society as a whole thinks about beauty, such that each individual can then be more comfortable in his or her skin. Method's brand ideal, as we will see in the next chapter, is "to be a catalyst in a happy, healthy home revolution." That ideal isn't only about how individual consumers feel about their products; it's about improving the whole category of cleaning products and changing how people clean their homes.

Leaders can use these five areas of fundamental human values to evaluate whether their own brand ideal is clear and strong enough, and aligned well enough with their business's core capabilities, to power significant growth. I have used these five ideals areas in dozens of consulting engagements and have found they always lead to productive and mind-opening discussion and action in elevating each brand's ideal.

STENGEL STUDY FINDING 3. THE HIGHEST GROWTH BUSINESSES ARE RUN BY BUSINESS ARTISTS, LEADERS WHOSE PRIMARY MEDIUM IS BRAND IDEALS.

There are countless ways to grow your business by centering it around an ideal. If what I'm saying about ideals seems too idealistic to be useful in business, take another gander at the Stengel Study top 50. As you look at these high-performing, high-growth businesses, consider this: the one sure mistake you can make is failing to aim high. If you are not ambitious enough to want to make a big positive difference in people's lives, you won't make a big positive difference in your business's bottom line either.

Sure, results can be juiced for a few quarters, but over the long term you need something more substantial to rely on and build your business. And there's nothing more substantial and powerful in this world than an ideal. For good or ill, ideals move millions of people at a time, and the actions of those people move mountains, politics, war and peace, art, technology, science—and markets! The most powerful and profitable tools in business are ideals—ideas for improving people's lives that speak directly to their instincts, emotions, hopes, dreams, and values.

The leaders running the world's fastest-growing businesses never forget that. That's the third major finding of the Stengel Study. The fastest-growing businesses in the world have a leader whose relationship to the business is not primarily that of an operator, no matter how savvy, but an artist whose primary medium is an ideal.

The business artists in the Stengel Study top 50 include the late Apple co-founder Steve Jobs; new Diesel CEO Daniela Riccardi; Discovery Communications founder and chairman John Hendricks; FedEx founder, CEO, and chairman Frederick Smith; Google co-founders Sergey Brin and Larry Page; Ernst Tanner, CEO and chairman of Swiss premium chocolate Lindt & Sprüngli; Method co-founders Eric Ryan and Adam Lowry; Red Bull co-founder and CEO Dietrich Mateschitz; Starbucks founder, CEO, and chairman Howard Schultz; and Zappos CEO Tony Hsieh.

Ernst Tanner has ensured that Stengel 50 brand Lindt fulfills its ideal of providing joy through small luxuries by orchestrating the activities of Lindt's *Maîtres Chocolatiers* (master chocolate makers). Lindt is one of the oldest Swiss brands. Created and manufactured thanks to a special process called "conching," developed by Rodolphe Lindt in 1879, Lindt was the first melting chocolate in the world. CEO Tanner attributes Lindt's steady growth to preserving Lindt's more than 165-year-long tradition of quality while innovating in new products, such as the Excellence chocolate bars with a high cocoa content, that Lindt introduced and popularized in the late 1980s.

Lindt's innovation also extends to its efforts to support environmental sustainability and the quality of life of indigenous cocoa farmers, such as buying all of its consumer cocoa beans at a premium through a local partnership in Ghana. This gives the *Maîtres Chocolatiers* the best possible ingredients to work with, and it gives consumers the best possible brand experience, including the knowledge that what went into the package was harvested responsibly. Thanks in large part to Tanner's combination of business and brand leadership, Lindt & Sprüngli's sales revenue has more than tripled since he became CEO of the company in 1993.

Bernard Arnault, CEO and chairman of French luxury conglomerate LVMH, has said, "Star brands only stem from an artistic and creative mind," and he insists that every one of LVMH's businesses must have an operator and an artist. I'd say that's a good leadership model for any business. Sometimes one person can fill both roles, as Dietrich Mateschitz does at Red Bull, but not often. Effective leaders must understand whether their strengths are those of the business operator or the business artist, and then find and empower a colleague who can fill the other role. Many observers of Apple in the late 2000s noted the partnership of CEO Steve Jobs, indisputably its business artist, and COO Tim Cook in running the enterprise. It will be fascinating to see how Cook evolves as Apple's CEO: Will he primarily be an operator? Or will he shift to more of an artist?

Today's world, again, is seeing the convergence of business leadership and brand leadership. In a global economy of excess supply and insufficient demand in every sector, it is not enough to have a product or service that plays a functionally useful role in customers' lives. That's table stakes and nothing more. The business case for ideals is about playing a role in the lives of both customers and employees at a much more important level than the competition does. It's about connecting with people holistically: rationally and emotionally, left brain and right brain. And that requires brand leadership at the highest levels of the business.

When I look back at the greatest business leaders of the

past, people such as William Cooper Procter (grandson of one of P&G's founders) and James Gamble, Bill Hewlett, and Dave Packard, I see amazing similarities with today's most effective business leaders. William Cooper Procter envisioned the way people come together in a business in almost spiritual terms. As I've already observed, Hewlett and Packard never used the word *brand,* but they were both consummate brand and business artists whose ideal of making a contribution to society through technology was an essential element of their success. In chapter 11, we'll take a look at how HP's current leaders are trying to seize that same ideal. IBM has been devoted to making business and technology systems work better since its beginnings in 1911. IBM's founder, Thomas Watson Sr., and his son and successor, Thomas Watson Jr., also exemplify the central lesson of this book: that a business leader's greatest leverage lies in rallying employees and customers alike to an ideal of improving people's lives. Later in the book, we'll also look at how IBM has refreshed its brand ideal as a key to renewed growth.

To guide category-leading growth, business artists and their organizations continually ask four questions:

- How well do we understand the people who are most important to our future?
- What do we and our brand stand for?
- What do we want to stand for?
- How are we bringing the answers to these questions to life?

These are simple questions. The power comes in the tough job of answering them and executing against them. That brings us to the fourth and most important major finding of the Stengel Study.

Stengel Study Finding 4. Business artists excel in similar practices that constitute an operating system for generating and sustaining high growth.

The Stengel 50 and their leaders have widely varying styles, from freewheeling to buttoned-down. Yet they all excel at five basic activities, which underpin the approaches they take to their businesses. I find that similarity absolutely amazing, and believe that it is the most important finding of the Stengel Study, a critical new benchmark for business leadership. The business artists in the Stengel 50 excel at:

- **Discovering**, or rediscovering, a brand ideal in one of five fields of fundamental human values.
- **Building** the business culture around the ideal.
- **Communicating** the ideal internally and externally to engage employees and customers.
- **Delivering** a near-ideal customer experience.
- **Evaluating** business progress and people against the ideal.

In its turnaround and growth in the 2000s, P&G concentrated with increasing insight and rigor on the same five activities. Based on these experiences, the Stengel Study, and my consulting, I am convinced that these five activities constitute an extraordinarily powerful business growth system.

To see what I mean, let's pay a deep-dive visit to fast-growing Method and observe how they work these five linked activities. Along the way, I'll also introduce you to a framework, the Ideal Tree, for building a similar growth system in your business.

3

The Ideal Tree Framework

A Method to Their Weirdness

I've found that the most effective way to convey and use the brand ideal framework is by visualizing it as a tree. I like the metaphor of the tree because businesses and their brands are living things. Much like a tree, they have roots that people do not see, they thrive with the right conditions, and they die without care, feeding, and freedom to grow.

I'm going to use the story of premium household cleaning products company Method to show how all the branches of the Ideal Tree come to life. But first let me give you some specifics on the way I will use this framework for the rest of the book, and how you can begin to think about it as a growth activity system for leveraging brand ideals in your own business.

FIVE MUST-DOS FOR LEVERAGING AN IDEAL: THE IDEAL TREE GROWTH SYSTEM

The root structure of the Ideal Tree has two elements: the beliefs of the people inside the business, which often draw on the heritage of the brand, and the values the business shares with customers and end users. Their dynamic interaction anchors and supports the base of the tree: the business's ideal.

The ideal—the higher-order benefit the business gives to the world—is rooted in its heritage, which begins with the business's initial reason for being, its founding vision for actively improving the quality of people's lives, and is continuously added to over time. Each generation of people inside the business, especially each generation of leadership, contributes its own beliefs, aspirations, and values to this heritage.

"Come off it, Stengel," I can hear some people saying. "Business isn't really about all this touchy-feely belief stuff. You see an opportunity and you jump on it with all fours and throttle it and break its neck. That's what business is about."

Businessperson as hunter. Sure. Just bag the kill, seal the deal, and move on.

All the evidence I know paints a different picture. The beliefs of a business's founders and people, especially their subsequent leaders, can be blinders that let them see only limited opportunities. Or those beliefs can be electron microscopes, night vision glasses, and telescopes that enable them to see the entire spectrum of a market's opportunities. You can bag a lot more game that way.

Above all, this means that brand ideals have to be genuine expressions of what you believe and who you and your people are as a business—you'll see this reflected throughout the Stengel 50. Genuine core beliefs and values aren't things you can pick up and discard without missing a beat. Beliefs and values are not tools; they shape your ability to use your tools.

That's why, at the very bottom of the tree, it says, "The people the brand serves: Be choiceful. Be sure the group is large enough to meet your goals." Win or lose, how big is your business's potential addressable market? If you're looking for a quick kill on a target of opportunity, that's one thing. If you're looking for big headroom in your market opportunities, you need to work in an area that is fundamentally important to people. That's where your brand and business have the chance to grow the most. Again, you can test that by assessing whether your ideal is rooted in one of the five fields of fundamental human values: eliciting joy, enabling connection, inspiring exploration, evoking pride, and impacting society.

THE IDEAL TREE

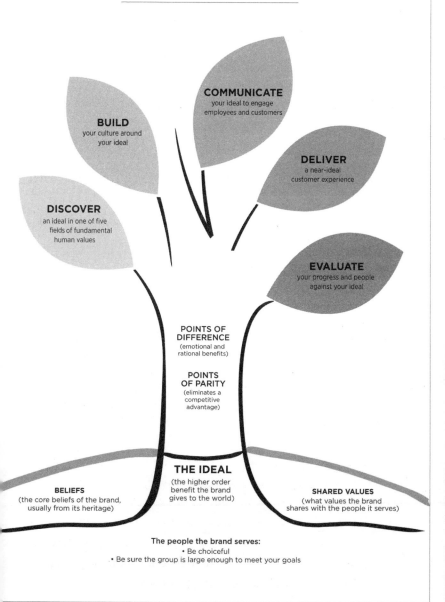

COMMUNICATE
your ideal to engage
employees and customers

BUILD
your culture around
your ideal

DELIVER
a near-ideal
customer experience

DISCOVER
an ideal in one of five
fields of fundamental
human values

EVALUATE
your progress and people
against your ideal

**POINTS OF
DIFFERENCE**
(emotional and
rational benefits)

**POINTS
OF PARITY**
(eliminates a
competitive
advantage)

THE IDEAL
(the higher order
benefit the brand
gives to the world)

BELIEFS
(the core beliefs of the brand,
usually from its heritage)

SHARED VALUES
(what values the brand
shares with the people it serves)

The people the brand serves:
• Be choiceful
• Be sure the group is large enough to meet your goals

■ ■ ■

The trunk of the tree illustrates the main ways a business achieves competitive advantage, its essential points of difference from its rivals. For Google, to take one example from the Stengel 50, it's the speed and quality of its search engine. Google never wants to lose this competitive advantage. It innovates against it and measures it rigorously.

The trunk also illustrates where a business can't fall below the competition, the points of parity that are the price of entry into a category, or that neutralize a competitor's advantage. For a time in the 1990s, P&G's Pampers diapers were deficient in fit, comfort, and aesthetics compared to Kimberly-Clark's Huggies. Pampers could not grow until it achieved parity in those areas. It is important for a leader to choose not only where to build competitive advantage (points of difference) but also where it is important to have competitive equality (points of parity).

The five main branches of the tree are the seed-producing and fruit-bearing parts of a business. As I explained at the end of the last chapter, this growth activity system of five must-dos for leveraging an ideal guides a business to:

- **Discover** an ideal in one of five fields of fundamental human values.
- **Build** your culture around your ideal.
- **Communicate** your ideal to engage employees and customers.
- **Deliver** a near-ideal customer experience.
- **Evaluate** your progress and people against your ideal.

The organic quality of the Ideal Tree goes beyond metaphor. It implicitly identifies all the people who are important to the future of a business and their relationships. Its roots, trunk, branches, and leaves capture the dynamic flow of all the elements that must work in harmony for a business to flourish, both those that are internal to a business (and hence almost always invisible to customers) and those that are or become external, such as communication strategies, products, and services.

Finally, the Ideal Tree graphically situates the business in a market ecosystem of customers, employees, and competitors.

"Well now," I can hear you saying, "that's very elegant, but how does it play out in the real world?"

I think you'll find the saga of Method, a self-styled David among Goliaths, an enlightening and inspirational story that brings the tree metaphor to life.

METHOD: KEEPING IT WEIRD

Since its brash appearance on the scene with the 2001 launch of its first products, a line of surface cleaners, San Francisco–based Method has achieved annual double-digit sales growth and been a game-changing innovator in a mature and highly competitive category. Method is small compared with giants such as P&G, Unilever, Clorox, and Reckitt Benckiser, but thanks to "green" products that work as well as or better than traditional ones, Method has achieved a rate of growth that has had an outsized impact on the entire household cleaner industry.

Method got on my radar screen in 2003 when I joined the P&G team devoted to the Target account at one of its regular meetings, at Target's headquarters in Minneapolis, with then chief marketing officer Michael Francis and his team. Michael and I often compared notes and served as sounding boards for each other, and on this occasion we walked through a Minneapolis Target together. As we passed by a display of Method's liquid hand soap, I asked Michael how it was doing for them.

Method was so new that I thought it was one of Target's private-label brands.

Michael said it was doing great. He told me how Method co-founders Eric Ryan and Adam Lowry cold-called him not just to pitch a new product but to fill him in on Method's unique philosophy. They said Target was their first choice as a national partner in the consumer retail world. Not only that, they revealed that they had also cold-called Karim Rashid, a world-renowned industrial designer with a host of A-list clients, and persuaded him to design the container for their liquid dish soap on a revenue-sharing basis, since they could not afford to pay him any fee at all, much less what he normally charged. The idea was to give the packaging a design as unique as the product itself, a natural plant-derived formulation that outperformed conventional liquid soaps in the total consumer experience.

"Some *cojones,* eh?" Michael asked me, and I definitely agreed. Impressed by the intensity of the Method co-founders' belief in the need and opportunity for "green that really cleans," something that Michael felt was right on trend, as well as their entrepreneurial zeal and their marketing flair, Michael's team agreed to meet them.

Eric and Adam knew they had to cover every possible objection. They arrived carrying not only Karim Rashid's prototype dish-soap bottle, but also the impressive, if so-far-only-regional sales results Method was having in California and neighboring states. They positioned both the design and the sales numbers in a compelling vision of their brand ideal. Target's buyers liked what they saw, and that, as Michael said to me, "was the beginning of a beautiful relationship."

These Method guys must be something special, I thought. When I got back to my office in Cincinnati, I alerted P&G's

mergers and acquisitions department to the potential of this fast-growing start-up. Ultimately P&G directed its M&A toward larger brands primarily in the beauty and grooming category. But from that time on I've continued to follow Method, especially because Eric and Adam share the conviction that ideals are the most important factor in business success. I've been fascinated to learn how they seized the power of ideals from the time they first began talking about starting Method.

Method's mantra is "Keep it weird." When you meet the Method folks, weirdness starts with the crazy titles on their business cards. For example, co-founder Eric Ryan, now the chief brand architect, is known as "Party Starter." Matthew Loyd, the vice president of brand experience, is "Brand Poobah." And Michele Hall, the general manager for fabric care, is "Laundress." Both tongue-in-cheek and serious, the job descriptions exemplify how Method approaches the hard work of building a great company with informality and a sense of fun, which are essential ingredients for the intense collaboration required to build a dynamic enterprise.

But don't mistake the forest for the trees. Many observers see the weirdness at Method, Zappos, Innocent, and some other brash, fast-growing young businesses and say to themselves, "That's not who we are. We can't be that," or "Oh. Just be deliberately weird, and that will attract customers."

Yes and no, on both counts. The thing to emulate is not the specific weirdness of a company such as Method, but what lies at the heart of its behavior. I can absolutely guarantee that you will not have enduring success if your people can't enjoy their interactions. So don't try to imitate the way Method encourages a sense of fun, if that's not true to who you are. But don't let that stop you from encouraging a sense of fun in your own way. Without it, your business won't hit the heights.

MUST-DO NUMBER 1:
DISCOVERING THE METHOD IDEAL

The first branch of the Ideal Tree is discovering your brand ideal in one of five areas of fundamental human values. Developing this branch actually means working at the base of the tree, in the link between your beliefs and the fundamental values of your customers or prospective customers.

Eric Ryan and Adam Lowry took the first step toward founding Method when faced with the task of cleaning the San Francisco Bay Area house they shared with three friends.

The house was as filthy as five young men not far removed from college and fraternity life could make it. But it wasn't only the dirt and mess that made the task unpleasant. It was also the cleaning products with harsh toxic ingredients that required wearing rubber gloves to use them safely and couldn't be left open if small children or pets were around. Eric, who worked in consumer packaged goods marketing, and Adam, who worked on environmental science issues for the Carnegie Institution, wished they had effective cleaning products that weren't poisonous.

When they went to the local supermarket to see if such things existed, they found shelves full of products from both long-established brands and new eco-conscious ones. Both groups, says Eric, had their "dirty little secrets." The established brands did a good job of cleaning up dirt and grime but were "full of toxic stuff that when used ultimately wind up on our bodies, in our bloodstreams, and in the environment." The problem with the eco-conscious products was that they didn't clean well. They learned that "If it's green, it doesn't clean" was a common joke among both manufacturers and retailers.

It should come as no surprise that a pair of twentysomething guys weren't exactly excited about cleaning. In fact, they still aren't. But they got and stayed jazzed about creating better cleaning products, and about people having a great experience using them. They felt that this "bigger idea" might be the basis for a philosophy that would be the anchor for future employees as well as the consumers they would serve.

When Eric and Adam started their business, they were very clear that their objective wasn't to create a product or service but to bring to life a transformational ideal. They wanted to articulate an ideal that people could rally around. "As human beings," says Eric, "we all want to be part of something bigger than who we are and what we are. When you articulate an ideal and create a cause, it gives people, including myself, the ability to do so much more. You're so much more excited to jump out of bed and go to work when you're doing something that improves people's lives. It's just so much more enjoyable and you produce so much more, because you're part of something bigger. Everyone—founders, employees, partners we work with, consumers—finds it motivating that there's this common ideal and common mission."

What Eric and Adam are saying about an ideal motivating higher performance is not a rote recitation of the wooden statements one frequently hears about mission and values. It is the individual expression of how Method's ideal enables people to bring all of themselves to work every day, all of their individual passion and creativity and energy. For Eric that means "bringing my passion for design into the context of the business," and for Adam it's "my passion for environmentalism."

Eric and Adam's ideal is a bold one: to be a catalyst in a happy, healthy home revolution that improves human health. It falls squarely into the ideals field of impacting society, with overlap in the area of eliciting joy by turning a dreaded chore into something that is actually pleasant.

The medium for the ideal of a happy, healthy home revolution is "people against dirty," a movement of revolutionaries that brings together those working inside the business with consumers who become fervent advocates for Method and its products. This gives Method's people a common focus for their actions and the ability to do things the competition can't or won't.

A revolution by definition involves radical change. As a newcomer in the home-cleaning-products category, Method had to distinguish itself from the dominant players in the industry. Even with unlimited resources, it could not differentiate itself by imitating the big market-share holders such as P&G, Clorox, and Unilever.

Imitation was impossible given the very limited resources Eric and Adam began with. They used up their savings, maxed out their credit cards, and solicited investments from family members before finally securing a first round of private equity funding.

Besides, although they had lofty financial goals—they unabashedly started with the aim of building a billion-dollar business—Eric and Adam did not want Method to become just another big company. They set their sights instead on creating premium products that could expand into the mass market. Their goal was not to dominate by volume but to move the market by example, and to eventually stimulate and build the entire category for premium green cleaning products that really do clean.

At first they were working pretty much by themselves, mixing up cleaning formulations in beer pitchers with some help from a few formulation experts. Eric and Adam kept pursuing a product with unique market attributes, one that was made of completely safe ingredients derived from natural plant sources and that worked as well as, or better than, conventional cleaners. Their breakthrough success was a line of surface cleaners. They managed to get it into a small number of upscale stores in the Bay Area and after that into regional grocery chains serving California and other western states. Success with these local and regional retailers enabled Eric and Adam to begin expanding Method's product line to include dish soaps and other cleaners. But they wanted to leapfrog to national distribution in launching these new products.

That's when they cold-called first Karim Rashid and then Michael Francis, as we've seen. The Target ideal, summed up in the slogan "Expect more, pay less" and exemplified by partnerships with famous designers such as Michael Graves and Missoni, was indeed a perfect fit for Method and its Karim Rashid–designed bottle. Target gave Method a trial in ninety Target stores around the country, and both Target and Method never looked back.

Method's maverick behavior became part of the company's MO as it has grown. Method's Joshua Handy, the senior director of industrial design (also known as "Disrupter"), says that everyone comes to the company because of either its environmental mission or its social mission. Together, Method's people strive to change the conversation with disruptive products in more and more household cleaning and personal care categories.

"Disruptive innovation is the goal we strive for on our best days. Big companies talk about economies of scale. We want to make the category about something else, so that all the money big companies spend is wasted."

Method connects its ideal with the willingness to do what the competition can't or won't through a very flat organization. One example of how Method's ideal permeates the whole business is its biodiesel truck fleet. More than 70 percent of Method's products in North America are shipped via biodiesel, more than any other company, with the goal of getting to 100 percent.

Nobody at the top said, "Hey, we should do this." It started with the operations team seeing the opportunity and taking initiative to act on it. The move to biodiesel trucks didn't hit Eric Ryan's radar until the operations team asked Ryan's group to design some graphics for the trucks, because they also had the good idea that they should use the side of the trucks to tell the biodiesel story. "Sweet," Eric replied. "Operations has trucks rolling with biodiesel, and on top of that they're already writing a great marketing story."

Eric Ryan shares this story, along with the first emergency phone call Method received from a consumer, when speaking to groups of new employees. "My cell phone number was on the product packaging and that first call came from a frantic mom whose son just drank our bathroom cleaner. She had poison control on the other line and was trying to find out what was in the cleaner. It was so great to be able to say, 'Relax. There's nothing in there that will do harm. Just have your son drink a glass full of water.' Stories like these are why 'People against dirty' is so powerful with both consumers and employees."

Hearing people talk about a soap company with words like *love* and *amazing experience* can only occur when a business lives its ideal on a daily basis, starting with its own organizational culture.

MUST-DO NUMBER 2:
BUILDING METHOD'S CULTURE AROUND ITS IDEAL

Building an organizational culture that aligns with your ideal is must-do number 2 for leveraging the power of ideals.

The heart of organizational culture is how you deal with human resources issues. If you don't hire, train, interact with, manage, promote, and reward your people based on your ideal, you will never bring the ideal to life for customers. Eric Ryan believes that "one bad hire is toxic. If you want to grow, it all starts with who you bring in to make part of your team. And the fastest way to screw things up is to bring in the wrong people. That's why we take hiring so seriously here."

Ideal-based businesses understand that organizational culture makes or breaks an enterprise. Of course, hundreds of books and thousands of consultants emphasize the importance of organizational culture, and business leaders commonly agree that getting the culture right is the hardest part of their job. What ideal-based businesses know that others don't is that getting it right comes from following their ideals. If Method was going to grow, it had to brand itself from the inside out— to "market ourselves as ourselves."

I have been part of, and known, businesses that are terrific recruiters. But in all my experience, Method sets a new standard. The percentage of time Method's senior team spends on recruiting and hiring is staggering. That's a competitive advantage. Most senior leaders spend too little time on recruiting and hiring and delegate the task too far down the management ladder. Nothing is more crucial to fulfilling a business's ideal than its people.

When a position has to be filled, someone is designated as the hiring manager. The hiring manager then builds a cross-functional interview team of seven to ten people. Every candidate thus has seven to ten interviews with people all across the business who see the candidate individually and as a group, not just with one or two people in the department with the job opening. After these multiple interviews, a short list of one to three candidates comes back for another interview, in which they are given a homework assignment to address a current Method business challenge from both strategic and tactical perspectives. In addition, each candidate must answer the question "How will you help keep Method weird?" when he or she returns the following week. The ultimate decision on which person to bring on board depends fifty-fifty on skill set and culture fit.

The homework assignment is Method's way of fast prototyping how people think and work, and what the chemistry with them would be in an actual work situation. Everything Method does, whether in product development, retail, marketing, operations, or brand experience, is accomplished through fast prototyping. "Design thinking" is the business buzzword for this intense prototyping, based on frequent consumer interaction and deep consumer understanding, and Method has studied well-known practitioners of design thinking such as award-winning design firms IDEO and Apple.

My experience at P&G, and as a consultant and researcher, is that ideal-driven businesses are exceptionally good at fast prototyping or design thinking. The more an ideal is built into the structure of an organization and woven into the fabric of its people's interactions, the easier it is to engage in collaborative innovation and the faster you can push the process.

The aim of the homework assignment for job candidates is to find people who can work collaboratively, within and across functions, in this system. So when the candidate presents to the whole interview team, it's about a real business issue that engenders a fast-paced and challenging dialogue. It's as if the candidate is already part of Method.

The first test, of course, is watching how a candidate responds to being asked to do a homework assignment. People are naturally enthusiastic when interviewing for a job, but the homework assignment is a good quick test of their readiness to join the Method culture. One CEO candidate (yes, *everyone* runs through Method's gauntlet) pushed back: "Why do I have to do this?" That was an immediate red flag.

During the forty-five minutes in front of the interview team, candidates can present however they want. PowerPoint, inter-pretive dance—the team simply wants to know how candidates approach solving a problem on their own and with others.

The homework assignment requires candidates to go deep into a category and assess Method's current position, or lack of position, and the competitive landscape. They have to find the opportunity for revolution—for Method's ideal of catalyz-ing a happy, healthy home revolution—and show what they would do with the business if they came to Method. That's an intense experience. But the third question—how the candidate will keep Method weird—is often the clincher. People have to show how much they're willing to open up and reveal them-selves.

So much is learned about people from these assignments. They're a much better indicator of success than the interviews. Real talent can't hide in a homework assignment, and some-one who only looks good on paper or just talks well can't hide that either. Sometimes the worst candidates look the best in traditional interviews, Method believes, because they've inter-viewed so many times.

The hiring team's interaction with the candidates during their presentations makes the hiring decision obvious. So when an offer is made, there is no anxiety as to whether the right choice was made. There are mistakes, but the success rate is 95 percent since Method started using this process.

It raises the bar for the designated hiring managers, but it also helps them clear that higher bar by supporting the time- and energy-intensive interview process. If a job candidate screws up a homework assignment, a hiring manager—usually one who hasn't served as hiring manager before—sometimes apologizes for wasting the time of people such as Eric Ryan. But Ryan's reaction is, "Why? I tell the hiring manager, 'That was great. We just dodged a bullet. That person looked wonderful in the interviews.' We save money by not hiring the wrong person. And we also save money on starting salary, if there are two finalists with varying experience and the homework assignment shows the person with less experience has more talent. Always bet on talent. Plus we get a lot of free consulting."

The best candidates see Method's lengthy hiring process not as a burdensome obstacle course but as a chance to make sure they've found the right place to work. Fabric care manager Michele "Laundress" Hall had only been at Method two years when she shared with me her perspective as both a fairly recent hire and a member of interview teams, noting that "keeping Method weird is really about bringing your authentic self to work every day."

Practicing a weird "Methodology" in a start-up with only a handful of employees is one thing. It's quite another sustaining it as the business grows and adds dozens of staff. CFO Andrea Freedman, "Chief Financial Person Against Dirty," helped establish some of Method's recruiting practices and cultural values and calls herself "the mother of our people and environment program," Method's moniker for HR. She recalls, "When Method had about forty employees we started to get feedback that they wished we would do more communicating about career development and company strategy. Suddenly it struck us that we needed an HR department. But we bristled at that, because HR typically makes people color between the lines, and that's not our way of doing things."

So the question became, "Can we 'Methodize' HR?" Andrea and others interviewed people at places with reputations for good culture, including Apple, Pixar, and Innocent. Method called HR the "people and environment program," borrowing from Innocent, the U.K.-based healthful food and beverage company. It was too good a fit with their ideal for Method not to use it.

The number one thing learned from these conversations was to continue focusing on recruiting the best possible people for Method. Nail that, and just about everything else would take care of itself.

Recruiting is indeed the magic formula. It's how you get people you can bet the business on. That and articulating your values clearly, so that when people come on board they're plugged into your values as soon as they join. Make people part of the conversation from day one, and make sure it's a two-way conversation where you listen well.

It seems like a no-brainer. But it's something most organizations struggle with, especially as they scale. It was easier, says Andrea, when Method was small and could communicate by simply all "sitting in the same room and yelling across at each other."

Method also builds its culture through a commitment to transparency, beginning with publishing product ingredients "down to a minute level" on the company's website. There is, additionally, a great deal of information shared with employees about the financial health of the company and what the leadership team is thinking. The level of financial transparency can be anxiety-inducing, says Josh Handy, so "we do a lot of work with people about how to think about what we're telling them, so that they don't get too worried about the financials of a business that has a lot of ups and downs."

Transparency about business issues extends to Method's open-plan office layouts, with the founders and senior leadership team sitting mixed in with everyone else. The walls are covered with sketches, mock-ups, project timelines, rough copy, slogans, and visuals of all sorts—more fast prototyping. In Josh's words, "Getting things visible and explicit allows different sorts of conversations to happen more quickly than in a formalized organization. So there's a collaborative transparency in developing projects."

The transparency at Method leads to a directness, a forthrightness of critique, that can shock newcomers. People new to Method, especially those coming from more sedate organizations, "aren't used to that sort of directness at that sort of speed," says Josh Handy, punching his fists together for emphasis. "I always tell new people that it's fast and bumpy here. It's tough to get hired at Method, and people are elated when they start. The first days are amazing, they're having a great time. But about six weeks in, they hit their low point. I'll see them come out of the bathrooms with their eyes red from crying, or I'll hear them on the phone with their friends hissing, 'What the hell did I do coming here?'"

Two things help new hires find their feet in the Method culture. First, Josh notes, "Because our intensive hiring process means there almost always really is a good fit for the new people, they usually figure out that it's up to them. They crawl out of the hole and they get up to speed with everybody else. We push people really hard to think for themselves and put themselves into the organization. Once they make that transition, they're fine."

Second, Method's leaders decided that they needed to put as much energy into onboarding new employees as they did into hiring them. Eric Ryan says, "We were so focused on hiring the right people, yet when they started we just threw them into the pool. A few weeks in, people who came from more traditional organizations were experiencing culture shock and becoming 'corporate homesick.' We realized we had to give people some support as they adjusted to working here." During 2011 Method began a comprehensive program for new hires, which starts with a welcome package delivered to their home and continues with a sixty-day personalized plan. Eric sums up the lesson he and his colleagues learned: "Thoroughly screening for the right people doesn't mean they will instantly acclimate into a unique culture. You have to work onboarding just as hard."

MUST-DO NUMBER 3:
COMMUNICATING THE METHOD IDEAL

The third branch of the Ideal Tree, the third must-do for leveraging your ideal, is communicating it honestly and compellingly both inside and outside the business. The story of your brand ideal is the story of who you aspire to be as a business, and every part of the business must express this in a unified way that is true to those aspirations.

Everyone at Method talks a lot about storytelling, and especially important to them is a unified story about the ideal of a happy, healthy home revolution and its links to category innovation and consumer experience.

"Brand Poobah" Matthew Loyd emphasized how Method entered "a low-interest category that doesn't have a great narrative attached to it and injected a really inspiring conversation." Many companies talk the talk about having a dialogue with customers and consumers, but few really walk down that path. For Method to start and sustain an inspiring conversation with retail customers and consumers, it had to speak honestly, remain true to its ideal, and be open to learning from external feedback and criticism. It had to live its ideal of bringing employees and others together as equal members of "people against dirty."

One of the most powerful instances, according to Loyd, came from what he characterized as a mistake that provided "incredible learning." Method can't compete with the giants in advertising spending, and so it uses "earned media" rather than "paid media." In November 2009 it posted a video on YouTube and peopleagainstdirty.com called "Shiny Suds."

The video parodies a television ad a big competitor did for one of its products. Method's video has cute little soap bubbles say endearing things to a mom who's cheerfully cleaning her family's bathroom with a fake product called Shiny Suds. The cute soap bubbles sing about doing a "Shinetastic job." The next morning the mom calls out to her family that breakfast is almost ready and goes into the bathroom to take a shower.

Only the soap bubbles are still around. The cute little soap bubbles of the day before are now sniggering Peeping Toms who announce that they're the toxic chemical residue from the cleaner. They ogle the mom while she's showering and say things like "Use the loofah. Loofah! Loofah! Loofah!" (A loofah, for those not in the know, is a type of bath sponge.)

There was a closing text crawl saying, "You deserve to know what chemicals are in your cleaner. Support the House-hold Products Labeling Act." The last thing on the screen was Method's name and logo and the URL peopleagainstdirty.com superimposed on the shower curtain and the embarrassed mom behind it.

The video was an amazing success, scoring a million views in one week. And many comments had the tone Method was looking for: a little bit shocked, but intrigued and amused.

Method saw the video as an extension of one of its first "people against dirty" images, which had shown an attractive couple cleaning their house in the buff, because they didn't need to protect themselves from the cleaners with coveralls and rubber gloves. But without realizing it, Method had crossed a line with "Shiny Suds." Some consumers reacted negatively to the video's Peeping Tom motif.

Doing anything provocative results in some people loving it while others don't. As Matthew and the rest of the Method leadership carefully monitored reaction in the "people against dirty" community, they were glad to see that it was generally very positive, as they'd expected. What they didn't expect was the extent of the dissatisfaction, and distress, that the video evoked in a small minority of people.

Equally surprising, however, and validating the concept of the "people against dirty" community, was that those who were offended did not rage broadly against Method as a corporate monster. Instead, they sincerely asked, "Why? Why would you do this? Why would you make this choice?"

Matthew says, "They were so deeply invested in Method. That was really powerful for me, because it felt so different from what I experienced working at other companies, where the consumer would simply say, 'I'll never buy your stuff again.' Instead people called and emailed and asked sincere questions. They wanted an answer why."

Method recognized that it had blundered across an important line, and quickly pulled the video. It was too harsh and had too many unintended connotations. The video's intent was to lampoon the product claims of a rival company. There was nothing wrong with that. But don't lampoon the competition with a video that makes some people think you're leering at the innocent mom you're trying to attract to join your happy, healthy home revolution.

It was Method's brand ideal that enabled it to quickly take the right business action and pull the video. As Eric Ryan summed up the incident, "When we decided to pull the video it was a very fast and easy decision, because our brand should never do harm to anyone. This is where values are so important. They guide you in making the right decision."

I hope it doesn't sound like I'm piling on, because I'm an absolute fan of Method's conduct throughout the whole situation. It shows their entrepreneurial courage and creativity, and the strength of their ideal. Thanks to their ideal, they were able to walk through the situation with people and say, "We're in the process of learning. We try to be provocative. It's part of who we are and what we do. But we don't always get it right. Thank you for being patient and helping us to get it right."

That was the first time, Matthew says, that he really understood how deeply people felt about belonging to "people against dirty" and how much heart people had invested in Method. "That empowers us to start a revolution in the category, rather than just hitting numbers. That gives us the opportunity to incite something so much deeper."

Method continues to be edgy and provocative in its messaging, but it's learned to calibrate this to keep a naughty-but-nice tone that is consistent with its ideal. For example, when Method launched a new, highly concentrated laundry detergent in the first half of 2010, a review of prospective ad copy led Michele Hall to blurt out, "It's so frickin' concentrated!"

The immediate reaction of her colleagues, Matthew Loyd told me, was, "Hey, why can't we say that in the copy? Our mantra is to do what the competition can't or won't do. Our ideal doesn't speak to everyone. Most brands want to speak to everyone, but that can be a dangerous ambition. We ask, how can we speak uniquely to our community of 'people against dirty'?"

With the word *frickin'* Method got upset emails and phone calls, but more frequently heard from people who loved it. And a lot of new consumers joined the "people against dirty" community after being intrigued by Method's putting *frickin'* in its copy. Method's people were still debating whether it was the right thing to do when Jay Leno picked it up and riffed on it. That, says Matthew, "validated to us that we were doing the kind of work we should be doing." The positive media Method earned in this way included the most important medium of all, word of mouth, within the community of "people against dirty."

Method's strategy of communicating with consumers has a parallel in the way it converses with retail customers. Just as Method is not for all consumers, so vice president of sales—or "Chief of Retail Health"—George Shumny emphasizes that it is not for all retailers. The company is serious about positioning Method products at the premium end of the mass market and does not want to be everywhere. Here is how George tells a prospective retail customer a brand ideal story that, by the way, hits everything a savvy retailer looks for: "I'm going to tell you a story about a new brand that can bring you differentiation, sales growth in the category, margin enhancement and profitability in the category, and image enhancement for you as a retailer. This is a brand that brings environmental sustainability to the shelf, and brings premium to mass. Is that something you're interested in?"

The four pillars of this story have made Method attractive to many retailers, but they have to be willing to join Method in breaking time-honored rules of category retailing. George explains: "We ask retailers to do a lot of different things, and some retailers said it wasn't right for them. As a master lifestyle brand, Method cuts across categories. When you tell retailers you want them to shelve hand wash with home cleaners, that upsets the territorialism in retail and spins to a whole political area. Who at the retailer gets credit for the sale?

"It's a challenging conceptual sell. But when we stick to it, it's a growth trajectory. Target is still our number one partner. Without going into any of Target's direct competitors like Walmart, we've grown the brand enormously outside Target without taking sales growth from Target.

"Like we tell retailers, Method also doesn't cannibalize sales within their stores. I say, 'Method will raise your profitability in the category and do it in a way that sends a message to shoppers that you're in the premium business and the sustainability business. You won't lose anything.' And they don't. It's a win-win situation."

Shumny adds that problems arise only when Method wittingly or unwittingly veers from its ideal, when it breaks its own rulebook to play by the retailer's or the category's traditional rulebook. When Method is true to itself and doesn't chase velocity and numbers, it does better, according to Shumny.

He cites experience with Costco, whose consumer demographics and psychographics are very similar to Target's: college-educated women, household income around $100,000. Method figured it should be in Costco. The feeling was mutual.

But Costco's format is "item at a price," and Method struggled to make that fit with the "Method home" merchandising model, showing all their products across different categories together. They decided to try one product, the flagship handwash product, in a jumbo size. Method packaged it beautifully in a jumbo version of the iconic Method bottle. Costco loved it.

Costco had an idea of what it should sell for to meet their hurdle rates and velocity thresholds. It was an incredibly low price, but Method agreed. However, when Costco put it on the shelf, it didn't meet their hurdle and velocity thresholds. Their reaction was to reduce price even more. But that didn't work either.

Costco threw out one of Method's competitors to put its product in. But Costco needed Method to play the game the conventional way, and they couldn't do it. As Shumny notes, "It takes discipline and investment on both the retailer's and our part to stay true to the Method story and make it resonate for consumers. If it's just one product in the store, or the products are shelved in different sections of the store with competitors' products, the big idea starts to diminish.

"We have to be completely honest with retailers at every stage of the process. It's a shame we're not in Costco. But it's better not to be there than to be there and disappoint them, our other partners, and ultimately the consumer. I believe we will be in Costco to stay one day. But we need to figure out how to tell our story there."

When retailers hear Method's presentation, George observes, they uniformly say, "Wow, that's a great story. How are you going to tell that story to my shopper? What kind of advertising do you do?" They are also uniformly shocked when Method responds that it does almost no conventional advertising. Shumny tells the retailers that Method has four pillars for the consumer in the store—the surface design and beauty of the package; premium fragrance (no lemon, lime, orange, pine, or industrial scents); efficacy; and sustainability—and this is largely conveyed through in-store marketing and word of mouth.

Pushing these four levers equally is the consumer magic behind Method. When it makes decisions internally, it advocates for every initiative to deliver on each pillar.

Method stands out in the retail aisle, with all its products grouped together rather than spread out in different categories. How the products look and smell is immediately evident. Once consumers buy the product and use it, and see that it works well, then they realize another benefit: that Method is green. When people experience all four pillars, Shumny says, "then we get the loyalty and advocacy of 'people against dirty.'"

Method's distinctive voice comes through in innovative graphics and copy in magazine and newspaper inserts that tell stories about "people against dirty." For example, Method worked with the advertising agency TBWA to detox an entire house with its products, and then to capture the experience and its results in a memorable multipage booklet.

That voice was also on display, as we will see below, when Method needed to educate consumers about a product they had neither previously encountered nor asked for: a supercon-centrated totally green laundry detergent.

Must-Do Number 4:
How Method Delivers a Near-Ideal Experience

The fourth branch of the Ideal Tree is the customer experience. The more this experience brings the ideal to life, the more advocacy and loyalty a business creates among its consumers.

Project Lighthouse was the name for Method's launch of a new laundry detergent, an 8x ultraconcentrate. Method had already had some success (and triggered some copycat behavior by the laundry product giants, as noted below) with a 3x concentrated laundry detergent. But introducing its 8x ultraconcentrated product in January of 2010 was a chance for Method to revolutionize the category in a much more thoroughgoing way. Project Lighthouse based its work on Method's belief in using plant-based ingredients and being as sustainable as possible.

Project team leader Michele Hall, a former Clorox marketer, says the team wanted to take laundry to the next level and bring change "by exposing the dirty little secrets of laundry such as rampant overdosing by consumers and synthetic toxic, petroleum-based ingredients." These were, says Michele, "things that are good for manufacturers' profits but not for consumers, their clothes, their budgets, or their washing machines."

The team rallied around the idea that it could create the product it wanted to create, something that the consumer "didn't even know she wanted or needed." By embracing risk, says Michele, "we freed ourselves up as a team. We ended up focusing on three things: great efficacy and scent for the consumer; a strong environmental benefit because of our core mission around a happy, healthy home revolution; and eliminating the lug factor of a heavy package and providing great ergonomics, which led to a pump dispenser. So we came up with the idea of giving the consumer the ability to dose with five squirts, and make doing laundry a clean, not messy, experience."

It took every piece of the company and the culture to make it happen. It was, says Eric Ryan, "a great collaboration story, moving from a nugget of an idea to everyone fully committing to it. And we love that it is the world's greenest laundry detergent and a radically different and more positive experience for the consumer. No single department scored the goal to make it happen. It was the formula, the packaging, the dispensing, the operational headaches, and the financial aspect of being strong and flexible enough to do it through the worst of the recession."

So far the new detergent is performing well in the marketplace. "We're doing really well at Target and other places where we're known," Michele says. In channels where Method is not known, the company has "bit[ten] off a really big story to tell" and needs to continue to raise consumer awareness of the company and its products.

Michele summed up the Project Lighthouse experience by going back to Method's ideal and "keeping it weird": "The revolutionary mission frees us up to be innovative. A lot of our innovation came from other functions: packaging, industrial design, formulation, and our creative people in the same room trying to solve an issue like, 'What should the capacity of the pump be to deliver the right dosing for the consumer?' It was so much fun to step back and watch the team cross-pollinating and trying to create a more revolutionary experience."

Method's commitment to delivering an extraordinary consumer experience extends to treating design as a strategic asset. I was intrigued to learn that the first thing this points to for Method's design leader is their culture, not the shape of the bottle or other packaging.

"Our biggest design innovation," says Josh Handy, "is the way we work with each other in our culture. That's our real competitive advantage."

Josh continues, "We come to the table with a point of view on modern, minimalist design. We try to keep it as simple, beautiful, and sculptural as possible. It is easy to disappear down a path of just being aesthetically driven, however, and leave the consumer out of it. It's also easy to be just operationally driven and make ugly bottles that run faster down the production line." Handy says that his role as design director is to weigh the influence of operations, marketing, the supply chain, the business side, and the retail and consumer experience, and massage them together. "It's about having a design discussion at the right level to make sure we're delivering on all our core pillars. That's what design is about for us."

While Handy insists that design is really not just aesthetics, he acknowledges that aesthetics is Method's Trojan horse. "If the bottle is beautiful, we'll get more people to try a green product," says Josh.

Handy's perspective reminds me of Apple. Apple's products look beautiful and work beautifully, but as Jonathan Ive, Apple's senior vice president of industrial design, has said, it's not about the surface appearance of fashion, as most of Apple's competitors seem to believe.

As I've already noted, ideal-driven businesses tend to have an edge in design thinking and prototyping. I believe that is because their ideals of improving people's lives help them understand design in the larger sense that Apple and Method do, as everything that contributes to the experience of buying and using a product or service.

MUST-DO NUMBER 5:
HOW METHOD EVALUATES ITS PROGRESS AND PEOPLE
AGAINST ITS IDEAL

Measuring what matters, the fifth branch of the Ideal Tree and the fifth must-do for leveraging an ideal, is one of the simple yet complicated truths at the heart of business success. However, where many flounder is by focusing on financial measures alone. They ignore or lose sight of vital measures of employee and customer engagement with the business, the things that ultimately determine its ongoing financial health. Ideal-based businesses grow bigger than the pack precisely because an ideal of improving people's lives serves as a GPS device for gauging progress toward long-term goals.

Measurement is the test of whether a business actually walks the walk, as well as talks the talk, of having a higher purpose or ideal. Method walks the walk. For example, the authentic story George Shumny tells to retailers includes the fact that "Method will never be the volume leader in the category. That's not even our aspiration." Accordingly, "units per store per week can't be our metric." Instead, Method measures the success of its retail partnerships in line with its ideal in terms of differentiating the retail partners from their competitors, enhancing their image, growing their sales in the category, and delivering "25–35 percent better retail sales margin in the category."

As CFO, Andrea Freedman keeps a rigorous eye on the financials. As "Chief Financial Person Against Dirty," she sees her role in a unique way: as a storyteller. "I tell our financial story with a passion for our ideal," says Andrea. She sees Method as a little ship that goes up and down on the bumpy seas of its category, and she keeps people motivated by reassuring them that Method is on track to meet its goals.

Everything Method does, says Freedman, "should be able to answer four questions with yes. Does it have style? Does it have substance? Does it create an advocate? Does it meet our gross margin hurdles?"

These are Method's ways of asking how well it understands the people most important to its future, what it stands for in their eyes, what it wants to stand for, and how well it is bringing those things to life. The style and substance of its products, the likelihood that these things will turn consumers into advocates, and the likelihood that the products will meet gross margin targets all go straight to the viability of Method's ideal of a happy, healthy home revolution.

Method's best products, Andrea says, hit all four pillars. "The test of getting everybody on board from a financial point of view is to get them to understand the key financial drivers of success in this business. We share how we make money and how that balances with our other goals."

For the first eight years of its existence, Method grew in what Andrea described as "lumpy and opportunistic ways." A major new retail customer or a new product launch "produced double- and triple-digit growth." More recently, Method has had to learn how to continue to innovate while growing its base business. A key forum for this is a weekly "product council" meeting where Andrea's four questions about style, substance, advocacy, and gross margin loom large. "It's a negotiation," Andrea says. "You're sitting in a product council meeting and going, 'This is such a sexy product, but it's five points below our margin hurdle. What do we do? Is there a path to improve the margin? How long will it take?' If I took a hard line on margin every time, we'd miss out on big opportunities. But as we continue to build our base business, that becomes our cushion to keep innovating."

A move that furthered the balance of innovation and growing the base at Method was its decision to concentrate on selling more to its passionate advocates, rather than on the extremely expensive proposition of marketing to new customers. The goal is that the totality of the cleaning products that each person purchases will more and more closely mirror the merchandising display of the complete "Method home" on retail partners' shelves.

In this way, Method grows its share of household cleaning and share of wallet without sacrificing profit margin. Equally important, it also grows its shares of trust and advocacy. Ultimately, the best way to grow a customer base is by word of mouth, and that is where Method puts its energy, creativity, and other resources.

In addition to regularly and frequently asking its four key questions about having style, having substance, creating an advocate, and meeting gross margin hurdles, Method has a one-page monthly scorecard and a longer quarterly one. Both scorecards incorporate financial, quantitative, and qualitative measures. The monthly scorecard focuses on building consumer awareness, developing the new product pipeline, and getting early insight into business trends. The quarterly survey "has a section on people and environment with questions like 'Have you gotten feedback from your manager in the last sixty days?' and 'Do you understand how your work contributes to our strategy?'"

Individual employee evaluations strike the same balance, duplicating the way the recruiting process is based fifty-fifty on skills and culture fit. "As we give feedback to people," Andrea says, "we use the same values language that we used in hiring and onboarding."

Method is one of an increasing number of companies moving to measuring a triple bottom line of financial, environmental, and social impacts. They are a Certified B Corporation, one of a consortium of businesses that evaluate success in this way. For Method this is not a matter of altruism apart from the core business, but rather a way of combining all the key measures that will determine the company's long-term viability. As Michele Hall put it, Method will be successful financially only insofar as they also have a positive social and environmental impact by influencing consumers to choose green products.

One of the most significant indicators of Method's financial, social, and environmental success is the extent to which other companies copy their safe, plant-based products and other innovations. Eric Ryan says, "The way I measure it is by looking for where we've pushed the industry as a whole. We have this tremendous list of firsts, and we get people in the industry to act faster. My favorite example is when the laundry people at Unilever told us they got board approval to launch All Small and Mighty because of our success with our 3x concentrated laundry detergent. Would they have done that eventually? Absolutely. They probably would not have gotten there as soon."

One number Method's senior leaders all have their eyes on is consumer awareness. It is a great idea to identify quantitative measures that can also be proxies for qualitative progress against your ideal, something I'll have more to say about in chapter 10. For Method, that quantitative measure is consumer awareness. As consumers become aware of the brand, Method finds that a significant percentage become passionate members and advocates of "people against dirty." But in terms of consumer awareness the Method story is still in its early stages; as Andrea Freedman says, "That's why one of the best barometers for us is building and measuring awareness."

Method has a long way to go to reach the $1 billion in sales that Eric Ryan and Adam Lowry have set as their financial goal. But basing their business around an ideal of improving people's lives has taken them very far, very fast. Given the passion for Method's ideal that I saw throughout the company, I'm betting they'll hit that mark, and then some.

Method is an inspirational example on many levels, but here is what I take away as their essential lessons for any business in any industry, organized around the five branches of the Ideal Tree:

- **Must-Do Number 1: Discover an Ideal in One of Five Fields of Fundamental Human Values**

  Method teaches us to never be complacent about our brand ideal. This company has been ideals-driven since its founding, in the ideals field of impacting society, but they continue to probe how they can execute better, based on a deeper understanding of their ideal.

- **Must-Do Number 2: Build Your Culture Around Your Ideal**

  Method shows us it's really all about the people behind the brand. So many companies say this; the way Method brings this to life is simply amazing. They urge everyone to "bring yourself to work," so that each person's individual personality can contribute to the brand ideal. The most powerful indicator of the way they focus on their people is the ideal-driven recruiting process. The percentage of time the senior team spends on recruiting and onboarding is the best I've seen. And they make very few mistakes in whom they bring into the culture. They realize one bad hire is toxic.

  Method always looks to learn outside its category. When I arrived at Method and walked into their lobby, there was a "class" going on. The teacher was Dan Germain, the communications director at Innocent, which is itself a fantastic story in brand ideal, mission, and outstanding performance. Dan was in the middle of teaching a writing class to several Method employees, and this was the culmination of a week he had spent at Method, learning from them and sharing his experience to help them be better. You will hear more about Innocent in chapter 8.

- **Must-Do Number 3: Communicate Your Ideal to Engage Employees and Customers**

Method knows how to win with compelling, mutually reinforcing stories for everyone in the value chain, from sales channel partners to end consumers. Method sells to retailers, as many businesses do. I had the pleasure of talking with "Chief of Retail Health" George Shumny, and he did a role-play with me, where I was the customer and he was the salesperson. His story hit everything a customer looks for—differentiation, image enhancement, margin growth, and collaboration.

Everyone at Method is a storyteller, with the CFO as chief storyteller. There are few CFOs who see their role as chief storyteller, but Andrea Freedman—"Chief Financial Person Against Dirty"—sees her role very much as keeping everything in perspective and making sure everyone's eyes stay on the horizon. Andrea sees herself as the person who keeps telling the story about what this brand is, what success is, and how they are making progress against it in the short, medium, and long terms.

- **Must-Do Number 4: Deliver a Near-Ideal Customer Experience**

Method delights customers and differentiates itself by only doing what the competition can't or won't

do. Method is all about differentiation in a category that previously had very few highly differentiated brands. Method's leaders differentiate on their ideal, design, fragrance, sustainability, and efficacy. And they get that balance right for their end consumers. Much as Steve Jobs as CEO at Apple did not go into a category he could not disrupt, Method never does anything the competition has done, or likely will do.

- **Must-Do Number 5: Evaluate Your Progress and People Against Your Ideal**

  Method is clear and consistent with everyone on what counts. Their clarity on the four key criteria for any initiative—style, substance, advocacy, margin— keeps the company growing sales and profits, and attracting customers to its special ideal.

Method is a superb example of the entire Ideal Tree framework coming to life in a business. Their results attest to the power of this framework: Method's market shares as this book went to press were at all-time highs, and their annual double-digit growth rate was continuing into their second decade.

But I have to say that one of the most remarkable aspects of my research for this book was that any of the businesses highlighted in later deep dives could also have served to illustrate the entire ideal-based growth system. As we'll see, what characterizes all the deep-dive companies is consistent excellence across the five must-dos for leveraging an ideal. In what follows, however, I'll be highlighting only one branch of the tree at a time, to provide a clearer understanding of its role in generating and sustaining high growth.

So let's now move on to the first branch of the Ideal Tree: discovering an ideal in one of five fields of fundamental human values.

PART II

The Five Must-Dos

4

Must-Do Number 1

Discover an Ideal in One of Five Fields of Fundamental Human Values

Where your talents and the needs of
the world cross, there lies your purpose.

—ARISTOTLE

DISCOVER
an ideal in one of five
fields of fundamental
human values

Every business in the world has a potential growth-driving ideal at its center. You discover an ideal for a business by finding a link between its central reason for being, the core beliefs of its people, including senior leadership, and the fundamental values of customers.

Most businesses articulate a vision (where they want to go), a strategy (what choices they are making), and a statement of what businesses they are in and what they are trying to achieve. The problem is that most have not articulated—and activated—this in terms of a life-improving ideal (why the business ultimately exists) that drives growth by inspiring employees and key business partners to innovate and to perform at a high level in all areas of the business.

Discovery or rediscovery of the ideal begins in the relationship a business and its customers have developed over time and how that reflects human aspirations in one of the five fields of fundamental human values. Building close customer relationships and gaining a holistic understanding of the customer will tell you where to look for your ideal, where you can best identify the higher purpose that is your business's fundamental reason for being and the higher-order benefit you can bring to the world.

WHAT CAN WE BECOME?

Pizza Hut, part of Yum! Brands, Inc., and the largest player in the $37 billion U.S. pizza category, lost touch with its ideal but then made a concerted effort to rediscover and releverage it.

Pizza Hut was conceived in 1958 by two college student brothers, Frank and Dan Carney. They borrowed $600 from their mother, purchased secondhand equipment, and opened the first Pizza Hut on a busy intersection in their hometown of Wichita, Kansas. Their ideal was pure, simple, and uplifting: provide a place where people could enjoy family relationships and friendships. Decades before Starbucks, they wanted to provide an environment that brought people together to build relationships. They realized that great-tasting pizza could play a huge role in relationship building, because pizza, all things considered, is the ultimate social food. And Pizza Hut grew enormously on the basis of the Carneys' vision of a brand ideal.

Fast-forward to the late 2000s, where Pizza Hut, now with 7,200 locations in the United States, found itself mired in shrinking market share, lackluster sales, and declining traffic, all compounded by the huge recession. Pizza Hut general manager Brian Niccol summed it up well: "We had put ourselves in a ditch."

Consumer research showed that Pizza Hut's value proposition was way off in consumers' eyes. Consumers felt that prices were too high and that there were better choices elsewhere. But these were symptomatic problems, not the main cause of the trouble. I began consulting with Pizza Hut in 2009, and the big question I asked them early on was, "Why do corporate and franchise employees want to work at Pizza Hut? Is there a higher-order benefit you give to the world? Is it articulated? Do you have a plan to activate it?" The answer was . . . silence.

Along with Yum! Brands CEO David Novak and other senior leaders, Brian Niccol and his leadership team began asking these questions of themselves and others throughout the Pizza Hut organization, and an interesting pattern emerged. When they asked corporate employees and franchisees and their employees what motivated them and made them feel good about coming to work, they kept hearing about the same sorts of things: delivering pizza to a family enjoying its weekly movie night together, a group watching a sporting event, or people enjoying other sorts of everyday moments together; giving a hardworking mom a night off from cooking; or interacting with groups of family members and friends when they came to eat in the restaurants.

Pizza Hut also looked back in its heritage. Brian Niccol and his colleagues quickly realized that their employees, many of whom knew little if anything about the Carney brothers, were echoing their founding vision. That realization brought an exciting new sense of the business's potential to regain that focus and so renew its growth.

After reflection and analysis they took action, beginning with leadership's very visibly reengaging the organization with its heritage and emphatically re-centering the business in the Carney brothers' brand ideal. This sent an important message to all corporate and franchise employees that Pizza Hut's leaders shared their belief about what made the business special. Brian Niccol's team also tapped in to the thoughts and feelings of employees, franchisees, and customers to glean ideas for improving the business's ability to bring the ideal to life in a fresh and appealing way. This in turn led to simplifying the menu and pricing, and to enhancing the look and comfort of their restaurants.

As part of this, Pizza Hut shot a good deal of video of employees talking about their work as well as actually making, serving, and delivering pizzas. Reviewing this video, they saw that the best advertising campaign they could create would feature real employees enthusiastically going about their work or talking about the satisfaction and enjoyment they got from it.

To lure back customers who had become disenchanted with the brand, Pizza Hut did a bold discount price promotion (any pizza with any topping for $10). To persuade those customers to keep coming back to the restaurants and having pizzas delivered after the promotion ended, however, Pizza Hut was relying on the ideal of enabling social connection that it had rediscovered and releveraged.

By early 2011, within fourteen months of our discussion about its ideal, Pizza Hut was a different business. Traffic and sales were up in double digits, and franchise employee turnover was at an all-time low.

Pizza Hut today is more in touch than ever with the essence of its heritage, its brand ideal, and its beliefs—held by current employees as much as by the founding Carney brothers—about the inherent value and ultimate goal of that ideal. Here is how Brian Niccol and his team articulate the Pizza Hut brand ideal in 2012: "We believe the world would be a better place if we could invest more time in the relationships that are important to us, and we exist to enable and support that."

Throughout my career I've gone back to the heritage of every business I've been involved with. What I've found time and again is that a great move for a leader in a new job is simply asking people to "look at our history and who we are now, and see what we can learn about who we can become and what we can do next."

As brand manager of Jif peanut butter, I wasn't thinking consciously about the core beliefs of the people who worked inside the business, the fundamental values we shared with customers, or discovering an ideal that expressed these beliefs and values. But I knew in my gut that if we could better understand what was important to moms with young children, it would be good for the business. I knew intuitively that doing things that made moms feel good about Jif would make Jif's people feel good about themselves and help them enjoy their jobs more—not only the marketing team, but everyone from finance to the plant floor. The power of the ideal extended to our advertising agency team, who were inspired to do extraordinary creative work.

A business never leaves its heritage behind, any more than a living organism leaves its original DNA behind. And like DNA, the heritage isn't static and unchanging. A business's leaders, employees, and customers—along with the outside environment—constantly influence and modify its ongoing heritage. The history of your business and the evolution of your cultural and organizational DNA over time will give you essential clues for discovering and evolving your ideal. Joey Reiman, the CEO of consulting firm BrightHouse, who works with companies to discover their higher purpose, sums it up by saying, "When I hear about a company moving backwards, I get excited."

THE FOUR QUESTIONS

In chapter 2 I described the four critical questions that business artists keep asking themselves and their people. No matter what your level of responsibility, you can use these four simple questions to acquire strategic insights like those I was fortunate enough to acquire with Jif and other brands in the P&G portfolio.

- How well do we understand the people who are most important to our future?
- What do we and our brand stand for?
- What do we want to stand for?
- How are we bringing the answers to these questions to life?

These questions go to the heart of how the customer relationship is evolving over time and thus what its growth potential is. They bring your heritage and organizational DNA into sharp relief. They show you how far you've come from your start and how far you have to go to achieve your current and future goals. They provide the best possible way to do a gap analysis, and they furnish critical tools for centering a business around an ideal.

It takes guts, discipline, and honesty to ask these questions and act on the answers. Doing so enables you to define and develop a compelling difference from the competition in the eyes of customers—and back it up!

Great businesses and great business leaders welcome these questions. They know it is folly to ignore them, or to try to answer them with mere wishes. Your answers have to connect your people's core beliefs and your customers' fundamental values in a genuine, significant way.

Those with the most trouble answering these four questions often have leaders who pride themselves on running "realistic," numbers-driven organizations. Ironically, these leaders simply aren't realistic enough to recognize the highly profitable top- and bottom-line growth that cascades from serving an ideal of improving people's lives.

Numbers alone can't be your North Star. It's too easy to game them, consciously or unconsciously. As nineteenth-century British prime minister Benjamin Disraeli and American author Mark Twain are both famous for saying, there are "lies, damn lies, and statistics." Set your sights on an ideal, however, and you can follow it to highly profitable top- and bottom-line growth.

One of the oldest businesses in the Stengel 50 is Jack Daniel's Tennessee Whiskey, founded in 1866. It is also one of the strongest examples of discovering an ideal and keeping it relevant and growth-inspiring. The ideal behind Jack Daniel's is virtually unchanged since its origin: Jack Daniel's exists to celebrate and evoke pride in personal authenticity, independence, and integity. In so doing, it embodies the maverick personality of its founder and evokes the aspirational pride of its loyal consumers.

Through seven generations of management, as the business has expanded to 135 countries and grown to be the largest whiskey brand in the world with 10 million cases in sales, it has remained true to its founding ideal, while continuing to find creative new ways to express that ideal. Let's now explore how Jack Daniel's has executed nearly flawlessly against its ideal throughout its history.

The Whiskey Everyone Asks For by Name

The character of Jack Daniel's, the whiskey with the iconic black-and-white label on the equally iconic square bottle, is inextricably bound up in the distinctive character of Jack Daniel, the brand's founder and first master distiller. A physically diminutive man only five feet two inches tall, Jack Daniel devoted his outsized personality to the ideal of making a whiskey that, thanks to charcoal filtering and other factors, he could be proud to sell and others could be proud to drink—at a premium price.

Jack Daniel never compromised on his recipe for premium-quality whiskey. For loyal fans of Jack Daniel's, he is an icon both of the independent American spirit and of universal values of independence, being your own person, and standing for something authentic.

From the start, Jack Daniel grew his business through astute brand leadership. He had lots of competitors around Lynchburg in distilling whiskey that was filtered through charcoal. He wanted his whiskey to be, and represent, something special. So he used only the iron-free cave spring water on his property and the finest grains, mellowed his whiskey by filtering it through ten feet of sugar maple charcoal, changing the charcoal more often to produce a more consistent and better whiskey. Jack liked to say, "Every day we make it, we'll make it the best we can."

Before his death in 1911, Jack Daniel passed his whiskey business along to his nephew Lem Motlow, who had long worked for him. After Lem Motlow died in 1947, his children increased sales with the brand's first national advertising, and then sold the business in 1956 to family-controlled Brown-Forman as the best way to maintain heritage and quality while expanding. Under Brown-Forman's ownership, and with the continuing involvement of Motlow family members, Jack Daniel's has seen a series of brilliant innovations that have preserved and extended the richness of its brand experience, while never veering off its hallowed ideal.

Until the 1950s, sales of Jack Daniel's grew almost entirely through word of mouth, boosted by occasional media attention and intermittent regional ads. In 1951 *Fortune* published an article on Jack Daniel's that chronicled its growth and appeal to such disparate figures as the 1950 Nobel Prize winner William

Faulkner, British prime minister Winston Churchill, and Hollywood director John Huston, whose movie *The African Queen* was then a big hit. A similar 1954 article in *True*, one of the most popular magazines of its day, put even greater emphasis on its being the favorite drink of celebrities, such as Frank Sinatra, Jackie Gleason, and Ava Gardner. Sinatra called Jack Daniel's "nectar of the gods," and he sometimes wore a blazer with a patch for an imaginary "Jack Daniel's Country Club."

"The first modern ad for Jack Daniel's," says Nelson Eddy, its brand historian, "done before the Motlows sold the business to Brown-Forman, was a small black-and-white ad simply pointing people to read a magazine article." What is especially interesting about Jack Daniel's beginning to advertise nationally in the 1950s is that demand then exceeded supply. "Until the mid-1970s, it was on allocation. The sales representatives would literally go into an establishment and let them know how many bottles or cases they could have."

In a situation like this, Nelson continued, "when other companies would pull back from advertising, Jack Daniel's advertised more. Those ads carried the message 'We'd rather ask for your patience than your forgiveness.' They spent money on ads to tell people they couldn't get it. What they essentially said is that like Jack Daniel and Lem Motlow before them, they're not going to compromise the quality of the product to meet demand, so customers can be assured that when they do get some, it's going to be the one and only Jack Daniel's."

The approach followed a 1955 one-page marketing plan drafted at the behest of Art Hancock, the brand's first marketing director, and Winton Smith, its first national sales director, who envisioned a future based on the heritage that Jack Daniel and Lem Motlow defined. The one-page plan, Nelson says, "codified Jack Daniel's as authentic, made by real people in an out-of-the-way place." Their ads are distinctive not only for what they say but also for what they show, evoking a premium brand experience that is unique in the marketplace.

Eddy notes that "if you look at liquor ads of the period, they're typically full-page, full-color with a big beautiful bottle shot and a man in a smoking jacket or posed by an expensive car, something that says luxury. Well, here comes this brand running smaller-space ads with black-and-white photography of these people in Lynchburg, Tennessee, who aren't in smoking jackets. They're in the work clothes they wear every day to make the whiskey."

This counterintuitive approach to marketing a premium brand—the one-page marketing plan included avoiding discounting the price—ran into skeptics along the way, who did not understand the universal values it evoked. "Going into the United Kingdom in the early 1980s," Eddy says, "there was pushback about small black-and-white ads showing people in Lynchburg, Tennessee. They said, 'That works in the United States, but it won't work here.' Guess what? It did." Today the U.K. is the second strongest market for Jack Daniel's.

While this decision now looks easy and smart in retrospect, I am sure it was gut-wrenching. I worked on dozens of global brands at P&G where this discussion happened in every new country as we expanded. There is a constant tension between the ideal of the brand and the drive to make the brand more local, more in tune with country-specific habits, practices, and culture. Like other top Stengel Study businesses, Jack Daniel's shows that if you are working a brand ideal at the fundamental level of eliciting joy, enabling connection, inspiring exploration, impacting society, or (in its own case) evoking pride, what makes you special, unique, and interesting will likely resonate wherever you take your business.

Ever since that one-page marketing plan, there's been a singular focus on telling the lore and legend around Jack Daniel's.

The stories use Lynchburg and its people but the takeaway isn't Lynchburg. It's those universal messages about pride in being independent, making your own way in the world, and standing for something authentic.

When Jack Daniel's went on allocation in the mid-1950s, the Jack Daniel Distillery began to receive letters from people asking when and where they might be able to buy Jack Daniel's in their communities. Jack Daniel's sales and marketing staff wrote back in a friendly way about how sorry they were to disappoint them and how much they valued their love of the whiskey. They wished they could make more, but they couldn't because it would hurt quality.

In 1956 Winton Smith and Art Hancock established the Tennessee Squire Association, which continues in operation. Each member of the association gains title to "a square inch of the Hollow on the Distillery grounds" and receives regular letters about what is happening in Lynchburg. Nelson tells me, "We don't talk about Jack Daniel's. We correspond about the town."

The special role of Lynchburg in the Jack Daniel's brand experience led to officially opening the Jack Daniel Distillery to public tours with the building of its first tour center in the early 1960s. More than 200,000 people now visit the distillery every year, with more than 15 percent traveling from outside the United States.

While Jack Daniel's remained available only on allocation through the 1970s, popular culture continued to associate it with maverick independence. Paul Newman's antihero title character in the 1963 movie *Hud* drinks only Jack Daniel's, and rock musicians of the 1960s and 1970s gravitated to it just as Frank Sinatra did. Probably no celebrities have been photographed more often holding, or next to, a Jack Daniel's bottle than rock stars Keith Richards and Slash.

The pattern shows no sign of breaking down. The biggest-selling song of 2010, "Tik Tok," by the rapper Ke$ha, includes a verse about brushing her teeth with Jack Daniel's. Nelson Eddy says, "When Hollywood scriptwriters want to use shorthand to show that a character is somebody to reckon with, they still put Jack Daniel's in their hands."

Jack Daniel's made a positive out of having to go on allocation, but it didn't want to frustrate large numbers of customers permanently. The challenge was to increase supply of an artisan-made product. How they finally solved the problem in the late 1970s testifies to the strength of the Jack Daniel's ideal throughout the business. Over the course of several months, Brown-Forman expanded the existing distillery and built bigger facilities on the same site, while the distillery employees continued to go about their work in the open air, walking on temporary wooden catwalks built around the still.

The result immediately made its decades-old, supply-constrained business model obsolete. "Jack Daniel's went," Eddy explains, "from a brand that we couldn't make enough of to where demand was being fulfilled. The situation changed from the public slowly growing the brand primarily through word of mouth to the brand actively having capacity to grow to unprecedented levels."

Jack Daniel's then grew into a global brand, almost tripling sales from 1973 to 1986. To support this growth, Jack Daniel's invested more in its archetypal Lynchburg-focused advertising, which had continued to resonate with consumers. It also began to engage in an active way with popular culture through sponsorships that embodied its ideal. The now famous Jack Daniel's barbecue competition dates back to the 1980s. In 1995 Jack Daniel's became a continuing sponsor of Professional Bull Riders, Inc. This relationship fit the Jack Daniel's persona of the maverick, authentic individual exceptionally well, because the now very successful Professional Bull Riders tour had been formed only three years earlier by twenty bull riders who split off from the Professional Rodeo Cowboys Association. Each bull rider put in $1,000, and their original $20,000 stake has become a large, thriving business. In the 2000s Jack Daniel's began sponsoring motor racing teams in the United States and Australia.

More recently, Jack Daniel's has seized digital tools to represent and bolster its brand experience online. The brand has more than 2.2 million Facebook friends, and counting, the largest fan base of any spirit globally. If you have your picture taken at the Jack Daniel's Distillery, as all those who go on the free-of-charge distillery tour do, JackDaniels.com is where you can download the free photo. And if you can't get to Lynchburg, Tennessee, you can take a virtual tour online with commentary by your choice of one of three real tour guides.

The team at Jack Daniel's continually looks to its ideal for inspiration for growth ideas. They are among the best I've seen in driving growth through pure commercial innovation—ideas that grow sales without changing the product (I'll talk more about commercial innovation in chapter 9). In September 2010 they began a campaign to establish a U.S. national holiday in honor of Jack's birthday. The campaign included a bus tour from Lynchburg to Washington, D.C., collecting signatures along the way to present to Congress. The campaign increased Facebook friends by 200,000. And for July 4, 2011, Jack Daniel's launched a sweeping, multimedia initiative to celebrate the independent American spirit. My favorite poster from this campaign reads, "56 men signed the Declaration of Independence, one man put it in a bottle."

Jack Daniel's has grown with much less product proliferation than most brands. Jack Daniel's Old No. 7 remains by far the largest part of their global business. Guided by their ideal,

Jack Daniel's management has introduced new products over the years to keep their brand and their ideal relevant. Every new product emanates from the ideal, and most are actually derivatives of the special whiskey from Lynchburg.

In the 1980s Jack Daniel's introduced Gentleman Jack, a smoother, softer whiskey, the first new whiskey from the distillery in one hundred years. In 1997 Jack Daniel's successfully introduced Single Barrel Select, the equivalent of a single-malt scotch whiskey. It can be purchased by the bottle or the entire barrel, about 250 bottles' worth, which is specially bottled for the customer. Purchasers of whole barrels have their names added to the Single Barrel Society display at the Jack Daniel Distillery, and the experience includes the option to choose a barrel in person with the help of the current master distiller, the seventh in the history of the brand, or one of Jack Daniel's master tasters.

The late 2000s brought two major initiatives: Jack Daniel's Country Cocktails, a range of malt beverages, and the global expansion of ready-to-drink cocktails that contain Jack Daniel's and either cola, diet cola, or ginger ale. In 2011 Jack Daniel's introduced Jack Daniel's Tennessee Honey Whiskey.

Tennessee Honey is one of the boldest new initiatives from Jack Daniel's over the past twenty-five years, and one of the riskiest. But the current Jack Daniel's leaders understand the imperative that drives this book and underlies the value of a brand ideal: it enables a business to keep growing in alignment with the fundamental human values that the ideal expresses.

"When you have an icon like Jack Daniel's, you've got to grow it," says Kris Sirchio, Brown-Forman's chief marketing officer—especially when the market is changing on you.

If you want to dominate market share in any category, you have to dominate customers' entry into it. Jack Daniel's has long been the dominant favorite of young people entering the whiskey category, but young whiskey drinkers' tastes are evolving, and the flavored whiskey category is growing fast. "But when you think about Jack Daniel's," Kris Sirchio points out, "you need to ask, 'How would Jack launch a flavor?'"

Kris and his colleagues, including brand manager Jennifer Powell, began with their brand ideal of affirming each person's independence and authenticity. The product's positioning and introductory marketing plan had to be "Jack."

The inspiration for the positioning came from Arnold World-wide, Jack Daniel's ad agency. They captured it in the phrase "A little bit of honey, a whole lot of Jack." The product, while flavored, had to be distinctive, authentic.

"It is black label Old No. 7," says Kris Sirchio, "in its purest form. It's flavored, but man, it's the full thing. One of the key decisions we had to make is to keep the product consistent with the brand."

The marketing also had to convey that this new flavored whiskey was true to the storied Jack Daniel's ideal. It had to embody Jack's swagger. And indeed it did: in the fanciful ads showing the Jack Daniel's beekeeper, he is dressed in black, whereas the other beekeepers are dressed in white.

And although Jack Daniel's embodies independence and being your own person, it is also all about friendship. So the social networks were atwitter about Jack Daniel's Tennessee Honey. Two months after its introduction, Tennessee Honey had nearly 500,000 Facebook friends, the fastest ever building of a fan base in the alcoholic beverage category.

In all their new product offerings, Jack Daniel's has listened to and taken their lead from consumers: seeing how they like to enjoy Jack Daniel's, and gaining a deeper understanding of the position the brand holds in consumers' minds and hearts. The people who work at Jack Daniel's know that if they offer something that is not true to the original experience, consumers will reject it. Each product innovation must also be an expression of the initial brand.

Jack Daniel's could not have succeeded without the passionate engagement of their own people in the brand experience. The people of Lynchburg, where generation after generation of the same families make the whiskey, is the greatest quality-control element. People want to do a good job because they're preserving a job for their children and grandchildren. "We have scientific quality control," says Nelson Eddy, "but there's no greater quality control than pride."

As Jack Daniel's has grown from a U.S. brand to a global one, so the Jack Daniel's marketing team has grown from a small number of people to a global marketing organization. To ensure that employees around the world understand the brand experience from the inside, Jack Daniel's brings them to Lynchburg, Tennessee, in small groups for an experience it calls Camp Jack. Over several days, the participants learn the legend and lore of Jack Daniel's up close, including a day working in the distillery.

In a world of teleconferencing replacing in-person meetings, reduced travel budgets, and cutbacks in training, the Jack Daniel's management continues to invest in bringing its people to Lynchburg to emotionally and physically experience the Jack Daniel's ideal. This even extends to senior management at parent company Brown-Forman; Kris Sirchio recently attended Camp Jack so that he could also deeply understand the Jack Daniel's ideal.

He says that "at my Camp Jack we had Jack Daniel's people from Germany, Australia, the Czech Republic, and the U.S. We listened to stories from people who have been part of Jack Daniel's for decades and decades, seven people who had two hundred–plus years of experience on the brand."

The goal of Camp Jack is to ensure that everyone who attends it can forever understand the absolute authenticity of the brand—that a century after the founder's death, the whiskey that bears his name is still being made in the same way by the same kind of people. In this regard, Kris tells me one of the most special parts of Camp Jack is the bestowal of nicknames on the participants in a ceremony on Barbecue Hill, site of the annual Jack Daniel's Invitational barbecue contest. As a symbol of friendship, nicknames are really an abbreviated story, and the nicknames weave the Camp Jack "graduates" themselves into the lore of the brand ideal. After all, Jack Daniel's full and proper name was Jasper Newton Daniel, but his friends nicknamed him "Jack." How fortunate—can you imagine Keith Richards drinking "Jasper Daniel's"?

REDISCOVERING AN IDEAL

I have a personal experience that illustrates the business-accelerating power of an ideal centered in one of the five fields of fundamental human values.

The year was 1991 and the brand was P&G's Crisco, the vegetable-based shortening. I was charged by P&G's senior management to turn around its dismal trends. While I did not consciously know it at the time, I needed to place Crisco squarely in the area of eliciting joy.

Crisco was a P&G legacy business, founded in 1911, and had been a huge profit center. Although the business remained large and profitable, there were a number of disturbing trends in its performance and prospects, starting with the disarray of the Crisco organization.

P&G's then-CEO, Ed Artzt, was very upset about what had happened to the brand and was absolutely determined to fix it during his tenure. Although Crisco was not nearly as financially important as it had once been, Ed felt that the damage to a P&G heritage brand was shameful and that the problems at Crisco had to be put right for the good of the company as a whole.

My approach at Crisco was the same as at Jif. I asked the basic questions that I instinctively knew held the key to a solution. I went around the entire organization and asked about the consumers who were most important to the business's future and how their behavior was changing; what had made Crisco so successful for so long and what was limiting our current and future success; and how we could best respond to these things.

P&G introduced Crisco in 1911 as a healthful replacement for lard in baking. Its primary use is still as a baking ingredient, although now it more commonly replaces butter. Among P&G's marketing innovations in making Crisco a household word for decades was giving away cookbooks that featured it in recipes for cakes, pies, and other dishes.

Unfortunately, 1990s consumers were less and less inclined to see Crisco as a healthful food. And P&G was doing a poor job of communicating that part of the Crisco story; we weren't showing consumers that Crisco actually had a decent nutritional and health advantage compared to butter. Ed Artzt railed that we had screwed up, that we had taken a "life brand" and turned it into a "death brand." "We have," he said, "become lard."

Equally important, although the stay-at-home moms who baked cakes and pies from scratch were shrinking in number, our marketing remained focused on those consumers and those dishes. The working moms of the 1990s wanted to bake healthful, delicious treats for their families. But they only had time for simple, fast things such as cookies, brownies, and muffins, not elaborate cakes and pies from scratch.

Recognizing how Crisco and its customers were moving apart enabled us to bridge and close that gap. We repositioned

Crisco as a healthier choice, versus butter, for delicious baked goods that could be made quickly in the midst of working moms' busy lives. We packaged it more conveniently in sticks instead of big cans. We put cookie, brownie, and muffin recipes on the packages. We did ads that compared chocolate chip cookies made with Crisco to ones made with butter. And the business and its people found their stride again.

In hindsight, what my team and I did was refresh Crisco's long-standing ideal of helping women bring their families together through favorite foods. We were working, I would now say, squarely within the ideals field of eliciting joy, with a touch of enabling connection.

There were other aspects to making Crisco a healthy business again. But they all depended on rediscovering the business's original ideal, thanks to gaining a better understanding of the people who were most important to the business's future, what we had come to stand for in their eyes, and what we could stand for—and then bringing this deeper understanding to life with employees, retail customers, and consumers.

As you begin the journey to a brand ideal–based strategy in your own business, must-do number 1, discovering an ideal in one of the five fields of fundamental human values, is your first priority. You must start here. We have just seen three examples of businesses—Pizza Hut, Jack Daniel's, and Crisco—that discovered, or rediscovered, their ideal, and then accelerated momentum as they activated that ideal.

Here is my simple advice for you in applying the learning from these three cases:

- **Express Your Ideal Explicitly.** Write it down, and your rationale behind it. Share it. Get input from people you respect, and then refine the ideal and your rationale for it. The Jack Daniel's ideal is explicit; it was the core of the 1955 one-page marketing plan that is still driving the business's growth today. Pizza Hut made their ideal explicit, after a business slowdown caused them to look back at their history, while also looking forward to what kind of company they wanted to be. For inspiration, review the ideal statements of the Stengel 50 in the appendix. Your own ideal statement should be unique to your brand's heritage and your organizational culture, but the brand ideal statements of businesses that have grown remarkably over the 2000s are a great place to start.

- **Be sure your ideal is in one of the five fields of fundamental human values: eliciting joy, enabling connection, inspiring exploration, evoking pride, or impacting society.** A key finding of the Stengel Study is that the ideal should be dominantly in one of these ideals fields, with perhaps secondary emphasis in another field. Pizza Hut's ideal—"We believe the world would be a better place if we could invest more time in the relationships that are important to us, and we exist to enable and support that"—is clearly about enabling connection, but it has a secondary emphasis on eliciting joy.

- **Make someone in your organization your business artist, responsible for the ideal and for the actions, systems, and behaviors that emanate from it.** This may be the CEO, or someone trusted with the freedom and decision-making authority to direct the organization accordingly. Without a business artist to hold everyone accountable to your brand ideal, it won't have the impact it could have. The business artist at Pizza Hut is Brian Niccol. At Jack Daniel's, it is CEO Paul Varga. At Method, it's co-founder Eric Ryan. Throughout this book, we will see many examples of business artists bringing brand ideals to life in their businesses.

• **Regularly assess the strength of the ideal in your organization.** You need to be sure the ideal remains strong and relevant over time. I like to use the following criteria with clients to be sure the ideal is resonant with stakeholders:

> • Is your ideal consistent with your heritage and cultural DNA?
> • Is your ideal actively impacting lives?
> • Is there leadership commitment to your ideal and does it inspire employees and customers?
> • Is your ideal spawning continuous, diverse, and growth-enhancing innovation from your organization?

> I have tested these pragmatic criteria dozens of times with clients in real situations, and they work. If you cannot say yes to these questions, you may need to evolve your ideal. We will cover that in the last chapter, "Keep It Going."

Of all the Stengel 50 brands, the one I feel most clearly exemplifies how discovering and rediscovering a business's ideal can help drive sustained high growth could not be more aptly named: Discovery Channel, the flagship channel of Discovery Communications. Discovery's founder, John Hendricks, rooted the business deeply in the growth area of inspiring exploration, and he and his colleagues have kept their brand ideal—satisfying curiosity—fresh and relevant for almost three decades. We all can learn a lot from Discovery and the other media brands in its portfolio, and the next chapter describes what I found on my deep-dive visit there.

5

Discovery's Endless Business

Satisfying Curiosity

DISCOVER
an ideal in one of five
fields of fundamental
human values

I was struck by the fact that Discovery Communications was the only media business in the Stengel Study top 50. Then I thought about how often my wife, Kathleen, and I and our children have clicked on the Discovery Channel over the years. No matter where in the world we were living, we knew we could always find something both entertaining and worthwhile to watch on Discovery.

Eager to learn exactly how Discovery was setting itself apart from both broadcast and other cable networks, I got in touch with Joe Abruzzese, Discovery's president of U.S. advertising sales. Joe and I had done business regularly when I was at P&G and he was running ad sales at CBS. "Jim," he said, "satisfying curiosity is not only the filter for Discovery Channel, the flagship network, but for everything we do."

Discovery's journey from an entrepreneurial vision in founder and chairman John Hendricks's mind to the largest nonfiction media company on the planet demonstrates that finding your ideal is not something you do once and you're done. It's an ongoing process that you must get right not only during takeoff and initial growth but in every phase of the evolution of the business. It becomes especially important during inevitable periods of stress. That includes both times when your business stumbles, as all businesses do, and times when your business is booming and you and your people risk becoming complacent.

Abruzzese continued with his explanation about the roots of Discovery's ideal: "It really stems from twenty-nine years ago when John Hendricks saw a void. John's vision was that Discovery could be a place in people's minds, a way of making people better physically, mentally, and emotionally."

John Hendricks first got the idea for a documentary television channel in 1975, the year HBO expanded from its initial base in New York and Pennsylvania and acquired a national audience. John says, "That started me thinking, well, gee, there may be potential in having very simple channels that address major categories. My own favorite television was documentaries about science, nature, and history, and I wondered why that couldn't be available all the time." In 1979 ESPN was born, and in 1980 Ted Turner created CNN as a 24/7 news channel. MTV followed in 1981, and the Weather Channel in 1982. "By 1982 I was obsessed by the idea that a documentary channel would work, and I was astonished that seven years after HBO launched nationally there still wasn't one. If no one was going to do it, then I was."

In fact, someone had done it. The Learning Channel, which Discovery would acquire in 1991, had launched in 1980 as an outgrowth of the Appalachian Community Service Network, which was founded in 1972. But it was dull fare. It did not hit the sweet spot that Hendricks saw for nonfiction storytelling with great production values, drama, and humor. His models were miniseries such as Kenneth Clark's *Civilisation*, Alistair Cooke's *America*, Jacob Bronowski's *The Ascent of Man*, James Burke's *Connections*, David Attenborough's *Life on Earth*, and Carl Sagan's *Cosmos*.

Intuitively, Hendricks knew he was not alone as a television viewer. He backed up this hunch by researching the ratings for documentary programming on both PBS and the commercial broadcast television networks. Hendricks was then working full-time as a fund-raiser for the University of Maryland. Showing his growing entrepreneurial spirit, John left the university to start a full-time consulting business called the American Association of University Consultants. To win new business he published newsletters for various academic disciplines, such as *The Chemistry Funding Newsletter*.

In 1982 Hendricks threw himself into a quest to launch a documentary television channel that would go far beyond the Learning Channel's thus far ho-hum results. He incorporated as the Cable Educational Network, a name he chose simply as a placeholder, and set about raising money.

It was a tough sell. For one thing, there was the lackluster performance of the Learning Channel, much of which did not rise far from the level of recorded classroom instruction. Many potential investors found it hard to imagine that a documentary channel could consistently attract big audiences.

Flying home to Maryland from a December 1983 trip to pitch a cable system operator in Florida, Hendricks knew that the placeholder name for his venture had to change. His friends had reinforced that he had to find something more exciting, and truer to his own vision. He jotted down possibilities and by the end of the flight had narrowed them down to four: Horizon, Vista, Explore, and Discovery. By the end of the weekend, he knew Discovery was it. "As a species, we love puzzles," John told me. "Curiosity drives our advancement."

Over the next year and a half, Hendricks raised $5 million, just enough to launch Discovery in a small way. The cable pioneer John Malone and Advance Publications, publisher of many newspapers and Condé Nast magazines, such as the *New Yorker*, were among his chief backers. But none of the broadcast television networks, station groups, or production companies, such as Time-Life Films, took a stake. Time-Life Films shied away even though it had co-produced and/or distributed successful documentary series including *The Ascent of Man*. Its most recent experience with such programming, the arts-focused series *The Magic of Dance* (1979) and *The Shock of the New* (1982), had been disappointments. As for related media, I think Time-Life Books could have found the entire $5 million in its party budget. But as I mentioned earlier, its leaders never asked themselves how to extend their organization's capabilities in nonfiction infotainment beyond selling multivolume book sets by direct mail.

Hendricks wryly recounted how he had failed to convince the established television powers to invest, noting that they also passed up chances to get in on the ground floor of every other nascent cable channel. A decade later, as cable television revenues surged, the broadcast networks had to pay huge premiums to buy their way into the industry they'd scorned.

John was determined never to make the same mistake. "I witnessed the broadcast networks and stations defining themselves narrowly in terms of their current business model and technology," he told me. "When we launched in June 1985, I told everyone, 'Let's not say we're in the cable business.' I didn't want us to limit ourselves."

One of the evergreen benefits of centering your business around an ideal is that it continually has new opportunities. Improving people's lives and connecting with their fundamental values can never become obsolete, and there will always be new ways to express your ideal. However, even the most successful product, service, business model, or technology platform can become a suffocating trap.

The better you understand the people who are most important to your business's future, the more you can stand for something fundamentally important in their eyes and the closer you can come to being an indispensable part of their lives. The less you understand, the less you stand for and the closer you come to being obsolete.

Indispensable or obsolete? It's a stark choice that every business faces every single day. Discovery's quest to become indispensable by continually finding new ways to satisfy curiosity is reflected in Hendricks's belief that "we're all on a mission here. If people are a little more enlightened about themselves, other people, and the planet, that's a good thing." Clark Bunting, one of Discovery's earliest hires and now general manager of the Discovery Channel, stressed how Discovery has always tried to reflect Hendricks's understanding that "viewers are smarter than they're given credit for. We never tell viewers what to think. We say, 'Here are some things to think about.'"

In considering programming for any of Discovery's thirteen networks, Hendricks, CEO David Zaslav, COO Peter Liguori, and the different networks' general managers have four questions. It is Discovery's version of the four basic questions:

- Does it satisfy curiosity?
- Does it have quality?
- Does it make an emotional connection with the viewer?
- Does it push the viewer's next question?

In one form or another, every great business probes for the same insight. *How well do we understand the people who are most important to our future? What do we and our brand stand for? What do we want to stand for? How are we bringing the answers to these questions to life?*

Discovery's ability to make an emotional connection with viewers depends on deep understanding not only of them but of everyone important to the business's future: employees, production partners, and cable system operators and advertisers. Discovery brings that understanding to life through quality programming that satisfies and stimulates curiosity. And in turn, the emotional connections Discovery develops with viewers grow its dual revenue streams from cable system operators and advertisers.

WHY "STANDING FOR SOMETHING" LEADS TO GROWTH

Discovery's growth has convinced John Hendricks of the power of being "a business that stands for something" in the eyes of everyone important to the business's future. In addition to employees, for Discovery that group includes advertisers, cable system operators, and viewers. "If you can connect to improving the human condition, that's a great place to be as a business. If your people are excited about your product, that's reflected in their work and in the viewers' response. I tell our employees, 'This business could be forever.' Because we're appealing to something at the core of human nature: their curiosity and their love of storytelling."

Focusing on the ideal of satisfying curiosity and constantly searching for new ways to reveal it has driven extraordinary growth for the Discovery Channel. On its June 1985 launch, it was available in 156,000 homes. By the end of that year, it reached 7 million. Its growth since then has traced an ever-rising arc. In 2011 it had 100 million subscribers in the United States, and almost 300 million more in the rest of the world.

In addition, the ideal and new ways of expressing it have grown Discovery Communications to thirteen profitable networks, including Animal Planet, Investigation Discovery, and TLC, as Discovery rebranded the Learning Channel in 1998. Taken together, Discovery's networks had 1.5 billion cumulative subscribers worldwide in 2011. The company's dual revenue streams from cable system operator fees and advertising have grown accordingly, and in 2011 totaled more than $4 billion.

That's not the end of the story. Discovery has also established thriving online extensions for its cable networks. And during my talks with Hendricks, CEO David Zaslav, and their colleagues, they shared their excitement over finding ways for Discovery "to live on the iPad and other mobile devices," in Hendricks's words.

It's important to recognize how they've done that, as I'll explain. But you shouldn't miss the fact that they've sometimes stumbled along the way. Mistakes are part of life, and no business is immune to them. But businesses whose leaders can reveal an ideal of improving people's lives—and not lose sight of it under pressure—have a much better chance of surviving tough situations and outperforming the competition as markets change. Regularly clarifying your business's ideal and finding fresh ways to reveal it internally and externally will help you make better decisions and be faster on your feet.

When serious mistakes and unintended consequences occur—and they always do—the best response you can make is to go back to your ideal. If you peel away the layers of your business's current practices, so that you can take a fresh look at the ideal, you'll then be able to reveal it to others in a fresh way. That provides invaluable direction for both midcourse corrections and fresh departures. It's like checking your compass, sextant, or GPS, or taking a new bearing on your North Star.

Two examples from Discovery demonstrate this need to never be complacent about your business's ideal, even when everything seems to be going great.

One took place in the mid-1990s, during one of Discovery's biggest growth phases, when they were developing plans for a history-focused channel. This initiative was personally important to Hendricks, a history major in college, and held great potential. But the distractions and challenges of managing explosive growth caused Discovery to miss a beat. Before they knew it, A&E stole a march on them and launched the History Channel (now branded simply History) on January 1, 1995. "When the History Channel outmaneuvered us in the marketplace," John says, "we learned we had to be more vigilant about what other channels there might be for satisfying curiosity."

Ten years later, success brought Discovery to an important crossroads. Having established Animal Planet as a cable channel for varied nature programming, it shifted the programming mix on the flagship Discovery Channel to include shows such as *American Chopper*, which took viewers inside biker culture and a family-owned custom motorcycle shop owned by mechanic Paul Teutel Sr. and his sons, Paul junior and Michael. *American Chopper* itself fit within the Discovery Channel framework, each episode combining a how-to-fix-it-and-upgrade-it technology story with the colorful dynamics of the Teutel family. But the success of the show led to similar reality TV programs that began to subsume the original Discovery focus on nature, science, technology, and history.

"Editorially and creatively," says Bunting, "people rightly said we were 'tattoo TV.' The ratings were great. And ad revenue was wonderful. We brought in a lot of new viewers, concentrations of young men eighteen to thirty-four we hadn't had previously, who were buying products we hadn't seen before in our advertising mix. We were getting 3s—at that time 3 was a very big number—against *Monday Night Football,* spanking ESPN. By any rating measure, that's a good night. By most metrics of success, by most television standards, it would be high fives and popping champagne corks. But it was too much, in too many time slots. It began to compromise the brand. Because what do you stand for? It got a number, but it wasn't us."

John Hendricks's view of the situation was that in 2004 and 2005, "the fundamental essence of the Discovery Channel started to drift away. We neglected science, nature, and history. Because we had created Animal Planet, some people internally thought that Discovery Channel didn't need to do nature programming. We should have stayed true to Discovery Channel's being the very best of science, nature, and history documentaries."

In addition to their personal reservations about the flagship network's programming mix, Hendricks and Bunting saw a worrying trend in the otherwise highly positive ratings. Qualitative and quantitative research indicated that Discovery Channel's traditional core viewers, especially parents and their children, were tuning in less often. Hendricks, Bunting, and their colleagues soon concluded that they were in danger of abandoning a sustainable recipe for success in exchange for short-term returns.

Hendricks and his team moved to correct the shift that was taking place in Discovery's brand by focusing on big, mission-defining specials. The first was the eleven-part *Planet Earth,* co-produced with the BBC. The original narration was by David Attenborough, the longtime head of the British broadcaster's Natural History Unit and the usual narrator of its big event programming. Discovery had used Attenborough's narration on three previous nature series it co-produced with the BBC, and would also use his narration on later nature series. But for this effort to reestablish Discovery's fundamental essence as a business, Hendricks and Bunting decided to engage Sigourney Weaver to narrate *Planet Earth*.

Changing the narration was not a trivial decision. It signaled to employees, the creative community, and the television industry as a whole that Discovery Communications was asserting its identity as a producer and originator of the best in nonfiction programming, not just as a distributor.

Planet Earth performed beautifully. Along with other programming in science, nature, and history, Discovery Channel successfully re-centered itself around satisfying curiosity. But this did not mean becoming bland, or simply returning the channel to what it had been before tattoo TV. Re-centering the Discovery Channel around its ideal also required updating the ideal. *Planet Earth* played its part by pushing the envelope on film and video technology and presenting the natural world in ways that had not previously been possible.

Continuing series such as *Deadliest Catch* also pushed the technological envelope, and together with new reality shows such as *Man vs. Wild* and more recently *American Loggers*, Discovery Channel as a whole remained far more high-energy and edgy than it had been before tattoo TV.

Discovery Communications also executed a transition of TLC from a narrow emphasis on home improvement shows to many facets of home and family life, including different kinds of families and marriage- and family-related situations. This focus has generated popular, long-running shows about families with very large numbers of children (*19 Kids and Counting; Kate Plus 8*), family businesses (*Cake Boss; Say Yes to the Dress*, which features young brides-to-be choosing their wedding dresses), families whose members have dwarfism (*Little People; Big World; The Little Couple*), and working mothers and young couples buying a first house (*My First Home*).

"TLC," Peter Liguori says, "strives to satisfy human beings' eternal curiosity about one question: 'Can love really conquer all?' More often than not, the answer on TLC is yes, but it's a realistic yes, with families doing their best in sometimes trying circumstances."

With this programming strategy, TLC became a good place to show *American Chopper*'s train-wreck-riveting mix of family dynamics and the creation of custom motorcycles. More recently, after further adjustments in the program rosters of both channels, *American Chopper* has been taken off TLC and put back on the Discovery Channel, but it is now simply another show in the programming mix, rather than the channel's dominant tone-setter. Instead of heading a block of tattoo TV programming, *American Chopper* now serves the role of helping keep an important audience segment, male viewers with endless curiosity about technology, engaged with the Discovery Channel. "It's a matter of degree," Clark Bunting says. "You can do shows like that, but you can't do them morning, noon, and night."

Crucially, for all the unusual aspects of some of the families that appear on TLC, the network manages to present them in a respectful, nonjudgmental way that shows what they share with families everywhere. Peter told me, "The thing about these families is that they may not look like you or me, but they all kind of work."

I am struck by this myself when I see one of TLC's signature programs. Whereas reality television elsewhere on broadcast and cable television often smacks of the freak show, TLC and the other Discovery networks have managed to build bonds of community between themselves, the people who appear on their shows, and viewers. This has made the Discovery networks essential properties for cable system operators. And it has also made the Discovery networks highly desirable environments for mainstream and upscale advertisers, including Apple, GM, HP, Intel, P&G, Mercedes-Benz, and Lexus.

Great Brands Know When to Say No

Even before deciding to move away from tattoo TV, Discovery's leaders turned down an opportunity to produce what they believed could be, and in fact became, a blockbuster show. Bunting had a dinner meeting in Las Vegas with Frank and Lorenzo Fertitta, owners of the Ultimate Fighting Championship, who pitched him on a show that would take viewers into aspiring fighters' lives as they trained.

"They said, 'This is a great idea. Why don't you do it?'" Clark recalls. "I said, 'I can't do UFC. As great an idea as this is, as big as this could be—and I have every faith—this is not a show I can do.'"

The Fertitta brothers' show, *The Ultimate Fighter*, soon became a huge hit for Spike TV. But it could never have fit Discovery's way of satisfying viewers' curiosity about the wonders of the world. Summing up Discovery's decision about the show, Clark Bunting says, "Great brands say no."

Let me put that in broader terms. Great businesses make great choices. And when they make the inevitable mistake from time to time, they recognize it and correct it quickly.

Business leaders face tough yes-or-no questions every day. The connection with revealing your business's ideal is that you have to have in your organizational culture and in all your teams (more on this in the next chapter) the commitment to never cede the leading edge of your category. You always need to be planting seeds for new business, and they've got to be the right seeds. Regularly re-committing to your ideal in fresh ways helps you get on the leading edge and grow significant new business there. The better you understand how your ideal connects with people's fundamental values and aspirations, the better sense you have of where to take the business next.

Sometimes leaders have to say no to moves that could pay off financially because there's too much collateral risk. P&G has always said no to contract manufacturing for private labels, whereas some competitors said yes. When I was at P&G, we got this question practically every week. Sure, it could have helped the financials. But it was also a slippery slope. What do you do if you have a new technology? Obviously if you're manufacturing for private labels, they'll want it and you won't be able to commercialize it on an exclusive basis as long as you would otherwise. The more you profit from private-label manufacturing on the side, the more you have an important set of customers whose agenda is not totally consistent with what you're trying to do overall. So we said no to private-label deals again and again.

P&G has likewise always said no to outright buying shelf space and paying for distribution. In emerging markets in particular, there were temptations every day to do that.

One of the toughest calls my team at P&G and I had to make was which environments to advertise in. When we looked at U.S. television network schedules, a large percentage of it was programming we would not be in. We felt these environments were not upholding P&G's most important values. We didn't think they were attracting the audiences that it would be most profitable for us to build affinity with over the long term, just as Discovery thought that tattoo TV was not a sustainable environment for them in the long term.

It's no coincidence that as Discovery grew, so did P&G's advertising across all its networks. Over the years—except for the tattoo TV phase!—Discovery's ideal-driven businesses have become better and better environments for P&G's advertising.

Uncovering your business's ideal, or revealing it in a new way, is an inherently entrepreneurial activity that will accelerate growth. Its impact on employees and customers alike is profound.

For the leadership at Discovery Communications, revealing the company's overarching ideal of satisfying curiosity, and the complementary ideals of each Discovery network, has long since proven its worth as a growth engine. Peter Liguori summed up the challenges and opportunities ahead as further developing Discovery's "creative courage" and its ability to produce "lean-forward programming," innovative programming that is based on "digging down to viewers' fundamental emotional needs as well as rational ones." Each time Discovery does so it has a positive impact on employees as well as viewers; it makes "our people get excited about what's next, so no one rests on their laurels."

To guide this process, Liguori has formed a "creative council" of senior executives from Discovery's production and marketing teams. The aim is to boost the ability of Discovery's global networks to generate more of their own programming and spark each other's productive juices.

Two recent examples of creative courage at Discovery are *Sister Wives*, about a polygamous family in Utah, and *Sarah Palin's Alaska*, both of which aired on TLC. Liguori recalls that both sparked controversy before they were on the air, adding, "You definitely want people leaning in on some level. But you don't want them leaning in because you're just doing something to make them look. You have to have some depth to the reason why you're putting that show on. Both of these shows are so bang-on for TLC, because TLC's greatest successes come from exploring a specific area of life through the eyes of a family." No matter what viewers might think of polygamy, Peter predicted that they would identify with one or more of the characters in *Sister Wives*. Likewise, *Sarah Palin's Alaska* is "a family living in an extreme part of America that isn't overly explored."

In terms of creative courage, Peter added, "These are shows where we reached a bit, and people here did have to go outside their comfort zone. I think they're pleased with the creative results."

In addition to these shows, which were pitched to TLC by outside producers, Peter Liguori pointed to an extraordinarily ambitious project that John Hendricks has initiated and will personally oversee. Beginning in 2011 and extending for at least sixty episodes over the next five years, Discovery Channel will air *Curiosity: The Questions of Life*.

Describing the premise of the hourlong series, John Hendricks told me, "It goes back to Aristotle asking, 'What is justice?' It goes back to Socrates' feeling that if you could answer a few core questions, you would have a better life. We still ask the same questions about life, consciousness, time, and so on, but we have new versions of them. Like what is artificial intelligence? What can it be?"

Clark Bunting speaks in much the same vein when he says, "There are still mysteries. There are still things we haven't seen and can't explain. I am Ahab when it comes to the giant squid. That sense of quest is what all of us here share with our viewers."

When I spoke to Discovery CEO David Zaslav about how the ideal of satisfying curiosity generated and guided the company's growth, he told me, "The great thing about curiosity is that it is universal. That has allowed Discovery to expand beyond the core genres that Discovery Channel inhabits. I try to remind our employees that Discovery is different from other media companies. We have a clear and defined mission, to satisfy curiosity, and we simply have to ask ourselves what we and our viewers are curious about in each of the new genres that we enter."

David also stressed the importance of "empowering employees to innovate and take big swings," just as John Hendricks had originally done in starting Discovery and was continuing to do with *Curiosity: The Questions of Life*. I took the opportunity to ask David about his own two biggest swings as CEO so far: partnerships to create the Oprah Winfrey Network (OWN) with Oprah Winfrey, and a children's channel, the Hub, with children's programming producer and toy manufacturer Hasbro.

Both OWN and the Hub launched in 2011, and neither was an immediate blockbuster success. Critics sniped in particular at the low ratings for OWN, but these ratings really weren't surprising in light of the fact that Oprah Winfrey herself was still shooting the last season of her syndicated talk show and was not yet fully involved in the new network. Frankly acknowledging that OWN's programming did not yet reflect her personal brand ideal of hope, aspiration, and self-discovery, Winfrey also dryly observed that a good portion of her existing audience didn't even know where to find OWN in the channel lineups of their cable television providers.

The surprising thing was really that both the Hub and OWN got off to solid starts in attracting new communities of viewers. And both fit well within the sphere of satisfying curiosity: about the world in general for the children watching the Hub, and about how people can live their best lives—an Oprah Winfrey refrain—on OWN.

I hope you can now appreciate why I think Discovery so beautifully exemplifies the power of finding a viable ideal within the five fields of fundamental human values. By planting itself firmly in the field of inspiring exploration, Discovery is continuing to build the "endless business" that John Hendricks envisioned when he founded it.

I hope you are beginning to see ways you can reveal a similarly powerful brand ideal in your own business. But after you've discovered the brand ideal you want to center your business around, you've got to solve the toughest growth problem of all: getting your culture right. That's where we turn next.

6

Must-Do Number 2

Build Your Culture Around Your Ideal

BUILD
your culture around
your ideal

"One team, one dream."

I love the idea expressed in this simple phrase. Kevin Roberts, worldwide CEO of Saatchi & Saatchi, hammered it over and over as I worked with him during my time as P&G's global marketing officer. By living this principle, Kevin and Saatchi had an extraordinary impact on P&G in the first decade of the 2000s. Saatchi & Saatchi was our largest advertising agency, and they helped define the ideal of some of P&G's most important brands: Pampers, Tide, and Olay, to name a few. Then they created advertising that drove awareness, trial, and loyalty.

Kevin rallied Saatchi & Saatchi around a higher ideal of "creating bold ideas to help brands," and quadrupled the value of his firm. He also coined the term *lovemarks*, for brands that elicit love from people. Lovemarks became Saatchi & Saatchi's mantra, and differentiated them from their competition.

The evidence from the Stengel Study is that nothing builds a higher level of trust, and the great teamwork that comes with it, than the shared meanings and emotional bonds that a life-improving ideal generates. Over the long haul, ideal-inspired collaboration always trumps command and control or rule by fear and manipulation. The ideal is the spark that really gets a team firing on all cylinders.

That's true for any size team, and a crucial guiding principle for managers at any level. John Smale, P&G's CEO from 1981 to 1990, once told me, "The job of senior management is to sustain the enterprise through continued investment in people." That points to the overriding importance of getting an organization's culture right. But even if you only have a few people reporting to you or you're assuming your very first leadership role as head of a small project, you've got to get your team right. You can't accomplish significant business goals single-handedly. By the same token, nothing will accelerate your career like being able to get people to work together enthusiastically.

My career and the careers of the most successful business leaders I know have hinged more than anything on building high levels of trust and rallying people to a common cause. My friend Fabrizio Freda left P&G in 2008 to become president and chief operating officer of Estée Lauder. Many questioned the choice. Fabrizio had been president of P&G's Pringles business, a far smaller business than Estée Lauder and, obviously, in a very different business category.

Hiring Fabrizio has turned out to be an inspired choice. The Estée Lauder company has tripled its stock price since he was named CEO in July 2009. The $9 billion company has grown sales at about triple the rate of the global prestige beauty category, thanks in part to how Fabrizio has leveraged his skills at inspiring and energizing people to work toward a common strategy with shared goals through a common purpose, or ideal. His organization accelerated growth on all brands, including the biggest ones such as Clinique, Estée Lauder, and MAC, with locally relevant innovations, while they focused on dramatically improving each brand's in-store service and experience.

This book's deep dives into several Stengel 50 businesses reveal the same pattern at work. Although good leaders naturally have their own individual styles, they all practice common behaviors when it comes to the culture of an organization or a team. They all have a knack for unleashing the potential of people. They demand high standards of behavior in bringing the ideal to life, but they put into place the capabilities to achieve it.

Over the years, I've kept running notes on the culture and teamwork practices of leaders I admire and that I've seen work well in different situations. As I recount two watershed assignments of my career I'll weave them into the narrative. The most powerful of these practices for building an ideal-centered culture is *being clear and explicit about what your ideal is and what you stand for.*

STAND FOR SOMETHING

Your organization can't move in the right direction if people don't understand what you believe in. For maximum positive impact your beliefs need to be consistent with your brand ideal, and the ideal must address fundamental human values if it is going to drive growth. My friend Roy Spence, co-founder of GSD&M, the advertising agency that helped grow Walmart and Southwest Airlines, likes to say, "It's not what you sell, it's what you stand for," which is also the title of his bestselling book.

One of the great practical benefits of bringing an ideal to life in your business is how it helps you be a leader with a clear, strategic focus. If you don't push to reach the high ground and hold it relentlessly, your people will get distracted and your programs will get overly tactical. Strategy (what to do) must always precede tactics (how to do it), and an ideal helps you keep your organization focused on strategy first, preventing it from getting bogged down in tactical issues. Tactical confusion and stagnation always reflect and flow from problems in clarifying an effective strategy.

Getting your ideal crystal clear opens up new strategic possibilities and new opportunities for competitive advantage. That has certainly been the case at Method, Jack Daniel's, and Discovery, as we have seen. Without an ideal-centered strategy at Jif, our tactics would have been hit-and-miss, and I doubt we would have seen the record growth that we achieved. Likewise, at Crisco, my assignment after Jif, I found a fearful organization clinging to an obsolete positioning, until we envisioned a new way of delighting consumers and improving their lives.

You have to reveal your ideal to your internal team as well as to a wider constituency. To win acceptance and support for the moves we were making at Jif and Crisco, many of which broke with P&G conventions at that time, I also had to show my bosses and internal colleagues what I stood for—and never waver. And I had to show it to ad agency partners, to retail customers, and most of all to consumers through our advertising and marketing. As you rise to higher management levels and your responsibilities broaden, you must reveal your ideal even more broadly, across business units and functions and to more and more outside partners, customer and consumer groups, and investors. They all want to know what you stand for and are working toward, and they want to see you expressing that in everything you do. And in 1993, about midway through my career at P&G, I was certainly given the opportunity to place what I stood for on the table.

Little in a business goes right when its culture is flawed. But when the culture is on track, aligned with an ideal of improving people's lives, the business soars, as I discovered during my time as marketing director at P&G's cosmetics subsidiary Noxell.

My Life as a "Spy from Cincinnati"

P&G bought Baltimore-based Noxell, home of Noxzema, Cover Girl, and a fairly young brand called Clarion, in 1989. Two years later, P&G acquired Max Factor and folded it into the Noxell portfolio. At a total cost of almost $2.5 billion, these acquisitions were "fully priced," as the mergers and acquisitions people say, and P&G needed to see them grow.

Cover Girl was the leader in the high-quality mass-market cosmetics category it invented at its 1960 launch, with substantial market share advantage over number two Maybelline. But the trend lines were disturbing. George Lloyd Bunting, the son of the founder and president of Noxell, had envisioned Cover Girl's purpose, or ideal, as helping teenaged girls and young women feel more confident, healthy, and radiant through its "clean, fresh, natural" positioning. But the brand had drifted away from this ideal. And Clarion had never really gained traction since its 1986 launch. My mission, if I chose to accept it, was to address a persistent culture clash between P&G and the marketing organization at Cover Girl and Clarion and make some changes. In the four years since the 1989 acquisition, several P&G executives had tried and failed to resolve that conflict.

I was then in a tough assignment with Crisco, and my wife, Kathleen, and I expected that, following usual P&G patterns, I would have another brand management job in Cincinnati for the next two years or so. We had recently started to remodel our 1920s-vintage house in Cincinnati's Mount Lookout neighborhood, and found ourselves in a situation familiar to many homeowners: the initial phase of work revealed bigger issues than we or the contractor had foreseen, including no foundation under the kitchen, and the project had tripled in cost and complexity.

Disentangling was going to be a hassle, and the Noxell job was another in what was becoming a series of high-risk, high-reward career opportunities. Any rising leader wants such assignments. They're where you earn your stripes. But they do make you stop and think before saying yes.

Kathleen and I decided we would take the Noxell challenge. So early one Sunday morning I began the all-day drive to Baltimore, while Kathleen stayed behind in Cincinnati with our two young children to sort out things with the contractor, the movers, the real estate agent who would be selling the house, and the hundreds of details that come with relocation.

This was still the era of dictating machines at P&G, and all through the nine-hour drive I filled up fifteen-minute-a-side minicassettes with memos to close loose ends in my previous job and to set expectations with my staff and the advertising agencies we would be working with in the new one. I recorded a dozen tapes by the time I pulled into the parking lot of a Residence Inn, my home for the next several months, near Noxell's facility in an industrial park. It was dark, and I couldn't see the Noxell buildings, which included both offices and a manufacturing plant. But I could smell them.

Wafting everywhere was the unmistakable medicated scent of Noxzema. Not a bad smell, really, but I had it in my nostrils 24/7 until Kathleen and the kids could finally join me and we moved into a house in the Baltimore city neighborhood of Homeland.

Given P&G's early-to-work culture and my own eagerness to get started, I made the brief drive over to Noxell by 7:30 a.m. with my dictating-machine tapes in a little box on the passenger seat. My new secretary, who had worked for several of my predecessors over the previous four years, came in at 8:45. We introduced ourselves and chatted briefly, but I couldn't help feeling her reserve. Was it the normal nervousness of meeting a new boss, compounded by having had so many bosses over such a short period of time, or was it also discomfort with another interloper from P&G? I filed the thought away for the moment, pointed to the open box of tapes on my desk, and asked if she could start transcribing them soon.

"I don't do dictation," she said.

"Oh," I said. "Is there someone else here who could transcribe them, or could we get in a temp or send them out to a service?"

"I guess we can find someone," she said, looking dubiously at the tapes. Then she brightened up a bit and said, "The general manager left word on Friday that he would be in early today, and that he'd like to see you in his office as soon as you get settled."

The general manager was a man who had started at P&G in manufacturing and then moved into marketing, because it was the best route to senior management. He had a reputation as a very empathetic guy, but we hadn't been talking for more than a few minutes when he said with a smile, "I think you're a spy from Cincinnati." He kept smiling for a moment, as if to underline that his comment was facetious, just a harmless bit of fun with the new kid. But I felt a level of suspicion I had not yet experienced in my career.

Uh-oh, I thought. P&G had sent me to make changes in the marketing organization, sure, but I wasn't a spy, even if my childhood fantasy was to be James Bond. And for Pete's sake, the GM and I were supposed to be on the same team. But apparently he had drunk the Noxell Kool-Aid, or maybe he'd inhaled too much Noxzema, because he strongly advocated creating "a third culture" that was neither P&G nor Noxell, but a synthesis of both. When one company acquires another one, you do want to leverage existing strengths and best practices. But unless you are going to operate the acquired company as a stand-alone enterprise, one or the other culture has to encompass the new whole. Otherwise you've got internecine conflict.

By the time I got back to my new office, it was 9:30 a.m. Except for the secretaries and mailroom people, there was still no one around.

"Where is everyone?" I asked.

"They're at the photo shoot for the new Niki Taylor campaign," my secretary said. Supermodel Niki Taylor had become the youngest-ever Cover Girl spokesmodel the previous year.

That threw me for a loop. P&G had a long-standing rule against brand management people attending photo and commercial shoots. P&G felt it was the responsibility of the advertising agency to produce and deliver excellent advertising. The very good reason for the rule was that it supported more objective judgment from P&G brand leaders about the quality and effectiveness of the finished advertising.

"Where is the shoot?" I asked.

"Santorini."

What? My mind raced with how much it was costing to have twenty marketing people at a photo shoot on Santorini, in the Greek isles. When my new colleagues returned to the office later that week, I came down hard on them about attending the photo shoot.

That was a mistake.

All of your actions as a leader are symbolic of what you stand for and value. And you have to look for ways to proactively influence the culture. Yes, Cover Girl, and Noxell as a whole, needed to become part of the P&G culture. But I should have respected their existing culture more, and recognized that this was something they needed to retain. Interacting closely with their advertising agency, photographers, and makeup artists on the shoots was part of how the Cover Girl people kept up with what was happening in the beauty category.

I learned a tough lesson. I sure did something symbolic with my new staff, but it was the wrong thing to do so early in our relationship.

At the same time, though, the people at Cover Girl had become much too cozy with their longtime ad agency people and much too focused on competing on image with prestige brands. The business had drifted away from the higher ideal—helping teenaged girls and young women feel more confident—that George Bunting had established.

Thanks to this ideal, Cover Girl had virtually owned the ideals field of eliciting joy, as far as mass market cosmetics were concerned, for most of its history. But having lost sight of their ideal, the Cover Girl team had lost contact with consumers. That was evident in the new advertising, which had abandoned the product-demo approach of the business's best growth years. The Cover Girl team claimed that consumers were bored with product demos and that beauty advertising had "moved on." But the truth was that consumers weren't bored with them, the team was. And the team was complacent and resting on its laurels.

I had to figure out how to bring this team to a place where it was more demanding of itself, and I had to be a little bit of a tough cop to do that. I had to set my standards high, but in a way that would be accepted by the Noxell culture.

A winning culture is a demanding culture. To build a winning culture, I have learned, it is vital to pick a few areas that are critical to meeting your goals for the business, such as the initiatives you approve, whom you promote, and which competitors or companies you benchmark. You have to get clear in your own mind what *your* standards are and how they serve the business's ideal, and then begin communicating them with your words and actions. You will almost always be amazed at how positively your organization responds.

I had to walk a fine line every day, showing how P&G's methods could help Cover Girl be more consumer-inspired and -guided, but not running roughshod over an organization that was extremely egocentric, very sensitive, and highly distrustful of me. It was like being in the Vatican four hundred years ago, as Dan Brown describes it in *The Da Vinci Code*. I didn't know who was going to stab me in the back, starting with my colleagues and going all the way up to my management.

The long-standing Noxell leadership lifestyle was 180 degrees different from that of any other P&G business unit. It included apartments in New York that were paid for by the business. Periodically, Noxell's brand leaders took the first Monday-morning train to New York, stayed there all week to comparison-shop beauty trends and hang out with their ad agency pals, and then caught the last Friday-evening train back to Baltimore.

Are you getting a whiff of the martini-fueled culture on the television show *Mad Men*? That's pretty close to the truth on these Noxell weeks in New York, I'm afraid.

My immediate boss was not the general manager but a Noxell executive who had come up through the ranks. He recognized the need for many of the changes I was pushing, but behind my back he whispered to the ad agency and others, "Don't worry about what Stengel is saying and doing. Nothing too major is gonna change around here."

It was a hard assignment, but it was great for my growth as a leader. It worked parts of me that hadn't been worked before. When I went to Jif, it was a healthy business that didn't realize how much new growth it could achieve, but everybody was receptive to learning how. Crisco was dysfunctional, but the people in the business were grateful to have new leaders who wanted to strengthen it, and they too embraced the new opportunities that came with focusing on improving the lives of consumers and customers. The team at Cover Girl had their heels dug in, and a lot of them wore stilettos—an Italian word, as Dan Brown might point out, originally used to describe daggers, not shoes!

So I had to be tough with Cover Girl's people about their

own and the business's performance. And I had to be tough with the ad agency, which saw me as an outsider threatening to take away their cash cow. But I didn't want to split up Cover Girl and its agency, because I felt they were capable of doing great things. So I also had to take them all on a journey with me.

My assigned task was to bring P&G's approach to brand building to the Noxell subsidiary's marketing, and improve results. I wanted to excel at that. But I also wanted to do something more. Even though I was only a marketing director at the time, a level below the general manager, I wanted my legacy at Noxell to be that the brands I worked with became as strong, competitive, creative, and profitable as any in the P&G portfolio. I wanted to infuse the Noxell brands with a deeper meaning, a higher ideal. Although I was not using that language then, that was what I was trying to do. Getting this done meant building trust, creating one team, one dream.

I started, once again, by asking lots of simple questions about the Cover Girl cosmetics business—variations on the four essential questions about the people most important to a business's future, what the business stands for and wants to stand for in their eyes, and how it is bringing that to life. Two things I did here made a big difference. One was that I asked these questions in a very open, inclusive, transparent way, insisting that we all look at the answers and evaluate them together, including the ad agency. The second was that I appealed to their pride as market leaders.

"Come on," I said, "Cover Girl should not only have the most beautiful and stylish ads. As the market leader, our ads should also have the strongest positive impact on sales. They should build our emotional brand equity [my language for brand ideal at the time]. They should set a new standard for the whole industry."

What I was trying to do was both set high standards and train informally all the time by overtly and explicitly using everyday encounters as training moments.

Every conversation, every meeting, every visit is an opportunity to train. Good leaders train by example, and bright, observant people pick up on it. I've done it throughout my career. It adds a few minutes to each meeting or visit, no more. In addition to a positive cumulative effect, regular informal training also improves immediate results. Right after a meeting ends, when everything is fresh, replaying the meeting outcome with the team or an individual shows ways to enhance it and triggers better follow-up. I learned the value and importance of this from my first brand manager at P&G. He used to group our team together after every advertising agency meeting and ask, "What did we learn? What could we do better? Are we excited about the outcome?" People love the message that building their talents and inspiration enables the business to win with customers and consumers.

Training is not just for others but for yourself as well. You must hold yourself accountable, in good times and tough times, day in and day out, for the capabilities you build in your culture. Again, being clear about what you stand for, discovering and activating your ideal, and then doing a gap analysis via the four questions (*How well do we understand the people who are most important to our future? What do we and our brand stand for? What do we want to stand for? How are we bringing the answers to these questions to life?*) will show you where you need to strengthen capabilities for competitive advantage. You must then develop a formal training program accordingly, and constantly measure and improve it. The magic in great companies—like many in the Stengel 50—is that they practice a blend of carefully chosen formal training and daily informal training.

The nub of the conflict between the P&G and Cover Girl

cultures was not in training but in how P&G measured advertising. P&G had a massive database of advertising test scores on things such as consumer recall and trial potential. P&G could predict with a fairly high degree of confidence that if an ad scored well above the norms, it would do great things in the marketplace. If it hit on the norms, we would go forward with it, but start immediately to improve it. If it hit below the norms, we almost always scrapped it or completely redid it.

Cover Girl's people ran the P&G measures on their ads because they had to, but they largely ignored the results, even though those were too often below normal. When I persuaded my new colleagues to try an updated product-demo approach, one that was supremely beautiful and stylish, it scored through the roof—and sent sales through the roof too.

The key was not just having the hard data. It was also bringing everyone together with a clear understanding of mutually agreed-upon goals and a shared vision of what success would look like. And then we had to hold ourselves accountable to the goals, celebrating milestones as we made progress.

My acid test on Cover Girl gave me a foundation for tackling the Clarion problem. Clarion was the Noxell organization's pride and joy, but it was a problem child. It had no brand ideal that drove its business operations. As a premium-priced brand compared to Cover Girl, it was not really a response to what consumers wanted or trends they were adopting. It reflected the Noxell organization's desire to have a premium brand for its own sake, something that this Baltimore-born and -based business could hold up as the equal of anything coming out of New York, Paris, or Milan.

Noxell had been investing a ton of money in Clarion since its launch. P&G had always had doubts about the brand, but it is hard for any business culture to sacrifice sunk costs and avoid throwing good money after bad. Over the four years since buying Noxell, P&G had continued spending on Clarion repositionings.

As I had on Cover Girl's advertising, I put together a team to assess Clarion, and I posed the four basic questions. We needed to establish once and for all whether Clarion had a viable platform, a brand ideal that was unique in its category, that gave us a compelling reason to invest in it, and that gave consumers a compelling reason to buy it. Did Clarion stand for something truly desirable and valuable in consumers' eyes? Did it have an aspirational ideal that was motivating to employees and consumers? Did it have a strong point of difference from the competition, emotionally and functionally? Did the business model make financial sense?

The first time the team sat down together, I think we could all see that the answers to these questions were negative. But the team wasn't ready to admit it. So I asked everyone to agree to a timetable. Then I encouraged them to articulate compelling positives, as well as the negatives. Over the next several months, we met regularly, and step by step the team faced up to the facts.

There were certainly no celebrations on the day we decided to discontinue Clarion. We didn't feel like winners. But we were. By coming together as a team and agreeing to operate with transparency and trust on a set of shared goals and measures, we found closure on one of the toughest issues in business: when to shut down a faltering enterprise.

In the months following the decisions on Cover Girl's advertising and Clarion, the spirit at Noxell grew more and more positive. Cover Girl's results rose on a new growth trajectory, and Clarion was no longer a drag on that growth. The Noxell way was becoming the P&G way, but still retained its distinctive flair. Things improved even more when Beth Kaplan came in from Cincinnati as Noxell's new general manager. I had worked for Beth on Crisco, and we were a good team.

Beth soon asked me to shift as marketing director from the flagship Cover Girl brand to the smaller Max Factor, a very troubled business, but also a classic brand that P&G was not ready to abandon. That was a tough move to accept as part of an upward career path, and another high-risk, high-reward opportunity. Max Factor had been relaunched just before I went to Noxell, but it was hemorrhaging money. If my team and I could stop the bleeding and make it profitable again, it would be quite a coup.

Max Factor, named for its movie makeup artist founder, had always positioned itself as the professional makeup artist's makeup. The team responsible for the relaunch had jettisoned all that. Ignoring Max Factor's history and its iconic packaging and product lines, the team basically wiped everything out and introduced new products, new advertising, new packaging, and a new in-store presence. In one fell swoop, they basically told all of Max Factor's loyal consumers, "Get lost. This is the new Max Factor."

The team felt they needed to do something this dramatic to reframe Max Factor's old-fashioned image. But it just bombed. When I took it over, Max Factor was losing more than $20 million a year, a huge hit for the division.

Some of those responsible for the failed relaunch lost their jobs. But Beth and I put together a leadership team that was about half existing Max Factor people and half newcomers from elsewhere in P&G. With these leadership changes we quickly put the right people into the right roles as the foundation for rapidly turning the tide at Max Factor. One of the most important additions was Mike Burnett, a supply chain expert who managed the liquidation of the massive inventory of products that weren't right and the installation of a new supply chain.

We agreed as a team on an aspiration for what we wanted Max Factor to be, what our principles were, what success would look like, and a scorecard to measure our progress. Again, although I wasn't then using this language, we were resolving what the business's brand ideal would be, what higher-order benefit it would bring to the world. We did a detailed diagnostic on the business to determine its strengths, assets, points of difference from competitors, and most of all its brand ideal.

We decided that Max Factor had to return to its original brand ideal—bringing the romance and glamour of Hollywood to women everywhere—but with a difference. Max Factor could still be the makeup of movie makeup artists, but the reference had to be new Hollywood, not old Hollywood. We started making heroes of current movie makeup people in our advertising, such as Gary Liddiard, who was working on *Up Close and Personal,* Tina Earnshaw of *Titanic,* and Michele Burke of *Austin Powers.* We told stories about the colors and formulas they were using. We also brought back some of the formulas and updated some of the iconic packaging that consumers loved.

These steps were consistent with the brand. They made sense to consumers. They returned the brand to a track it never should have left, but freshened it. Within a year we were breaking even and back on a growth curve.

Right before I left Max Factor and Noxell, there was a huge P&G sales meeting in Phoenix, Arizona. The Max Factor team and I put on a big show, with comic and dramatic sketches on a James Bond theme (yes, I was Bond, James Bond, fulfilling that boyhood fantasy, at least for a few minutes onstage) about restoring Max Factor's heritage as a business in a contemporary way. It was a lot of fun, pumped up everyone at P&G about the new direction, and boosted a great team spirit inside Max Factor and Noxell.

I had been at Noxell now about two years, and was charged up to continue to accelerate our momentum. But P&G then asked me to take another leap into the unknown and tackle an even bigger opportunity in getting a business culture right.

THE PRAGUE POSSIBILITIES

Twelve years after I joined the company, P&G promoted me to the job of general manager of its operations in the Czech Republic and Slovakia, the young democracies that had replaced communist Czechoslovakia. It was an early shot at being a general manager, a big jump from being a marketing director at Noxell into a strategically important situation for P&G.

The Czech and Slovak subsidiary, headquartered in Prague, had been established only five years earlier, under then chairman and CEO Ed Artzt, shortly after the fall of the Berlin Wall in 1989. His successor, John Pepper, who was chairman and CEO from 1995 to 1999, made growing P&G's operations in the emerging economies of Asia and post-communist Eastern Europe one of his top priorities.

The Prague operation had achieved strong growth, and P&G had made a sizable investment in it. But the group president offering me the job felt that the organization needed some rethinking as it grew. Its original general manager, who had taken the assignment after several other people had turned it down as too difficult, was moving on to another business development role in Central Asia. Did I want to replace him?

I was eager to move into general management, with its wider scope of responsibility. I felt ready to take what I had learned about building and leading a team to the next stage: creating and leveraging a higher sense of purpose in an entire organization. I wanted to elevate our brands in the Czech and Slovak republics to fulfill higher ideals, although once again I was not yet using the term *brand ideal*. In addition, I was inspired by John Pepper's vision of P&G's potential business growth and societal impact in the new Eastern Europe. I got pumped up imagining my own goal as general manager and my legacy in that role: growing the business and further establishing P&G's principles, vision, and purpose in Prague. Finally, Kathleen and I were intrigued by the prospect of spending the next four or five years in one of the world's most beautiful cities and in the midst of one of the biggest economic, political, and cultural transitions of our time. We thought it could be a great experience for our family and a rare opportunity for my business life.

Every assignment in your career is an opportunity to "live your legacy" and make a significant business contribution with a lasting impact on the people you work with, if not an entire organization, through the way you work day to day. Since the start of my career, I have wanted every business I worked in to be better for it, and for my colleagues and employees to remember our work together as positive and growth-filled.

Living your legacy starts with being clear about what you stand for. It goes beyond that, however. It means focusing explicitly on what you want to be remembered for, and then acting on it. Without conscious thought and energy, it simply won't happen.

John Pepper wanted to establish the purpose, values, and principles of the rapidly globalizing P&G so that it would never lose its special culture. In particular, he wanted to enter China and post-communist Eastern Europe in a way that would not only lead to enduring growth for P&G in those markets but also serve as a beacon for how businesses should operate in these emerging economies.

What a legacy—to influence the business practices and

principles for countries such as Poland, Hungary, Russia, and Ukraine as they rapidly transitioned to free market economies. John encouraged all of us to get involved not only through our businesses but also through the region's new regulatory agencies, emerging trade associations, and a variety of new government task forces and initiatives. John, along with Herbert Schmitz, the head of Central and Eastern Europe for P&G, believed this was simply the right thing to do. They also knew that transparent economies, with rational rules of law, would be a far better environment for P&G to compete in over the longer term.

"IS THIS GUY FROM MARS?"

When I went into the Prague office for the first time on a Monday morning in August 1995, I called the heads of the finance, marketing, public relations, manufacturing, customer service, sales, and human resources departments together in a meeting. We were a virtual United Nations. The head of finance was from northern England and had a thick Yorkshire accent. One of the marketing directors was Dutch. The incoming HR head was French. The people running public relations and regulatory affairs were native Czechs.

I said that I was delighted to join them at a moment of great opportunity for P&G and the whole region, that it was essential for us to become one team, with one dream, and that we would meet like this every Monday morning to ensure that we did so. I briefly shared my career story and my early feelings about our opportunities. I said we would agree on very clear goals and standards in the P&G spirit, that we would operate with a high level of trust, with mutual respect and accountability. We would work together to build our portfolio of brands into brands with higher ideals. In short, I began my first day on the job wearing "be clear about what you stand for" on my sleeve.

The department heads were sneaking looks at one another as I spoke. But the impression I got was not of them against me, as I had found and had to overcome at Noxell. To the contrary, the people sitting around the conference table seemed uneasy about one another. They seemed to be glancing out of the corners of their eyes, in order to see if anyone was already clued in to my plans and had an inside track with me.

One thing was clear beyond a doubt: they were looking at me not as a spy but as if I came from Mars.

It soon emerged that in the five years of the subsidiary's existence, there had really been no leadership team. Most meetings were one-on-one, closed-door encounters with my predecessor. The department heads never got an opportunity to question this practice. In any case, they were all rather young and fairly new in their roles. Those who were not native Czechs and Slovaks were part of the wave of adventurous young people who had come to Prague because it was the cultural center of the new Eastern Europe, a breathtakingly beautiful city bustling with creative energy, even if P&G's subsidiary there was not always full of that energy.

The subsidiary had lots of energy, but it was too often the destructive kind. Fueled by the pent-up dreams and ambitions that the fall of communism unleashed, all the local employees wanted desperately to improve things for themselves and their families. But they had no concept of working together to achieve this. Each and every one of them was out for him- or herself alone. The communist regime had always lied to them about the solidarity of the people while the party bosses enriched themselves, and the organization reflected the damage done to Czech and Slovak society by decades of repression.

The organization also reflected my predecessor's management style. He had a very different style from mine—he worked issues one-on-one, and this resulted in some misunderstandings and, at times, suspicion and jealousy.

At the most basic level, the organization displayed its dysfunction in such totally non-P&G behavior as pilfering office supplies and machinery, from paper and pencils to office microwave ovens, and lying on expense reports. Even more disturbing was how ready people were to undercut one another, just like neighbors reporting on each other to the secret police.

My clear standards, along with open decision-making lines and a consistent emphasis on teamwork and shared principles, vision, and purpose, had a positive effect. So did the introduction of an employee stock-ownership plan. But our progress in becoming one team, one dream was frustratingly slow. I could feel the immense potential of the organization, but I couldn't harness it. People were still harshly competing against one another rather than joining forces, developing a sense of personal ownership, and investing all of themselves in their work.

My philosophy of transparent organizational leadership and building a high level of trust among employees and with outside partners and retail customers struck the organization as very strange. Some of my department heads in particular didn't like my team concept and accountability. But there was no bench team ready to put into those people's roles, and I couldn't simply replace them all. In the meantime, their resistance was gumming things up inside and outside the organization. On the latter score, we had time-sensitive opportunities to build distribution and retail partnerships with long-term strategic value and competitive advantage. I was determined not to let those opportunities go to waste.

My head of HR, Pierre Rebour, had been in manufacturing in P&G's French subsidiary, and he really had a sense of the

P&G way. He was also very new to the Prague organization. Discussing things with me one day, Pierre suggested that I bring in Agnès Sangan from P&G's Paris office as an internal consultant. I knew vaguely of Agnès by reputation. She had an MBA from Harvard Business School and had developed expertise in both consumer understanding and human resource areas.

It was worth a shot. Pierre and I planned an off-site meeting for the leadership team, and Agnès came from Paris as facilitator and workshop leader. Agnès turned out to be the classic French intellectual, imperious, brilliant, and with a biting wit, but also with a deep reservoir of empathy and kindness. We were completely different personalities, but we hit it off right away.

Over the week with my very troubled team in a dank castle turned conference center in the hills outside Prague, I marveled at Agnès's highly developed gift for listening to people, sensing underlying dynamics, and telling a story back to them. In a series of intense sessions punctuated by chances to unwind together outside the office, Agnès led the team members to recognize and acknowledge blocks to trusting me and one another and to signing on to a shared sense of purpose. These dialogues gave me priceless opportunities to show that I was really serious when I talked about making our operation the best company in the Czech Republic and Slovakia, that I was serious about focusing on our brands' underleveraged ideals, building the best customer and consumer relationships, and a work culture that our people enjoyed and that others wanted to join; and showing that all these things went together with the principles, vision, and purpose that made P&G special.

It was a pivotal experience for the team, and it had a huge impact on me personally. It made a night-and-day difference in our ability to communicate and work together. It was also another great lesson for me on being clear about what I stand for. While I thought I was being clear from my first day in Prague, my organization did not internalize it. Only after these sessions with Agnès improved our communication did the organization really understand and begin acting upon a shared vision for the future.

The week also marked the start of Agnès's becoming an important mentor and colleague for me throughout the rest of my career at P&G. It's important to realize that mentors are not necessarily always people who are higher up in an organization than you are. Never let ego or hierarchy get in the way of learning from people who are true masters of their crafts.

The Prague leadership team's breakthrough was genuine. But it was just a step, albeit a crucial one, in a long journey. I quickly had to consolidate that breakthrough and extend it throughout the Czech and Slovak subsidiary.

One important venue for doing that was a distribution infrastructure innovation. The Czech Republic and Slovakia then had a very fragmented retail picture, with some 35,000 small retail outlets for a total population of about 15 million people. The idea, piloted in Poland and already in progress when I came to Prague, was to enlist local entrepreneurs in getting our brands out to all the little shops in the region's towns and villages. We bought Mercedes-Benz vans for them, becoming Mercedes-Benz's largest corporate customer, fronted them other funds, and taught them good business practices. The vans and the start-up money weren't outright gifts, but advances to be paid back.

We had regular headaches keeping that distribution network ethically clean—on occasion we discovered that someone had emptied a P&G warehouse overnight, or was trying to extract kickbacks at some point in the supply chain. These were all occasions to demonstrate that our principles, vision, and purpose were real, that we walked the walk as well as talked the talk. We set our standards high and did not compromise. The return on our investment of time, money, and high ethical standards was that this distribution network became a huge competitive advantage. Before long, it extended from Poland, Hungary, and the Czech Republic and Slovakia to Ukraine and Russia. And it had a huge positive impact on our local employees and their sense of pride and ownership in working at P&G.

We had the chance to create an equally important partnership at the other end of the retail spectrum. There was as yet no Walmart effect in the region, but big Western European retailers were starting to move in. Tesco and Carrefour had a foothold in consumer retail. Another potential entrant was Makro, a top-five global retailer with a cash-and-carry discount warehouse model for local businesses that originated in Holland and then became part of the German retail-wholesale giant Metro Group.

I reached out to Makro's new general manager for the Czech Republic and Slovakia, Levine Oggel, when they were in the idea stage. Emulating P&G's retail customer teams in the United States for Walmart, Target, Kroger, Costco, and others, but on a much smaller scale, I immediately put a multidisciplinary team together in my organization, the first such team it had ever had. I said that I would personally sponsor the team, and that we would help Makro get started in the region by sharing everything P&G had learned about the Czech and Slovak market over the previous five years.

We helped them find locations for their warehouse outlets. We advised Levine and his leadership team on where to find good apartments. We consulted on hiring. We shared our intellectual property on local consumers' shopping habits and preferences, whether or not they were for P&G brands. Over the course of our partnership with Makro, P&G brands won massive shares in their stores because of the growing strength of the brands and our willingness to share our intellectual property. When I left Prague, Levine Oggel presented me with an amazing piece of Czech crystal, an intricately carved wine carafe, etched with the date August 1, 1997, and the words, in Czech, "To Jim Stengel. You are a true friend of Makro's."

The customer team on the Makro account was a great leadership model for the subsidiary. It demonstrated that we were not about a transaction, but about a win-win relationship. That prepared the organization to build relationships with other Western retailers as they came into the region. We also created smaller teams to work on distinct sales channels, such as regional supermarkets.

Earlier I spoke about the importance of planning and carrying out a few highly symbolic actions. Leading the Makro account team was one such action during my time in Prague. Another was becoming personally involved in recruiting, including speaking at universities and interviewing recruits, and having my leadership team do the same. In keeping with its practice of promoting from within, P&G has a long tradition of senior management involvement in recruiting and hiring to ensure that the company always has plenty of top talent. The Prague subsidiary had to adopt this practice to share the larger P&G culture, and it was an important part of what I wanted my legacy as GM to be. Many of the people I personally recruited to join the Czech and Slovak business continue to have very successful careers at P&G and beyond.

Equally important symbolically was how I dealt with visits from P&G leaders. As a hub in the new Eastern Europe, Prague was a frequent destination for senior P&G managers. I told P&G visitors, "It's great that you're coming to Prague. We'll do our best to make sure it's a productive visit for you. In return, I expect you to spend time with my people. I expect you to go into the field and visit stores with them and give them the benefit of your expertise. Train them."

On my side, whenever I spent time with P&G visitors, I had as many of my department heads with me as possible. I wanted the visits to be both training experiences and showcases for my team, stretching them and allowing them to shine. I made it clear that those who got this opportunity to interact with P&G senior managers also had to share the learning from it with others in the Prague organization.

One occasion in particular that stands out was a visit in the summer of 1996 from Durk Jager, who was then president and chief operating officer of P&G. We started on a Saturday morning by taking him into a variety of Prague shopping areas and stores so that he could get a good sampling of the market. Then we went back to the office, and I had all of my department heads in the room with Durk to discuss business challenges and opportunities.

We had a lunch planned at Prague's oldest continuously operated brewery-restaurant, dating to the 1400s. We didn't get there until almost four o'clock because we were having such a great discussion.

We broke for a couple of hours after this late lunch, and then I brought the whole leadership team back together with Durk at dinner on the balcony terrace of a restaurant in the heart of old Prague, near the Charles Bridge. I made a toast to my team, and Durk followed that with a beautiful little impromptu speech. It was a magic moment on a golden summer evening, when we could all feel a part of realizing John Pepper's and Herbert Schmitz's vision of P&G's contributing to, and sharing in, the growth of the new Eastern Europe.

By Monday morning it had become a magic moment for everyone in the company, not just the relatively small number of people at the dinner. Everyone was talking about how I had included the entire leadership team in the whole day of activity with the president of P&G.

Over the following months, the Czech and Slovak operations made major progress on multiple fronts. My role as general manager had really stretched me as a leader, but I had seen once again how powerful a shared vision of improving people's lives can be in a business. From Jif to Crisco, Cover Girl, Max Factor, and the Prague subsidiary, I had progressed from a largely intuitive to a more conscious understanding of how uniting people around such a vision could supercharge a business.

There was still plenty of work to do in Prague. One thing I really had to improve on in my leadership was optimizing my focus on different parts of the business and conveying the right emphases to the organization. I was getting a lot of pressure from my bosses to build P&G's global brands. But I had also inherited a large number of important local brands, dating to the communist era, which my predecessor had smartly acquired. In my first year in Prague, I didn't pay enough attention to these small brands, and the growth and profitability of the business as a whole suffered. In my second year, we began to figure out how to accelerate growth on the local brands—by revealing and activating their brand ideals—to the point where they generated the majority of our profit.

I was still working on balancing big and small businesses in the Prague subsidiary's portfolio when I became involved in an extraordinary adventure with Pampers, P&G's biggest business, and at that time its most troubled. It was in many ways the signature brand and business leadership challenge of my career, and a real test of building a business culture around a brand ideal of improving people's lives. It set the stage for my time as global marketing officer at P&G, and for my developing the principles and practices in this book. But before telling you about that experience in another deep dive, I want to sum up my learning over my career on how to build a culture that emanates from and amplifies your ideal.

THE TEN CULTURE BUILDERS

Here are ten culture builders that have been integral to all my leadership experiences. They continue to serve as my guideposts for addressing organizational issues as I work to help others be more ideals-inspired in all they do.

1. Reveal your inspirational brand ideal and operationalize it. This is where you always must begin as a leader. Discovery's founder, John Hendricks, showed us a near-perfect example of a leader keeping his brand ideal relevant and inspirational for decades, and operationalizing it in every function of the business. When I became the marketing director at Max Factor, my first priority was revealing its ideal, harking back to its roots as the glamorous makeup for Hollywood stars. We then operationalized it and turned the business around within eighteen months.

2. Be clear about what you stand for, inside and outside your company. From day one of my P&G assignment in Prague, I tried to be clear about my priorities, values, and principles. I engaged employees, distributors, regulators, and suppliers constantly. But I learned it sometimes takes an intervention to really embed your principles into the daily business priorities, and to change behavior accordingly. Not until a pivotal off-site with my leadership team, about a year into my assignment, did my organization really embrace the direction I was setting.

3. Design your organization for what it needs to win. This includes the specific work your organization must do, the capabilities you need to build for competitive advantage, and the career path to bring this to life. The Cover Girl story is a terrific example. I needed to shift the work in that organization from an obsession with executional work, such as traveling to Greece to shoot television ads, to work on ideals-inspired brand strategies, marketing spending analytics, competitive assessment, and team leadership. We achieved that and the business got stronger and more sustainable.

4. Get your team right and do it quickly. Most of my management mistakes stemmed from not moving quickly enough to reshape my team. I moved quickly when I took over the leadership of Max Factor, and we turned around the failing business far faster than my management expected. It is one reason I was promoted after only twelve years at P&G to a general management position in Prague.

5. Champion innovation of all kinds. You must visibly champion a portfolio approach to innovation, emanating from your brand ideal. Every business needs a mix of product or service innovation, pure commercial innovation, and disruptive innovation that redefines a task or a business model. I will talk more about these three kinds of innovation in chapter 9, but my Prague experience clearly shows the benefits of a portfolio approach to innovation. We created a disruptive innovation by making our brands available to far more people through the Mercedes-Benz van sales distribution program. Meanwhile, we had a steady flow of product improvements and commercial innovation, such as new sampling programs.

6. Set your standards very high. One of the most powerful leadership actions I took at Noxell was to raise the standards for our business growth expectations and our advertising results. Setting standards high is one of the most powerful daily opportunities a leader has. You make decisions every day about what meets your standards when you agree or disagree with recommendations from your people.

7. Train all the time. This is simply a mind-set shift. Every interaction every day is a training event, and you can capitalize on it or not. I showed in the Noxell and Prague stories how I trained constantly, including frequent debriefings after sales calls and management meetings to coach my people on how to improve the outcome next time. Training all the time is fast and efficient, and a hallmark of great leaders and great companies.

8. Do a few symbolic things to create excitement about what is important. Focus on one or two symbolic events a year, major actions that will be meaningful to your organization and other stakeholders. When I formed a special multidisciplinary team in Prague to help Makro succeed, it reverberated among our employees and our customers, and with our competitors. It symbolized that I wanted us to win big with modern retailers as they entered the Czech Republic and Slovakia.

As a leader, you get to decide who the heroes are. Your choices are symbolic, and they speak volumes. When my team and I took Jif to record sales and profitability, P&G chose me to make a presentation at the global management meeting held every November in Cincinnati, the corporate headquarters. More than 5,000 P&G managers from around the world attended, and my bosses said my presentation would send a signal about taking an entrepreneurial approach to brand management.

Addressing this meeting was a huge honor, especially because I had been with the company only a little over six years. I was elated! But I also wanted to send a signal of my own about how my team achieved its success. The format for these presentations was staid, to put it mildly, with senior managers standing stiffly on a podium reporting mostly numerical results and discussing supply chain initiatives, corporate restructurings, and the like in dry, bureaucratic jargon. For visual interest, there would be a few static slides.

The segment of the meeting including my presentation was headlined "Maximizing Consumer and Customer Satisfaction," an absolute imperative for any business, no doubt about it, but not very inspiring language. I wanted to tell the story of how Jif achieved new growth in a much more personal way. And I wanted a cross-section of people from throughout the business to join me onstage in telling that story. Several weeks before the November meeting, I got together with my team and planned a presentation that included two music videos, one with lyrics I helped write. MTV had been around a few years, but for P&G this was a revolutionary idea. The first video showed children of Jif people, from managers to plant employees, having fun slathering peanut butter on bread, bananas, and other foods, and getting it all over themselves as they ate their favorite concoctions. My young daughter, her face covered in peanut butter, was one of the little kids. The second video showed Jif people "playing" instruments, dancing, and lip-syncing lyrics in locations that included both our peanut butter plants.

The lyrics for the music video won't put me in the Songwriters Hall of Fame, I'm afraid. Here's a snippet from one of the videos: "Everyone across the nation, join our family celebration . . . Consumers helped us see the light, we listened and we did it right."

A bit corny? Yes. But it also sent a signal that we were a team that broke records *and* had fun.

It took some persuading before the presentation was approved. But it was worth it. We began with the video of the little kids. The audience was surprised and delighted, but they weren't quite sure how to react, because they'd never seen anything like it at these meetings before. Then I emphasized that our record growth resulted from our caring deeply about moms and building that emotion into the business. That led into the second video. By this time the audience had relaxed enough to enjoy itself, and the arena filled with laughter and applause.

Then I turned over the rest of the presentation to other members of the team: one of my marketing colleagues, a woman from P&G's toll-free food product information line, a plant manager, and an assembly-line worker from one of our two peanut butter plants. The visuals were not just slides with numbers, charts, and diagrams, but also featured photographs of Jif people and consumers. The energy and confidence my Jif colleagues showed in addressing the audience gave me goose bumps. The last words of the presentation, spoken by the plant manager, were about Jif's future, one in which "every member of the Jif family will be having fun."

We really did have fun, and that's what stayed with all those who saw the presentation. I demanded a lot of the Jif team, and we worked as hard as any group at P&G. But I've always found that people do their best work when they believe in it, enjoy it, and feel they are advancing. Ever since my Jif days, I've made it a priority to build a work culture with these attributes. And I've also made it a priority to find symbolic, memorable ways to communicate them. It's an important part of making your organization a magnet for the best and most talented people.

9. Think like a winner, act like a winner. Several years ago I discovered an obscure study on a P&G European detergent brand with declining market share. The study found that consumers didn't buy the brand because they sensed that the people behind it were uninspired, unhappy, and disengaged. Consumers did not think about it consciously in this way, but they did not want to put their money into something that wasn't backed by the full faith and credit, so to speak, of the people who made it.

Wow! I had never explicitly thought of looking at the root cause of a business's malaise being the experience of the people in it. As I'd been trained to do in business school, I looked at product data (is the offering superior or inferior on key benefits?), distribution (again, better or worse than the competition's?), and so on.

Important questions, but this study made me realize that the answers point to a larger issue: the motivation and inspiration of the people behind a business. I had always believed that happy, motivated people drive better business results. There is a boatload of research on that. What I had not known before this obscure study was that customers can sense how motivated a business's people are just from seeing the product and how it's presented to them. If you looked at the brand in the study, there was no obvious clue that its people didn't believe in it. But customers and consumers knew that this was so.

People want to buy into a winner. They want to be part of something that is making a positive difference. So be sure that you think and act like a winner, especially when your business is going through a rough patch. Otherwise, your people won't act that way, and customers will spend their money elsewhere.

One reason we shut down the Noxell Clarion brand was there was simply never a winning attitude on the team. And a big reason Max Factor turned around and Cover Girl accelerated was the winning attitude on those teams, which their consumers noticed and rewarded.

The difference between what was possible with Clarion and what was possible with Max Factor and Cover Girl had everything to do with brand ideals. A brand ideal is a huge plus in building a winning attitude, because it charges everyone up about contributing to something that really matters, something of fundamental human value.

10. Live your desired legacy. I always write down what legacy I want to leave in every assignment I have. I do this in my first 100 days. It keeps me focused and centered, and provides a North Star, if you will. Earlier in the chapter I talked about P&G CEO John Pepper's legacy in Central and Eastern Europe: establishing business practices in those markets for P&G and indeed for other businesses to follow.

To paraphrase Mick Jagger, you can't always get where you want to go. But if you don't know your ultimate goal, you'll never get there.

My experience at Noxell and Prague vividly illustrates that the so-called "soft stuff" is really the "hard stuff." Nothing is harder to get right than a culture change, and nothing pays such huge dividends. In the next chapter, I will develop this idea further with the story of how Pampers rebuilt its business culture around a rediscovered ideal, giving P&G a template for category-leading growth throughout the first decade of the 2000s. Pampers is the story of how an everyday business in an everyday category set out in a small way to change the world, and how, because of its culture, its impact turned out to be not so small.

7

How Pampers
Changed the World

How an Ideal Transformed a Culture and a Business

BUILD
your culture around
your ideal

Working in my office in Prague one cold morning in March 1997, I received a mysterious phone call. Larry Dare, one of P&G's most senior vice presidents, was on the line. That was normal enough, because I was in frequent touch with leadership at P&G's European headquarters in Brussels about our young, expanding presence in the new Eastern Europe.

Larry wasn't calling about business as usual, however. He wanted me to meet him that very night at the Frankfurt airport, subject to be disclosed only face-to-face.

On the flight to Frankfurt, I couldn't help wondering what Larry was going to say. Moving to Prague and becoming general manager for P&G's business in the Czech Republic and Slovakia had been a huge step up in responsibility, and lots of work remained to be done. I wasn't itching to move on to something or someplace new. It was exciting to be part of the development of democratic societies and free market economies in post-communist Eastern Europe.

In the Lufthansa lounge at the Frankfurt airport, Larry said, "Jim, we want you to move to Frankfurt and take over Pampers Europe." Pampers was P&G's flagship business, its largest revenue producer. But it was also a business in serious trouble. Reflecting that, Larry added, "We want you to run Europe and make friends with North America."

One of Pampers' many problems was that its regional groups and 80-plus country teams were all acting independently, competing with one another as much as with other companies' offerings, especially Kimberly-Clark's Huggies and Pull-Ups. P&G knew it had to begin fixing that in Pampers' two biggest organizations, Pampers Europe, which was then being run by an Austrian, and Pampers North America, which would continue to be run by an American. The two executives were not collaborating, and that was stifling any potential for their organizations to cooperate in solving the global challenges Pampers faced in every area from research and development to design, manufacturing, and marketing.

A STATIC BUSINESS, A FLAT IDEAL

Although my understanding of the importance of a brand ideal was a work in progress in 1997, I had seen more than enough evidence to show me that no business ever really takes off without an inspiring idea at its core. I had also seen again and again that the heritage of a business holds vital clues to the potential for such an idea to drive success in the present and the future. So from the moment Larry Dare offered me the chance to run Pampers Europe, I started looking for the clues that would help drive Pampers' success.

Launched in 1961 as the first mass-marketed disposable diaper, Pampers quickly became P&G's fastest-growing enterprise and subsequently its largest. When I joined the business in mid-1997, Pampers had global annual sales of $3.4 billion. Yet although the category it had originated continued to grow significantly, with no end in sight, Pampers had become P&G's

poorest performer in terms of profitability and market share growth. Wall Street saw Pampers as the biggest drag on P&G's overall financial results.

Although it remained the world's biggest diaper business by far, Pampers faced increasing competitive pressure. The much greater size of the Pampers business compared to the competition should have been a scale advantage. But we were squandering, not leveraging, that advantage. Kimberly-Clark's lower-priced Huggies had taken the number one spot in North America. In response, P&G had cut the North American price of Pampers closer to that of Huggies, but its market share kept eroding along with its margins.

Pampers dominated the European market, where it enjoyed premium pricing and substantial profit margins. But Kimberly-Clark had just introduced Huggies in the United Kingdom and soon would be selling them in the rest of Europe, threatening the same market share and profit erosion Pampers had suffered in the United States. Additional competition loomed in both Europe and North America from private-label brands and smaller diaper businesses.

Paying attention first and foremost to what we could learn from moms (dads in every market followed their wives' choices about which diaper to purchase), my team and I began to analyze Pampers' slowdown and potential for recovery. We started by reviewing Pampers' heritage, and its existing strengths and weaknesses.

With the introduction of the disposable diaper, Pampers gave families, and moms in particular, unprecedented convenience, time savings, ease, and confidence in dealing with the large amounts of you-know-what that healthy babies produce at unpredictable times throughout the day and night. As the category grew and copycat disposable diapers appeared, Pampers emphasized the most important benefit of the disposable diaper for the first generations of mothers and babies to use them: they were far more absorbent, and thus kept baby much drier and more comfortable than cloth diapers.

Everyone in the Pampers business strove to ensure that they stretched a lead on the competition in absorbency and dryness. The success of their efforts, along with the residue of first-mover advantage, meant that most hospitals used Pampers, a significant fact for all moms, but especially those having their first child.

As the category matured, focusing so closely on dryness gradually led consumers to see Pampers solely in terms of superiority in that single functional benefit. Meanwhile, Kimberly-Clark's Huggies provided adequate dryness, the standard of entry into the category, while adding better fit and more appealing aesthetics as well as a lower price.

Kimberly-Clark was not just a follower in the market. In 1989 it introduced Pull-Ups training pants with an "I'm a big kid now" tagline. They became an immediate hit. Because training pants commanded a significantly higher price and profit margin than diapers, Kimberly-Clark soon had 90 percent of the market segment with the most profit. It also gained increasing support from big retailers such as Kroger and Walmart because of the new sales and profits that Pull-Ups generated.

It took Pampers five years to introduce its own training pants, with the unimaginative name of Trainers. They failed so miserably that Pampers killed the product two years later, in 1996.

Meanwhile, Pampers R&D, design, manufacturing, and marketing continued to emphasize dryness first, last, and always, even though Premium Pampers introduced breathable side liners in 1996. This innovation offered more than dryness; it made baby more comfortable from the moment the diaper went on, before any wetting occurred. But we couldn't convey that benefit to moms distinctly when we ourselves didn't appreciate its wider meaning.

P&G invented the multibillion-dollar disposable diaper industry with Pampers, but North American moms now saw Kimberly-Clark's Huggies and Pull-Ups as the products that best addressed their preferences and their children's needs. We had to halt and reverse that decline in North America, and prevent it from happening in Europe and the rest of the world.

To succeed in doing so, Pampers needed a unified organization, but its business culture had fragmented over the years. As P&G's biggest revenue producer, Pampers was valuable territory, and many fiefdoms had arisen to claim and protect different pieces of it. I've already mentioned how the regional groups and country teams were operating virtually independently. The largest countries all had their own advertising agency teams and marketing partners, so each could create whatever it needed from scratch. There were multiple product designs, multiple marketing campaigns, and multiple packaging formats. This built heavy duplicate costs into the business and stymied any effort to present the product and communicate with consumers in a coherent way.

Fragmentation and turf guarding characterized all the functional areas of the Pampers business. Amazingly for P&G, Pampers had no single brand or marketing leader. There was a manufacturing leader, an R&D leader, a finance leader, a human resources leader, a market research leader, an information technology leader, a strategic planning leader, and a president of the business. But Pampers had no business artist who held everyone accountable to a core brand ideal and strategy.

The president of baby care at the time, Mark Ketchum, could have potentially done it. But truth be told, the dysfunction at Pampers was symptomatic of problems throughout P&G. Within a year, Wall Street would begin hammering our stock price as it lost confidence in the company's ability to solve these problems. Mark was mired in trying to simplify severe supply chain complexity, and also dealing with the inevitable fires that happen every day when a business is in crisis.

Although the functional leaders and the regions generally agreed that dryness was Pampers' big selling point, they weren't working together to deliver this. Each had its own separate initiatives and communication plans on the dryness benefit. It was a "not invented here" culture, where people thought the only good ideas were the ones they had. In particular, manufacturing and R&D on one hand and marketing on the other might as well have been on separate planets. This was especially problematic because complexities in manufacturing, supply chain, and distribution make disposable diapers a business with a long lead time. New products were often in development for years, and might even be on the verge of being launched into the market, before marketing people became involved.

As one Pampers employee told my team, "There is a leg cuff guy in R&D. He works on nothing but leg cuffs, in his own world. While diaper leg cuffs prevent leaks, the leg cuff guy isn't talking to anyone in marketing or design about what might signal to a mom that the cuff works."

You might assume that a baby care business attracted moms and others with a passion for babies to work on it. Pampers had a very male, engineering-led structure, however. It made little effort to recruit people who wanted to work on products for babies, or to build an organization that embraced moms and babies and inspired employees to want to help improve their lives. Far from having more women and moms working on it than the average P&G business, Pampers had a lot fewer. The women who were working in the business didn't want to stay there, and turnover was much higher for women than for men.

The male-dominated leadership of the Pampers business

reflected all this. A. G. Lafley, who as P&G's CEO from 1999 to 2009 constantly emphasized "the consumer is boss," said that Pampers' boss in the 1990s was not the consumer but "the machine," the factory. In head count, budget, and priorities, the organization was dominated by what the engineers thought would improve absorbency and dryness.

Worst of all, the Pampers culture had degenerated into finger-pointing. If a new product or product upgrade didn't do well, the departments blamed each other for the poor performance.

Pampers' external relationships with consumers had also deteriorated. When Pampers first put disposable diapers on store shelves, the business became moms' best friend, freeing them from constantly washing and drying soiled cloth diapers. Pampers no longer interacted with moms as a friend, however. The marketing and ad campaigns simply talked at them. Despite the fact that moms' buying decisions in the stores, and their direct comments to P&G researchers, said loud and clear that this was counterproductive, the business was not listening.

The communication was all one-way, a tired advertising format with an expert endorsing Pampers with a product demonstration. It was the last thing moms wanted: one more voice telling them what to do. The packaging was equally dated, a pale green plastic bag with a picture of a perfectly posed Caucasian baby, but no cues to help a mom easily pick out the right size or product features for her child. In focus groups, moms described Pampers as the brand their mothers-in-law told them to use, while their friends were using something else. Ouch! But rather than change what it was doing, Pampers just talked back at moms about dryness.

Being the leader in dryness wasn't enough, given the fact that Pampers failed to deliver an excellent product experience in other ways. Pampers diapers now looked and felt generic to moms. If you took different brands out of their packages and put them all on the same table, you could not tell which one was a Pampers. In fact, Pampers had serious deficiencies to Huggies in terms of important design features such as texture, playful graphics, and fragrance.

It's an old business adage: you get what you measure. For many years Pampers had been measuring R&D, design, manufacturing, and customer satisfaction on—you guessed it—dryness. The measures became ever more precise and particular, homing in on independent elements of dryness such as leg cuff leakage. Missing the change in consumer attitudes as every disposable diaper came to offer adequate absorbency and dryness, Pampers completely failed to measure the subtler things that now had moms' attention.

Instead the organization looked at its data, saw its numbers on customer perception of diaper dryness rising, and congratulated itself on doing a great job. It's an all too familiar recipe for failure in every industry, and a hallmark of businesses without brand ideals to guide them: staying loyal to the wrong measures, evaluating what you think is important rather than what matters to customers and makes a positive difference in their lives.

The bottom line was that Pampers had become a stagnant business. It could not evolve to keep in step with moms, the people most important to its future, because it did not have a clue what moms really wanted. The only thing Pampers could evolve was its dryness.

If Pampers could be about more than skin dryness, however, could it regain its preeminence in the market? Could the business grow beyond diapers to become a force in toddler care with training pants and other products?

Only moms could help us answer those questions in detail. But the more my team and some colleagues on the global team discovered about the heritage of Pampers' relationship to moms, the more I felt the outcome could be positive—provided we learned from the example of Pampers' creator, Vic Mills. He hated changing his three grandchildren's diapers as much as his daughter and son-in-law did, and he wanted to improve the lives of the whole family.

Mills naturally concentrated on the biggest problem with cloth diapers, their wetness. But dryness was never his ultimate goal; rather, he wanted to improve the lives of babies, moms, dads, grandparents, and everyone else who interacted with babies in hospitals, nursery schools, and the rest of the world. Again, on their introduction Pampers offered not only dryness, but a level of convenience, time savings, ease, and confidence that had never been available before.

Dryness was the most important factor for the first generations of mothers and babies to use disposable diapers, and Pampers was right to concentrate on it. But dryness was only a marker and a symbol of the real purpose of the product: improving the lives of babies and those who loved and cared for them. Dryness was a means to a great end, not the end in itself. Over time, the symbol took on a life of its own at Pampers, and the people in the business and throughout P&G forgot what it originally stood for. Made complacent by success, P&G had come to misunderstand the reason for being of its most important business and the true basis of its competitive advantage.

This happens in good companies in every industry. One of the hardest challenges business leaders face is to prevent or recover from it. As with Pampers, the way to root out complacency and renew a business is through a viable brand ideal. The Pampers team that began this journey—Bruce Bader, Gianni Ciserani, Mathilde Delhoume, Elizabeth and Karl Ronn (a married couple: Elizabeth was in marketing, Karl in R&D), and myself at P&G, along with Barbara Boyle and Toni Helleny at

Pampers ad agency Saatchi and Saatchi—had to emulate the inventive creativity and entrepreneurial vision of Mills and figure out how Pampers could help families on the eve of the twenty-first century and on into the future. We had to discover how Pampers could improve the lives of moms and babies not only in mature markets such as North America and Western Europe but also in developing markets around the world.

The effort became a proving ground for brand ideals–centered principles and strategies. It involved rediscovering the Pampers brand ideal, building the Pampers business culture around the brand ideal, communicating the brand ideal, delivering a near-ideal product experience, evaluating the entire business against the brand ideal, and evolving the brand ideal to ensure that Pampers remained in step with consumer needs and preferences.

In short, Pampers needed major work in all the branches of the Ideal Tree, as is typical of businesses in serious trouble. The five branches of the tree are a linked activity system, and they all influence one another all the time. But as I reflect back on the journey my colleagues and I went through with Pampers, it is always culture that comes to the fore. As we're about to see, every inch of progress we made on this journey depended on hard-won victories in aligning the Pampers culture and the Pampers brand ideal.

(Re)Discovering the Pampers Brand Ideal

To gain a full understanding of how to adapt Pampers' original brand ideal to new generations of moms and babies, the Pampers team sought answers from moms themselves. We immersed ourselves in moms' lives at home, work, the supermarket, and wherever else their daily routines took them.

Spending intensive personal time with consumers was not a new activity for P&G or Pampers. But we dramatically increased the amount of it, the number of countries and cultures in which we did it, and the participation of senior people in the business. I signaled the importance of these consumer immersions by playing an active role in them whenever I could, and my leadership team did the same. In fact, on my very first day on the job in August 1997, I spent it immersed with consumers in downtown Frankfurt.

In addition, we analyzed all our rivals in the diaper business, including private-label and local brands that had caught the attention of moms. We also benchmarked Pampers against leading non-diaper child care businesses such as Gerber, Graco, and Johnson & Johnson. This enabled the team to gauge Pampers' relationship with moms in the context of the entire baby care competitive landscape.

The effort had to proceed quickly but carefully. Given Pampers' $3.4 billion in global revenue and importance to P&G as a whole, the downside risk of choosing the wrong direction for the business was big.

Whatever we did to reactivate the Pampers brand ideal had to work in multiple geographies around the world to cut costs and leverage scale. I had already experienced how the most powerful brand ideals transcend cultural differences, and I knew we had to replant Pampers in deep human values that were equally meaningful to moms in Mexico City and Manila, and in Manhattan, Kansas, and Manhattan, New York City. We could not confuse or disappoint moms, whether they were new to Pampers or loyal users. It's tough for consumers when a brand they love and trust makes an unwelcome change. The brand ideal had to strengthen Pampers' relationship with current users, bring new moms into the fold, and last but not least inspire the Pampers organization around the world.

The time we spent with moms in low-income as well as more affluent communities in varied countries revealed their common priorities and concerns. Moms everywhere cared above all about their babies' development, and they were enormously sensitive to the stages of that development over the first three-plus years, from newborn to sitting up to crawling to toddling. Pampers had not addressed the subtleties of these transitions in a baby's life, but neither had any other disposable diaper business. By the same token, no disposable diaper business had yet shown that it appreciated the extent of moms' devotion to helping their babies make these transitions, no matter how abundant or meager their resources might be.

Taken together, the consumer immersions provided a rich three-dimensional picture of how moms viewed their babies at each early life stage. As moms talked to us, we heard a common language across cultures about the stages from newborn to potty-training toddler. The Pampers team became excited about the possibilities to innovate against these stages, matching moms' care and concern with the best new learning about baby and child development.

A higher brand ideal began to emerge. What if Pampers could be more than just a diaper that absorbed wetness and odor and protected the skin? Moms' number one concern was their babies' physical, social, and emotional development. What if Pampers could be moms' partner on that journey, with the right product for each stage of a baby's growth? This would be a diaper with the right shape and fit, the right texture and feel, the right materials and designs.

It was a great brand ideal vision. As we stepped back from it, however, a glaring fact emerged. This brand ideal vision was light-years away from where the Pampers organization was looking. We were going to have to change our culture's perception of moms and their needs in a major way, and we had a culture that was on the whole very resistant to change.

One very helpful circumstance was that Pampers' heritage

of category-leading absorbency and dryness did not become unimportant in this context. It gained new relevance, if only we could get our people to recognize this and act accordingly. An absorbent diaper that kept babies dry improved skin health and helped them sleep through the night. The fact that moms and baby care professionals saw Pampers as number one in dryness and skin health gave us a great foundation to build on.

So the seed was planted. Pampers' expanded brand ideal would build upon the life-improving ideal of its inventor, Vic Mills, but would elevate it to a new place in the lives of moms and babies. Pampers would become more than moms' convenient, time-saving friend. Pampers would aspire to be moms' partner in every stage of their babies' development, to help mothers care for their babies' and toddlers' healthy, happy development. That became the inspirational brand ideal of P&G's largest brand. And it placed Pampers in the field of inspiring exploration, because babies develop by exploring their world, and Pampers wanted to be a partner with mothers in that journey.

HOW BUILDING THE CULTURE AROUND THE IDEAL INSPIRED HIGH PERFORMANCE

To deliver on what became the Pampers Baby Stages of Development lineup of diapers, we had to make many organizational changes to enable the best and brightest minds to collaborate and unify the fragmented Pampers culture around a higher brand ideal. Chief among them was quickly getting the right people in the right roles. Deb Henretta, one of P&G's best general managers and marketers and the mother of three children, became vice president of Pampers North America, and eventually succeeded Mark Ketchum as global president of baby care in 2001. Mark had begun the ideal-inspired baby care turnaround, and Deb would continue the momentum.

Deb intuitively grasped the essence of the higher brand ideal and the competitive advantage it could win. Jane Wildman, a P&G general manager who excelled at consumer understanding, became Pampers' global vice president of marketing and the Pampers franchise leader, its business artist, as I became global marketing officer in 2001.

Together Deb and Jane reconstructed the Pampers organization to realize the ideal of becoming partners with moms in their babies' development. Without their thorough organizational reengineering around the heightened brand ideal, Pampers would never have grown as it did or sustained that growth into the present.

With Deb's backing, Jane pulled together the Pampers regional leaders and gave them the task of working much more interdependently. Jane also carefully selected a core global brand franchise team with fresh perspectives from throughout the Pampers organization. The goal was to combine the benefits of global scale in knowledge and cost with the best in local insights and execution. This was a new behavior in Pampers and to a great extent in P&G. The success of Pampers' global brand franchise team was one of many ways in which Pampers served as a proving ground for building organizational cultures around brand ideals throughout P&G's portfolio of businesses.

"We had a small but incredibly talented team," Jane recalls. "Debbie Kokoruda in design, Mathilde Delhoume and Susan Convery in advertising development, and Frances Roberts in global marketing worked closely with our regional marketing directors and our partners at Saatchi & Saatchi and LPK, our global design agency. We traveled together not only to work with Pampers' people but also to share interactions with consumers."

Jane also strove to stimulate communication between Pampers' people in developed and developing markets and between the technical and commercial sides of the business. She and her core team traveled around the world, enlisting everyone working on Pampers to live the brand ideal in everything they did. Over time, the organization morphed from a narrow focus on product benefits to a broad focus on delighting moms and enhancing their babies' development.

For example, Pampers increased the number of design staff to address its weakness in that area. But equally important was that the new designers worked in close collaboration with manufacturing and marketing people, so that the design, the materials, and the presentation of the products would all come together effectively.

Likewise, marketing partnered with R&D to ensure that the renewed brand ideal guided the innovation pipeline. This helped gain quick new product wins, as well as kill bad ideas before we invested precious capital.

"The partnership with R&D was a turning point for Pampers," Jane says. "Bruce Brown, head of baby care R&D, set the tone to make the partnership a close one. Like Deb Henretta, Bruce was an early supporter of our new design efforts, and he always made sure that marketing was represented at any major innovation or technical review. Bruce [now P&G's chief technology officer] and his successor, Kathy Fish, even funded marketing positions to make sure we had the right resources."

The rebalancing of leadership roles that began with my taking over Pampers Europe meant that marketing became a far more important voice in key management decisions on Pampers. Historically, in the "machine is boss" regime, the manufacturing leader and the R&D leader set the Pampers agenda. Now, with the support of newly appointed global president Deb Henretta, marketing took an even stronger leadership role in setting the agenda. As the champion of the renewed brand ideal, marketing had to play a leadership role within Pampers on everything from innovation strategies to financial decisions to management reviews.

One of the common characteristics of the high-performing businesses identified by the Stengel Study is that they find powerful ways of focusing their organizational and individual attention on behaviors that support their brand ideals. For example, IBM brings its ideal of building a smarter planet to life for all 400,000-plus IBMers by expecting each and every one of them to have a work plan for furthering that goal within their areas of responsibility. Equally symbolic, the Minneapolis headquarters of Target, shoved just outside of the Stengel 50 because of the Great Recession's impact on retailing, is a shrine to design, the business's most important point of difference from other discount retailers. From the giant red Dale Chihuly blown-glass sculpture in the lobby to the red-and-white design theme in their cafeteria, Target just screams, *We love design!*

On one of my own benchmarking trips as GMO, I saw the positive impact Nike's campus was having on its culture. When I told Deb Henretta about it, she agreed to send Jane Wildman and Pampers HR director Dave Clark there to see for themselves how the right physical environment could inspire better business results. Pampers subsequently made its symbols and physical environment all about babies and mothers. Whereas the old "machine is boss" Pampers culture had been actually unfriendly to the women working in it, Pampers now offered maternity parking spaces, gifts for new parents on the brand, and on-site day care for the babies of employees. As part of ongoing consumer research, Pampers brought new moms and their babies into the offices to interact with employees on a daily basis. The colors and décor of the office environment changed, and eventually the business moved to a new location that was even more parent- and baby-friendly.

These changes were not frills. They were worth every dollar

they cost, and then some. They helped focus everyone in the business on delighting moms and babies and becoming moms' partner in their babies' development. As I'll explain, they measurably improved productivity and innovation.

Hiring decisions represent a crucial aspect of culture change. Deb Henretta, Jane Wildman, and the entire baby care leadership team started recruiting people who were passionate about babies. They didn't have to be parents to join the business, and many were not. They included mothers and fathers, aunts and uncles, grandmothers and grandfathers, and even a pediatric nurse. What bound them together was the brand ideal and their zeal for improving the lives of moms and babies.

Within a remarkably short period of time, the Pampers organization underwent radical change. When dry diapers were its greatest good, the organization was dry as dust, fragmented, and divisive. When it embraced the higher ideal of partnering with moms in their babies' development, it rapidly became an exciting, cohesive, and even joyful place to work, a magnet for P&G's best talent.

The organizational work in bringing a brand ideal to life is never really done. Vestiges of the "machine is boss" and "not invented here" culture lurked within Pampers, and the organization's leaders had to root them out whenever and wherever they appeared. Equally important, continuing to develop the business value of the heightened Pampers brand ideal required many evolutionary adjustments and sometimes more extensive change.

The organizational progress was real and substantial. It plainly showed people in Pampers and elsewhere in P&G what building a business culture around a brand ideal could accomplish, and how quickly. The people inside the business felt as if they had discovered an entirely new brand ideal, and they buzzed with energy to realize and create products and services to fulfill it. The organization was reborn, and it was poised to change the world again.

HOW THE PAMPERS IDEAL-INSPIRED CULTURE ENGAGED CONSUMERS

Before we could change our communication to embody our new ideal, we had to do a better job of listening to moms and reading between the lines of what they said. As Jane Wildman put it, "Moms weren't going to tell us outright how the brand ideal could help them. While possible, it was unlikely for moms to ask for something they viewed as unachievable and unbelievable. It was up to us to listen, keep digging, and work closely with moms to provide them with a new reality."

Moms responded enthusiastically to our eagerness to talk with them about the stages of a baby's development. They loved talking about helping their babies develop better, and they welcomed the new research we shared about a baby's sleep and other developmental issues.

The marketing communications Pampers created to build on these dialogues with moms ultimately had an extraordinarily positive impact. They elevated Pampers' place in moms' perceptions and preferences, built the business, had a strong return on investment, and won awards. But at first, we stumbled badly. It's something anyone trying to talk about a new brand ideal should expect, since you're not likely to get it right the first time.

Pampers' progress toward a higher brand ideal almost came to a screeching halt, and the culture change it needed might have ended right here. The poor communication of the brand ideal in some of the early advertising we did really reflected a cultural problem. It showed that not everyone in the Pampers organization understood and accepted the expanded vision of the brand's relationship to moms and babies. Important partners inside P&G and at the communication agencies also did not fully understand or believe in it.

Some of the marketing communication overpromised how a diaper could help a baby's development. Moms didn't see it as authentic. As one said, "A diaper is not going to send my baby to Harvard."

Other early advertising did not overpromise, but it had everything to do with a baby's development and absolutely nothing to do with how Pampers could improve it. Another miss.

Pampers had reached a critical juncture. Many people inside the organization started to revert back to the familiar ground of dryness and distance themselves from the higher ideal of partnering with moms in their babies' development. Such a moment is a normal occurrence in organizational transformations, the time when those leading the transformation must show what they're made of.

A small group of early believers in the higher ideal, including me, remained steadfast and were willing to keep working to get it right. Jane Wildman's global brand franchise team first went back to moms to make sure the ideal was right. They then took the vision and the supporting data to the top of P&G and presented them to CEO A. G. Lafley. He agreed with the team's recommendation to keep working the higher brand ideal, and he became a vocal advocate for it with his senior management team.

What the team heard when they went back to talk with moms was consistent with the original learning and helped persuade A.G. and other senior leaders that the higher ideal was right. Moms, no matter what their income level or life situation, wanted to support their babies as they developed and were willing to invest and make sacrifices for their children.

When the Pampers team visited a poor neighborhood of closely packed little houses in the Philippines, they saw what might have been small carports in a better-off community serving as outdoor living rooms. Children and pets ran through paved sitting areas that ended at a one-lane street full of cars whizzing by.

One of the moms in the neighborhood said that she woke up every day hoping that no one was sick. Her husband's day began with hoping that someone would call his cell phone (there was no landline telephone service in this poor community) to offer him work for the day. It was easier for the mom to get work than her husband, and she was about to move to Hong Kong to be a nanny. Her mother would take care of her baby, and she would send money home. She was so proud of her little girl. Her face lit up as she described how her daughter would dance around when she could barely even walk. Although the mom did not want to leave her baby to care for someone else's, the sacrifice was worth it to give her child advantages they could otherwise not afford.

In another poor neighborhood in the Philippines, a mom showed the Pampers team her baby's crib in the small, crowded main living room. The mom had placed an English-language newspaper in the crib in the hope that her baby might learn a bit of English from it.

The Filipino moms reminded the Pampers team of a new mom they had met in Poland. Here too the grandmother was helping with the baby, in this case so that the dad could work and the mom could attend college. All three moms wanted to better their families' lives, and all three moms' aspirations centered around their babies. They would do everything they could for their babies, no matter what the sacrifice. Their babies were their future, and as they talked about their babies, the future looked bright.

Equally important, the brand franchise team went back on the road to talk to Pampers employees around the world. They personally conducted brand ideal training sessions in every region both to train and to gain feedback that could advance the ideal.

The most important part of these visits occurred after the training sessions. The regional marketing teams conducted a self-assessment of their work versus the baby development approach and presented it to the global team. The global team had to be accessible and receptive, yet stewards and guardians of the renewed ideal. This at times meant saying no to work that the regions liked, and at other times advocating that work developed in another part of the world be used globally. One of the important lessons from talking to moms around the world was twofold: it showed that how Pampers brought its brand ideal to life was as important as the brand ideal itself, and that moms in different parts of the world responded in much the same way to how we presented the brand ideal, which gave real impetus to the efforts of Jane Wildman and her team to unify Pampers' efforts in different markets.

Remember, this was very new behavior in the long-fragmented Pampers culture. As Jane summed up both the internal and external communication about the higher brand ideal, "Iterating and working an ideal can be life and death to a business. The notion of baby development continued to show great promise, but we had to refine our approach: more relevance and empathy for mom, more life improvement for babies, and more work getting people in our organization on board. We had a major rub with some senior managers and agency partners. They still felt that if it wasn't about dryness, it wasn't Pampers. We had to get a lot of people over the hump."

Fortunately, there were also early communication successes. It is important to score a few quick wins and share them widely, and one such win came from the Pampers website.

Pampers was a leader in digital marketing in the consumer packaged goods industry. From the start, the brand franchise team wanted the website to have global reach, appeal, and usefulness for women.

Besides telling moms about Pampers, the website featured lots of relevant information about baby and child care and development. The site also included information about how a healthy pregnancy and childbirth affect the subsequent health of both mother and baby and the baby's development. Expectant moms could subscribe to a free email newsletter with tips and reminders for the different stages of pregnancy and labor.

A first-time expectant mother in Great Britain signed up for the pregnancy and labor newsletter. When she received an email describing the symptoms of preterm labor, information that was new to her, she realized she was experiencing many of the same symptoms. She immediately sought help, and she and her baby received the emergency treatment they needed. When the crisis was over, she emailed the website to express her gratitude. Her email shot through the Pampers organization like lightning, inspiring employees to continue striving to improve the lives of moms and babies everywhere.

With encouragement from Deb Henretta and me, the Pampers brand franchise team adopted a one team, one dream approach to global marketing. The objective was to create an emotionally resonant advertising campaign idea that could be the centerpiece for the business in all regions and all types of communication. The team found the very rough kernel of an idea in Europe. Early executions had tested poorly, but the team felt that with the new understanding gained from moms, they could make it work. Make it work they did, and the "Inspired by babies, created by Pampers" campaign achieved outstanding results around the world. It became the backbone of all communication: advertising, direct mail, sampling, outreach to hospitals and baby care professionals, and digital marketing.

With a robust marketing idea that brought the higher ideal to life for moms everywhere, the regions could work together better. The contributions of the regions built off each other, and the work improved as it traveled around the globe.

A key element in this success was working with a single advertising agency worldwide. In the 1990s P&G followed a practice of using lots of different agencies on the same business, reckoning that this would increase the odds of getting great work. It didn't turn out that way, and I was frustrated by the confusion and duplication the practice created. We chose Saatchi & Saatchi because of the passion of people inside the agency for helping moms and babies. It was clear to Deb, Jane, and me that Saatchi & Saatchi's people, including CEO Kevin Roberts, account leaders Vaughan Emsley, Anne O'Brien, and Madeleine Miller, and creative leaders Barbara Boyle and Tris Gates, were as passionate about the higher ideal as we were.

Another Saatchi & Saatchi person with that passion was creative director Cliff Francis. Shortly after Jane Wildman joined the Pampers business, her telephone rang one day at 4:00 a.m. It was Cliff calling from the other side of the world while he was attending an agency meeting in Australia. He had only one thing on his mind: telling Jane about a Pampers television ad that he had seen just before getting on a plane from South Africa to Australia.

Cliff had messed up his time zones, but Jane realized he was too excited to have him call back later. Blurry-eyed, Jane got out of bed and staggered down the hall, out of earshot of her sleeping husband and kids. As she listened to Cliff describe the ad—it featured a real-life South African mom talking about her baby, speaking from the heart about how much better the baby was sleeping thanks to Pampers—Jane knew that its joyous, adventurous spirit conveyed exactly what the higher brand ideal meant. Cliff Francis's understanding of this was one of many indications, over the following months, that Saatchi & Saatchi should handle all of the advertising for Pampers. And for years after that, the marketing team showed the South African ad to new people on the business to give them a feel for what the Pampers culture was all about.

By the time Saatchi & Saatchi started to expand the "Inspired by babies, created by Pampers" campaign worldwide, Pampers had already made significant strides in delivering a better product experience. But the clarity and power of the new messaging helped accelerate that progress tremendously.

A New Culture of Innovation in Baby Development Products

The naysaying we heard when we first proposed these changes faded away as moms in North America as well as Europe embraced them. We very soon checked the erosion of our North American market share by Kimberly-Clark's Huggies, and we preserved our dominant share in Europe.

Inspired by the higher brand ideal of partnering with moms in their babies' development, the Pampers team went on to create the Baby Stages of Development premium product range. It launched around the world with great success and achieved continuing sales and revenue growth, because it delivered an experience that ever more closely approximated that higher ideal. From the basic diaper to the premium Baby Stages line, Pampers no longer looked generic. Meaningful design cues on the packaging and the diapers themselves made it easy for a mom to find the right product for her baby in the store, and improved the diaper-change experience.

The Pampers organization applied the latest findings in baby development, such as clinical studies about the importance of a good night's sleep, on both basic and premium diapers and increasingly on non-diaper products as well. Every Pampers product provided a baby development benefit and reflected the business's deep commitment to improving the lives of moms and babies. The lotion in Pampers Sensitive Baby Wipes, for example, was gentler than soap and water for a baby's skin.

As these efforts came to fruition over the course of several years, Pampers' stance in the marketplace went from defensive to offensive. Instead of protecting a declining position in North America, we rebuilt market share there, stretched our lead in Europe, and entered an explosive growth phase in developing markets.

Elevating the Pampers brand ideal and delivering products that came as close to the ideal as possible reestablished competitive advantage and total brand experience superiority. Keeping the Pampers organization on track through the stages of recovery and new growth required another crucial set of changes: the way we measured our activities over the short and long terms.

How the Brand Ideal Inspired Measures That Built a Winning Culture

Just as measuring the wrong thing, dryness as an end in itself, derailed Pampers, measuring the right things got the organization rolling along again.

Pampers leaked less than the competition. But leaking less wasn't winning in the market when moms' attention was elsewhere.

With measures such as a good night's sleep that showed meaningful life improvement for mom and baby, however, the business took off. Pampers started to measure elements of consumer satisfaction such as "This is a brand that shares my values. It is a brand I trust. It is a brand I would recommend to other moms."

The business did not stop measuring absorbency and reductions in leakage but incorporated these data into a set of measures that reflected the higher brand ideal. As time went on, R&D and manufacturing no longer sought to measure dryness in itself, but focused on how it contributed to moms' reporting that their babies slept better.

Refining our measures in this way depended on changes to the organizational culture I've already mentioned. In particular, it depended on the new, close teaming of R&D and manufacturing with design and marketing. This meant that the engineers had to get even more sophisticated and precise in their numbers, which they loved. Diapers that not only kept baby drier than the competition's but also fit, felt, smelled, and looked better; packaging that was no longer one-bag-holds-all; new non-diaper product lines—all this required much finer tolerances and more complex, inventive modeling at every stage.

The engineers no longer ruled the roost, and some never recovered from the shock. But the best and the brightest of them realized they could add more value to the business than ever before, and they responded to their new challenges and opportunities with rigorous skill and creative invention.

A telling example of this occurred in 2006, when the Pampers management team met to debate spending priorities. A powerful and vocal regional vice president argued for reducing the cost of making the Pampers basic diaper by removing the colorful character designs that moms and babies loved. The most insistent defender of the designs that day was the head of manufacturing, one of P&G's veteran engineers, who promised to find another way to save the money, rather than sacrifice the baby-friendly designs' contribution to the higher brand ideal.

Significant changes in human resources practices and measures motivated such responses in every area of the business. Career paths in P&G, as in most of the corporate world, had long meant a succession of two-year assignments with no inherent connection to each other. They were usually too brief a time to carry through an initiative that significantly improved the long-term growth of the business or the individual involved. The result was that P&G too often rewarded people for what they started working on rather than what they completed.

Typical of the "not invented here" syndrome, P&G tended to pay attention to homegrown ideas and innovations, ignoring the value of those from outsiders. The company said it wanted great teamwork, but it wasn't measuring and rewarding to foster it.

I had long been frustrated by these realities of corporate life, and as I took on bigger leadership roles I always tried to address them within my area of responsibility. As head of Pampers Europe, and then briefly as Pampers' first global business artist before Jane Wildman succeeded me, I asked my leadership teams to stay in the business longer than was usual at P&G. I made sure to reward their good results with raises, promotions, and recognition. I also put as much emphasis on reapplying and improving good ideas as on originating them.

It was still important for ambitious managers to gain experience in different functional areas and gain a broad perspective, but greater continuity within Pampers and the baby care category accelerated sustained growth for both the Pampers business and a new generation of leadership talent. After becoming GMO, I worked with Deb Henretta and Jane Wildman to continue these approaches within Pampers and baby care, and I began to duplicate them—with equally good results—with other P&G leaders in other businesses.

An early win in best practices came when Jane Wildman first succeeded me as Pampers brand franchise leader. While in a Tesco store in Britain, she learned that the recently launched Pampers Sensitive Baby Wipes were doing well throughout Europe. Jane assumed that other regions were also marketing the product. But when she got back to the United States and asked about results there, she found that the U.S. team had not even done test marketing. It was a reflection of the still fragmented Pampers culture, with countries and departments competing against one another more than against Pampers' rivals in the marketplace.

The U.S. brand manager at the time, Robert van Pappelendam, was relatively new to the Pampers business. Originally from Holland, Robert had no problem reapplying a successful European approach. He made a quick trip to Europe and brought back the product and the advertising. When pre-market testing showed very positive results, he quickly launched Pampers Sensitive Baby Wipes throughout the United States, where they became a big hit. That helped stimulate a whole series of successful reapplications and extensions of innovations and best practices within Pampers worldwide.

Mapping out extended career paths within Pampers and matching the business's needs with people who had a passion for its brand ideal also paid big dividends. Management transitions improved at all levels, and the results of the business as a whole got better and better. Jane Wildman's tenure as the Pampers global brand franchise leader was about eight years, and her core team had similar continuity. They scored impressive results on a whole range of measures: organic business growth, return on investment, and P&G surveys on leadership effectiveness. In fact, the Pampers team led P&G in over 90 percent of all measures. Its constantly increasing managerial expertise, business savvy, and market insight also contributed enormously to the success of P&G's entire global baby care team.

When Jane retired from P&G in 2008, her successor as Pampers global brand franchise leader, Frances Roberts, had been in the baby care category for ten years. She had acquired a full complement of functional and managerial expertise, but in a coherent rather than scattershot way. As a result of this continuity in her career path, Frances has been able to keep the Pampers business on an impressive path of sustained growth.

You get what you measure, and if you measure in terms of the brand ideal, you get great results.

A NEVER-COMPLACENT CULTURE: ALWAYS EVOLVING, ALWAYS IMPROVING

One hallmark of sustainability in a business is being able to expand into, and adapt to, a tough new market ecosystem. For U.S. companies of all kinds, no market has been tougher to crack than China, and its business landscape is littered with the remnants of hopes to sell Western products and services to its more than 1.3 billion people.

The Pampers brand ideal of baby development was not just for middle-class and affluent families in developed markets. In developing countries, Pampers had to deliver products that could serve its higher ideal at a lower price point.

In the mid-2000s the Pampers team looked closely at moms and babies in China and many parts of Southeast Asia. They learned that the tradition there was to use a piece of cloth between the baby's legs that was held on with a "split pant," a baby-sized pair of pants with an opening in the crotch where mom could change the cloth.

During its "the machine is boss" and "not invented here"

days, Pampers would have tried to lecture moms in China and sell them the same diaper sold in the United States. I am certain that although they might have listened politely, moms in China would have gone away thinking that 10,000 years of doing things the Chinese way couldn't be all bad.

Motivated by the ideal of helping moms and babies in every culture around the world, the Pampers team listened closely to moms in China, and R&D, manufacturing, market research, and marketing all worked together to create a Pampers diaper that met the needs of the Chinese consumer, and at the right price. The new diaper has won acceptance from millions of moms in China's burgeoning middle class, making Pampers one of the most significant Western business successes in China and positioning it for further growth there.

Throughout the 2000s, Pampers strove to improve coordination of its local and global marketing in order to take cost out of the business and increase return on investment through better work. Jane Wildman and her team crafted a global master planning process to address this need. They cut the number of marketing projects in half, achieving more focus on the remainder from the most talented agency partners, higher production values in advertising, and a dramatic reduction in total costs. They tested the resulting marketing rigorously around the world and found that the work tested better than when there were double the projects on the global planning slate.

The team truly found the right balance of global scale and local effectiveness. The marketing is not imposed on the regions, but developed with their input. Each region has ownership of at least one major marketing project, and all the regions can adjust the results for their particular needs. This "better and cheaper approach," as Pampers people nicknamed it, has improved return on investment and helped Pampers to roll out great ideas globally. Competitors are much less able to watch what Pampers is testing in one market and then race into another market with a copycat effort.

While creativity was abundant, the system set in place to support the work was equally important. The global franchise team had regular Monday morning calls with their agency partners to review creative briefs, and the franchise and agency teams had meetings each quarter to discuss the toughest issues, often at Wildman's kitchen table.

Vestiges of dysfunctional behavior can emerge in a destabilizing way at almost any point in the transformation of an organization's culture, including long after it looks like the transformation is complete. In fact, business leaders can never assume that work on an organization's culture is truly complete.

Whether off-ideal behaviors are well-intentioned mistakes or part of a rogue initiative from an overly ambitious manager, you have to be ready with a response. One afternoon the Pampers marketing directors from around the world were meeting in Cincinnati, as they did a couple of times a year. The agenda always included opportunities for the marketing directors to share their regions' most exciting new efforts, from print and television ads to interactive digital work. Following each director's presentation, the group discussed the featured work's strengths and weaknesses, with a special emphasis on ways to reapply great work from one region in other regions.

It came time for a marketing director from Latin America to present his team's best new initiative, a television ad. He pressed play, and on the meeting room screen appeared a group of naked little baby boys, all looking at their penises and singing "I'm so wrinkled" to show that competitive diapers just didn't keep them dry. A bit of whispering and paper rustling ensued. Finally someone asked the marketing director what the ad expressed about the higher brand ideal, which went beyond dryness, and why his team thought it was appropriate. The marketing director was at a loss but said that the ad had tested very well in Brazil.

At this point global advertising director Mathilde Delhoume, who had been with Pampers since the 1990s and was one of the early Pampers brand ideal pioneers, spoke up. She matter-of-factly but firmly pointed out that in addition to being sure to offend moms in many other markets, the ad had nothing to do with the brand ideal. The ad met its timely end that very day.

The problem was not local experimentation, but local experimentation that was out of step with the brand ideal. A great example of local experimentation that was leveraged around the world arose when Jane and her team began to look for a baby-development cause to partner with on a global basis. Pampers had a long history of supporting baby-related causes, and the team felt the business should take advantage of its global scale to make a bigger difference to more babies. During a global marketing meeting, the Latin American team shared news of a cause-marketing program Pampers was supporting in Argentina, which was slowly emerging from a devastating economic crisis. Pampers was partnering with UNICEF to help feed Argentinean children in need.

The Latin American team showed the television ad that was then running for this initiative. When the ad finished, there was no whispering or paper rustling. There was complete silence, but not from dismay. There was not a dry eye in the room, and the global brand franchise team knew that UNICEF was the perfect global partner for Pampers.

Since then, the focus of the partnership with UNICEF has changed. After testing in Belgium, Britain, and Japan, a new Pampers-UNICEF program expanded to virtually every region of the world in 2008. With the message "One pack = one vaccine," the program seeks to eliminate maternal and new-born tetanus worldwide. Moms love it because they know they are making a positive difference with every purchase of a product they trust and need. UNICEF loves it because it is helping to wipe out a highly painful yet preventable death. And Pampers employees love it because it truly embodies Pampers' higher brand ideal: to develop and explore, babies must be healthy, and tetanus was a disease Pampers could help eradicate.

The expansion of the UNICEF partnership from Argentina to the rest of the world seems like a no-brainer. From the start it has done lots of good for less fortunate moms and babies while growing the Pampers business and improving its image. What's not to like?

During one discussion with the Pampers team, they took me through recent Pampers-UNICEF results. I asked when the program was coming to our single biggest market, the United States, where it had already tested well. The team hesitantly explained that at the last Pampers global marketing meeting, the U.S. marketing director had announced that she and her country team were looking for a cause of their own.

It was "not invented here" all over again, but eventually the U.S. marketing group got on board with the program. The story has a happy ending: the U.S. team took the Pampers-UNICEF program to new heights, including the addition of actress and mom Salma Hayek as a spokesperson and being featured on Oprah Winfrey's show and at the annual meeting of the Clinton Global Initiative. But it wasn't easy, and it shows why you must never stop working the process of aligning your culture with your ideal.

The rewards are enormous, however. From $3.4 billion a year in global sales when I joined the business in 1997, Pampers grew steadily to $4 billion, $5 billion, $6 billion, $7 billion, and then $8 billion a year.

This is organic sales growth with healthy profit margins, not low-margin growth through expensive acquisitions of other businesses. The bigger a business is, the harder it is to attain this kind of growth. For a business the size of Pampers to double in ten years illustrates just how powerful ideals can be.

Pampers continues to achieve higher and higher performance through its commitment to a higher brand ideal. It has gone past $9 billion a year in global sales, climbing to $10 billion. Market share in North America has climbed back to near 40 percent, the business is completely dominant in Europe, and growth is skyrocketing in developing markets such as China and India. The most powerful engine for these financial results, my successors at P&G tell me, is the Pampers-UNICEF program's effect on sales. And for the all-important issue of leadership continuity, Martin Riant, a talented "whole brain" leader from the U.K., took over from Deb Henretta in the mid-2000s and is in his seventh year in the role as president of baby care.

As we've seen, the Pampers story involves all five branches of the Ideal Tree. But culture had the most decisive role, as it almost always does, in bringing the brand ideal to life.

Now let's go deeper into how to communicate your brand ideal, inside and outside your company, to everyone important to your present and future growth.

8

Must-Do Number 3

Communicate Your Ideal to
Engage Employees and Customers

COMMUNICATE
your ideal to engage
employees and customers

I often think about Tolstoy's famous opening line from *Anna Karenina*—"All happy families are alike; each unhappy family is unhappy in its own way"—when it comes to the ways businesses communicate.

The highest-quality businesses—the fastest-growing, most profitable, and most innovative—share a common thread: their high-quality communication. Everything—internal conversations, memos, and reports; business cards, office stationery, and email signature blocks; logos, product claims, advertising; employee, investor, and consumer communication via traditional channels and the latest digital social media—expresses and supports the brand ideal.

Mediocre or poor performers, on the other hand, communicate badly in their own uniquely incoherent way. Nothing—no voice, no point of view, no purpose—unifies what they have to say to each other or the world.

The branches of the Ideal Tree really do have an organic connection, and you can't have a highly effective business culture without highly effective communication. A business that communicates as one team with one dream can make beautiful music together. A business that communicates at cross-purposes is just a lot of noise.

Communication forms and touch points never shrink. They

continually increase as technology and social behaviors expand the channels and bandwidth available to the people—employees, customers, end consumers, investors—who are most important to the future of your business.

Communication is the lifeblood of any relationship, and the best model for a business is the communication in a loving human relationship. The kind of dialogue we seek and rely on in our personal lives is a dialogue of mutual trust, based on shared fundamental values, with honesty, respect, caring, warmth, and humor.

First and foremost comes trust based on shared fundamental values. As Disney chairman and former P&G CEO and chairman John Pepper puts it, "Trust is the antidote that overcomes fear—and fear is the greatest inhibitor of all to a relationship that welcomes and nurtures new ideas."

Trust, honesty, respect, caring, warmth, and humor aren't the criteria most companies use to develop and measure their communications. But they are the criteria the most successful businesses use.

When we evaluated the P&G businesses that were growing far faster than average, we found that those with a trust advantage over competitors had a huge market share advantage—brands such as Tide, Pampers, Downy, Crest, Always. Probing for the mechanisms that won trust and market share advantage, I kept finding superior communication based on a higher purpose of serving consumers.

The Stengel Study provides further compelling evidence on the impact that quality communication has on business results. Red Bull, Louis Vuitton, IBM, and their peers in the Stengel 50 excel at aligning their communication with their distinctive individual ideals.

A $100 billion behemoth with more than 400,000 employees

worldwide, IBM proves that large multinational companies can be united by an aspirational, growth-inspiring ideal. For IBM that ideal, centered in the ideals field of impacting society, is "building a smarter planet."

IBM's "Let's build a smarter planet" campaign is brilliantly conceived and masterfully executed. But it's not just advertising and marketing talent and resources, paid for from IBM's vast marketing budget, that make it so. Equal and even vastly greater budgets, employing the most acclaimed agency creatives, are squandered regularly by businesses who are just talking the talk and not walking the walk.

A brilliantly conceived and masterfully executed communication campaign may win awards. For a time, it may even favorably influence important audiences of customers, end consumers, and investors. But if the campaign is in any way dishonest, intentionally or unintentionally, the truth will sooner or later puncture its expanding balloon.

Who can now read or hear "BP, beyond petroleum," and not flash on images of the vast oil spill in the Gulf of Mexico in 2010 and its brutal impact on the environment and local communities? Hold those images in your mind a moment, and you begin to hear the wisecracks on television talk shows about "BP, bringing pollution." Think about them some more, and your mind reels at what the news media exposed about BP's environmental and safety practices leading up to the oil spill.

Whereas when IBM talks about IBMers helping to build a smarter planet, that beautiful copy simply states the truth. From its founding in 1911, IBM has been about making the world work better, from its first tabulating machines to the IBM 360 mainframe and the industrial breakthroughs it enabled, from the IBM PC's opening the floodgates of personal computing to integrated services for the world's most complex and sensitive systems. Every current IBM employee's work plan involves contributing to the goal of building a smarter planet.

In a long talk for this book, John Kennedy, IBM's vice president for corporate marketing, said, "The enduring idea that is the essence of IBM has meant different things at different points in our history. At one point, that meant automating the office. At another point, it meant helping put a man on the moon in the Apollo space program. Today it means all the systems that keep the world working in health care, transportation, the power grid, the infrastructures within industries. We have to talk with many audiences about these things, and what 'building a smarter planet' does is it enables us to engage all these audiences at the level of deeply held beliefs about the world. The conversations we have with our customers, for example, they start with a shared way of looking at the world, a common belief in how technology can improve the world."

IBM recognizes that it's not just an option to communicate with people in this way, it's a necessity. As John told me, "Because the world is so much more transparent now, we have to assume that our audiences have more information than we do. People have access to so much information, they know or they can find out so much about the world and the products and services that are available to them, and they have much, much higher expectations of the companies behind those products and services. If you want to win in this kind of environment, every part of the business has to meet a higher standard."

John gave me a great nugget to sum up this ongoing trend. "Social media," he said, "is word of mouth at scale."

That structural fact is what makes a great, authentic brand ideal so powerful today. You know you can't hide your true character from your next-door neighbors. The real word spreads fast over the backyard fence. And now you never know exactly who all your (virtual) next-door neighbors are. The backyard fence is now Facebook and Twitter, and social media have dramatically expanded and elevated the conversations that a business must have not only with customers and end consumers but also with employees and everyone else important to its future.

IBM's been an ideal-based communication leader there too, one of the first big companies to seize the power of social media internally. Its Innovation Jams (the first was in 2001), with tens of thousands of IBMers around the world participating over the course of a day or weekend via social media, have become an indispensable element in its innovation program.

It is often participants in the Innovation Jams who speak to us in IBM's ads. They're the ones who tell us what IBM is doing in health care informatics, power and transportation grid technology, and so on, and who then look at us and say, "I'm an IBMer. Let's build a smarter planet."

I am always moved by the way these messages honestly portray one team with one great dream, and invite us to be part of that dream.

Advertising is just one aspect of communication, but it's an important one. The Stengel Study team studied Millward Brown's advertising testing database, Link, which provides the best ad testing data in the world. We found two critical communication measures that scored above average for a sample of brands from the Stengel 50: active involvement in the advertising, and viral potential. In plainer language, people who experienced the advertising from a sample of Stengel 50 brands and their competitors felt more involved with the advertising of the Stengel 50 brands and found it more interesting, more distinctive, more positive. They were also more inclined to want to share the advertising with others.

What I've learned from my experiences and the research of the Stengel Study is that a business's communication must be holistic, an organic whole in every sense. The way to get there is through high levels of emotional intelligence, which begins with great listening skills.

Great communication begins with one party in a relationship seeking deeper understanding of the other party. But as you well know from both your personal and business lives, people don't always say what's in their minds and hearts. It's just like in your personal relationships with your spouse or significant other, your kids, or your close friends. Before they can explicitly articulate an issue, positive or negative, you can see that something important is going on inside them from their facial expression, their body language, and their tone of voice. Even pets know how we're feeling, often before we're consciously aware of it ourselves, because they observe us so closely.

Here again we have hard data, from Millward Brown's neuroscience practice, that confirm the more traditional measures in the Link database. Implicit, cognitive neuroscience-based measures also show that consumers find Stengel 50 brands to be more empathetic and more ideals-based, to be clearer and more memorable on what they stand for, than their competitors. The people behind these brands practice what you might call holistic listening: paying attention to all the signs, explicit and implicit, that affect how people think, feel, and act in relation to the business. Implicit communication constitutes a powerful early warning system, if you know how to read it. Over the next few years, cognitive neuroscience-based measures will continue to add hugely to understanding the people most important to a business's future, with insights on how to improve their lives.

These compelling data from Millward Brown validate what

we all intuitively know: the quality of our communication determines the quality of our relationships. Remember, if you're in business, you're in the relationship business. You're in the business of forging enduring bonds with the people who are most important to your future.

An ideal of improving people's lives is the only basis for achieving and sustaining communication with these qualities, for connecting with others on the basis of shared fundamental human values. Without a genuine intent to do well by others, communication inevitably breaks down, and sooner or later so does the relationship.

To see what a genuine intent to improve people's lives can do for a business's communication—and its financial results— let's take a trip "across the pond" to check in on Innocent, the English company (and Stengel 50 brand) with a thirty-year goal of becoming "the Earth's favorite little food and drink company" with products that "make it easy for people to do themselves good." This is Innocent's simple but profound brand ideal: to make it easy for people to do themselves good. They are clearly in the ideals field of impacting society, with a touch of eliciting joy, as we will see. After the Innocent story, we'll look at how ideal-based communication helped a much bigger company, Procter & Gamble, to drive accelerated growth.

INNOCENT AT HOME AND ABROAD

Founded in 1999, Innocent began by making fruit smoothies sold in the London area. It has since extended its reach throughout the United Kingdom and Europe, offering products that include fruit smoothies for kids, snack fruit tubes, thickies (fruit smoothies made with yogurt), juices, and microwave-heatable vegetable pots. Innocent has been so successful that Coca-Cola, another Stengel 50 brand, purchased a 58 percent stake in 2010.

Innocent's communications have always had a distinctive style and tone of voice. Initially it was simply the Innocent logo, a doodle-like, fruit-shaped circle with two squiggle eyes and a halo; presentation of the brand name with a lowercase *i*; and quirkily described product content information on its packages. It soon expanded to include online channels such as blogs as well as traditional television and print advertising. Enlivened by immediately understandable verbal and visual puns and jokes, Innocent's communication never takes itself too seriously. It matches the naming of its decidedly unostentatious offices in London and elsewhere as Fruit Towers, an echo of the television comedy *Fawlty Towers*, starring former Monty Python member John Cleese.

What is really striking is the ideal-based bond that Innocent has forged with consumers through its products and communication, and how that has given the business permission to try new things and learn from the results, good and bad. The Innocent voice remains unique, despite many imitators, because it is based on the friendship sustained by a common ideal between creative director Dan Germain and co-founders Richard Reed, Adam Balon, and Jon Wright. The friendship blossomed during their time together at Cambridge University and continued as the company prospered.

"We've known each other since we were eighteen or nineteen years old," says Dan. "Our voice comes from the friendship and the natural tone of conversation with someone you really know well and trust. When we started talking to the few people buying our product when the business started, we had to treat them as our most dear and precious friends. We wanted them to buy the stuff again, and it was fun."

One of Dan's very early jobs was manning the email inbox, opening the letters in the morning, and answering the "banana phone," an actual phone shaped like a banana. "The conversations I had with the people who discovered us really early on were my favorite Innocent conversations ever. Because it was just like having this good chat with a friend."

Innocent's desire to engage as spontaneously and directly with consumers as possible goes back to the three founders' first test-marketing of their smoothies, when they had jobs working in advertising and consulting but wanted to start a business of their own. In a stall they set up at a London music festival in August 1998, they put two large bins for the empty containers with a handmade sign asking people to vote on whether they should quit their jobs to make smoothies full-time. After selling out their supply of smoothies, they counted the votes: only three cups in the "no" bin (allegedly from their mothers), while the "yes" bin was overflowing.

When they started selling the product in bottles on supermarket shelves, the label included not only their telephone number and email address but also their physical address with an invitation to "pop round for a visit." They still invite people to pop round for a visit, and they still have the banana phone.

"The banana phone's always acted as our 'bat phone,'" Dan continues. "When it rings, it could be the biggest emergency in the business. It could be one of our biggest customers calling to order something. In the beginning, more often than not, it used to be my mum phoning to check if I was coming home at the weekend. But it could be anyone in our universe calling, and the great thing was I never knew. So I had to answer it with the same sort of enthusiasm and vigor that I'd have for anyone I really wanted to help out."

Now there are three or four people whose sole job is to handle the email and letters and to answer the banana phone and have those conversations with people. And if those conversations go on for a long time, then they go on for a long time.

"If all the regular banana phone people are on a call," Dan says, "then new calls start lighting up everyone else's phone. Everyone in the business has to be ready to answer those calls. Whether you're one of the founders, an intern, whoever you are, you've got to be poised to help whoever is calling. And if it's my mum, and sometimes it is, it's my mum."

So Innocent has a culture of finding multiple ways to talk to people because it feels like the natural thing to do. That is their communication strategy: to speak to consumers the way that they always speak to one another, to treat people buying their products as part of an extended gang of friends, and, uniquely, "to make sure that we're open to them, because if you want to call, call. If you want to pop into the office, pop in. There are always people wandering around, which can be a bit unnerving. We've had a few people outstay their welcome, let's say. One guy camped outside for four days in a van and treated the office like a soup kitchen."

Despite the occasional glitch, this openness has worked well for Innocent. Once a year, for example, Innocent has its AGM, or "annual grown-up meeting." About a hundred consumers come in on a Saturday, hang out, and invent some new recipes. They get to listen to the founders talk about the plans for the future and have a Q&A with the people who make the business tick. Customers have a chance to get under the skin of who the folks at Innocent are and what they do, and everyone leaves with the feeling that Innocent cares about what they think.

WALKING THE WALK

Ideal-driven businesses inevitably encounter skeptics who question their authenticity. One reason is that companies often mistake surface for substance in communication. They think that adopting the vocabulary and assuming the attitude of young consumers or other target demographics will do the trick. Tricks won't work for long. Consumers in all age groups grow up fast these days, and they quickly abandon false, fair-weather friends—and then tell all their Facebook friends how a brand betrayed them in a crisis.

You really can't just talk the talk. But it is amazing how many businesses and brands try to get away with spinning an appealing story in a currently popular "voice" and/or visual style without walking the walk. My colleagues and I occasionally saw this in faltering teams at P&G: internal and external communication didn't ring true, because the team's leadership didn't fully understand or commit to their brand's ultimate purpose. By contrast, the best teams learned to communicate as, and be, true friends with consumers through thick and thin, and so accelerated both their business results and their own careers. I see it as a consultant. And it looms large in the Stengel 50, whose varied, ideal-based communication styles are all consistent with the businesses' ideal-based actions.

Innocent's Dan Germain believes that being authentic is the differentiator. "You've really got to be prepared to bare your soul and show people what it's really like at your place. You can't just say, 'Hey, look! We did something crazy on purpose, so we could talk about it on the back of the package.' It needs to be consistent with who you are. And then people might grow to like you and develop a friendship with you. For Innocent it always relates back to the products. It always relates back to the fact that we strive for naturalness."

When Dan Germain talks to both his team and the wider business, the words he uses to drive its communication are *useful* and *interesting*. Conventional strategy says Innocent should be in stores giving away samples and handing out information about special offers that people just want to throw away. Neither makes Innocent relevant and useful in people's lives.

What is genuinely useful and interesting might not even be very good at selling people Innocent products directly, but it might make their lives a little bit better—which of course is the ultimate aim of the products in the first place.

"All of us at Innocent," says Dan, "are like the people who buy our stuff. We drink beer, eat pizza, and don't always eat enough fruit or vegetables. And we invented this delicious drink to help them and us. Having drunk it, now they can go and do all the other things that they need to do in their day. And while they're at it, they can read this little stupid thing we put on the back of the package, because that might give them another moment's enjoyment while they drink their smoothie or eat their veg pot."

Dan continued about the role of Innocent in people's lives: "People will forget about Innocent for a while. After all, how much time do people actually spend consciously thinking about companies and brands? Not much. That's why being useful and interesting, just staying friends with people, is a great long-term strategy, because when they stand in the store and look at the shelf or go online to shop, they'll prefer to buy the brands they feel friendly toward. Or they might buy the next thing that you launch."

The Innocent tone and voice might not work for everyone; after all, no one is friends with everyone. It won't work if you subscribe to the idea that businesses should make perfect bits of communication or perfect ads that will speak to everyone and not alienate anyone. Sometimes Innocent gets it mostly right, and sometimes they don't get it right. That's part of human nature, with all its flaws.

It also means that people know that the folks at Innocent are human, which is good. That relates back to the products and the fact that Innocent strives for naturalness. It's okay if people can see occasional flaws and understand that what's going on is natural, that it isn't coming out of a homogenous machine.

One example of not getting the communication right was the "plump nuns" saga. "We never mean to be rude and offensive in the copy on our packaging," says Dan, "but our labels do include 'comedy ingredients' such as 'a banana, an orange, and a lawnmower' or 'a ten-gallon cowboy hat'—just some things for people to have a chuckle over. On one of our early packages we put, 'The contents of this smoothie are: two apples, one banana, three strawberries, and two plump nuns.'"

The plump nuns thing didn't go down well with some nuns and other people—the bureaucrats at the local Trading Standards Authority, for example. Innocent got a cease-and-desist letter from an official, who actually said, "You must either remove that phrase from your label or start putting said items into your drink." Dan and others had a lot of fun writing a letter back saying that Innocent was changing the label rather than putting two plump nuns in the smoothie.

UNITY OF VOICE

Looking over the range of Innocent's communications—websites for adults and kids, blogs, television and print ads, even what it calls an "Orange Paper," a response to a U.K. government white paper on diet and public health—I was impressed by how consistent they are in style and tone. The vocabulary changes a bit from one audience to another, but an unmistakably Innocent voice unifies them all.

Innocent has just stuck with who it is and what it does, trusting the fact that all human beings share certain fundamental concerns and values. Dan drew a connection here to the greatest comedians and communicators and their ability to strike deep chords that all human beings respond to. "If you think of Laurel and Hardy or Steven Spielberg, it doesn't matter if you're five years old or eighty-five, there are basic human emotions and triggers that are in everyone, no matter what your age or your background. That's why a film like *Slumdog Millionaire* did so amazingly well. Pretty much anyone could watch that film and walk away thinking, 'That was joyous. That was good.' That's why *ET* is one of the greatest films of all time."

Accordingly, Innocent "tries not to have different voices for different audiences. Just because you're a nutritionist or a doctor doesn't mean that you don't like jokes. It doesn't mean that you don't like fun stuff. It doesn't mean that you don't like all of the usual Innocent repertoire. So I'm a great defender of keeping all our communication broadly the same."

This applies to Innocent's internal as well as external communication. "There isn't," Dan says, "a way that we communicate externally that is different from the way that we talk inside the business. If I think about what is on our Twitter feed and what is on our internal blog, there's a real blurring of the line between external and internal communication."

Like IBM's "smarter planet" success, this illustrates one of the greatest benefits of centering your business around an ideal: the ability to bring everyone important to the business's future into a common conversation, with shared values and purpose. Among other things, that makes it possible to have difficult conversations in a way that quickly addresses and resolves the underlying problem. We saw that with Method ("Did we cross a line with the video of the mom in the shower?" "Did we screw up at Costco?"), Discovery ("Should we really be tattoo TV?"), and Pampers ("Are we going to be a 'machine is boss' or 'consumer is boss' culture?" "Why is this ad so off-ideal?" "Are we going to let a couple of rogue managers derail a global partnership with UNICEF?").

Innocent bolsters its communication culture by bringing everyone in the office together on Monday mornings. In London that's about 220 people now, using the biggest space in Innocent's meeting hall, and electronically with their other offices. People from each team or department stand up and just say what's happening in a short minute or two. One Monday Dan stood up and showed a few shots from the latest TV ad. Another person talked about a sustainability project Innocent is supporting in Kenya. Someone else gave a few numbers on financial performance. In half an hour everyone quickly learned the headlines from all over the business. And it rotates, so over the course of a few months everyone in the business will have spoken at these Monday meetings.

Innocent fosters internal communication aligned with its ideal by, as Dan put it, "having people sit 'all mixed up.' We don't sit in departments or teams. If you're a graphic designer, you may be sitting opposite the guy that's working in logistics and making sure we've got the right amount of trucks on the road delivering the right products, and that guy might be sitting next to someone who handles invoices payable, and that person might sit next to one of the founders."

Recall that Method also has people from throughout its business sitting "all mixed up." This is not something only small companies can do, however. One of the defining culture-changing moves at P&G in the 2000s was to break the old rigid divisions between functions and locate technical and commercial people together in the same offices.

This goes to the heart of an objection I sometimes hear: that it is impossible for a big, complex company to be truly ideal-centered. The bigger the company, the argument goes, the more opportunity there is for people to establish fiefdoms and isolate themselves from other functions, other business units, or senior corporate management.

Sure, the risks of fragmentation and disunity increase as a company gets bigger and more complicated. But P&G proved that a global company with more than 300 brands, dozens of major business units, and 140,000 employees around the world can cohere around a shared ideal of improving people's lives, expressed in many ways by its many brands. My experience at P&G and working with other very large companies is that an ideal is in fact the one thing that can unify and drive growth throughout the biggest and most complicated enterprises. You can see this in the global companies in the Stengel 50, from Coca-Cola to IBM to LVMH and others.

There is obviously a limit to the number of people you can pull into the same meeting room. But digital technologies make it possible to erase physical boundaries and bring people together in the same virtual space. A well-planned and well-executed rhythm of actual and virtual meetings and of communication across all channels can build and sustain one team with one dream, whether you have 10, 100, or 100,000 employees.

Every quarter, as P&G's GMO, I held an all-hands webcast that I dubbed the Stengel Marketing Hour. It was a cross between a variety show and *PBS NewsHour*. In addition to an element of fun (I hosted one webcast in bicycling tights at Nike's headquarters), it offered a serious venue for rallying everyone to our higher purpose of improving the lives of consumers around the world, reporting results and setting expectations, and highlighting best practices. I devoted the feature segment of the hour to a best practice and celebrating those associated with it as heroes we all should emulate.

HOW DO YOU SAY "INNOCENT" IN FINNISH?

As George Bernard Shaw said, "England and America are two nations separated by a common language." So, as an American looking at Innocent's communications, I couldn't help but notice how the average American consumer would find the idiomatic terms and cultural references baffling, despite our common language. Yet Innocent has managed to translate its voice and style into entirely different languages for an increasing number of markets in Europe. When I asked Dan Germain how he and his colleagues had accomplished this, he answered in a way that again pointed to the way a business's ideal enables it to connect with people through fundamental human values.

"It was quite difficult in some ways," Dan says, "because I don't speak all the languages of the nations into which we've expanded. I don't speak Finnish or Norwegian, for example. When we took Innocent into continental Europe, I got really nervous, because so much of what we do is based on nuance and tone and the wit of using language. So when I thought of us trying to speak to people in German or in French or in Danish, I wondered, 'How are we going to be funny in those languages? How are we going to connect with people? How are we going to be amusing and useful and interesting?'

"Interestingly, I spoke with people at Apple about this question a few years ago. I was just doing a bit of research about how other companies retained the same tone for different audiences. And I found out that Apple did on a bigger scale what I was planning to do, and that reassured me. Because all they've done is gone out and find great people. And the secret of great businesses is simply finding the right people.

"So when we wanted to move the Innocent voice into Germany, into Scandinavia, into France, I went out and found these guys called Matt, Nicholai, and Christian. And they respectively wound up working in our new offices in Hamburg, Copenhagen, and Paris.

"I found them all not via traditional means. I found Nicholai, the Dane, by reading his English-language blog about publishing and literature and thinking it was really funny. I started talking to him via his blog, then interviewed and drank beer with him. And I tried to work out if in some weird way he was a bit like me and thought the same as the Innocent brand does about nature and so on.

"I still to this day don't know if Nicholai, Christian, and Matt respectively have been swearing profusely in Danish and being rude to people in French and boring people in German. But I know them and trust them enough to know that they're trying to give people the same experience that we've given people in the U.K. And our sales and the feedback from the people in those countries confirm that they're doing that very well."

Innocent's communication strategy is also bolstered by hiring skilled writers when opening a new office, because so much of what it does is communicated in text via packaging, the Web, and social media. This is a good idea for any start-up. Really skilled writers can straddle the line between external and internal communications. They can be the voice of the business internally, and can also write copy for ads. Innocent's writers are able to write and communicate in an Innocent voice in any area, blur the distinction between internal and external voices, and be consistent wherever communication is taking place. Good writing combines insight and passion, reason and emotion, in a way that everyone can understand and appreciate. If you want to win friends and influence people by expressing the essence of your business, your brand ideal, good writing will be invaluable.

Innocent began as a small company of friends, trying to help people "do themselves some good." Even now, at $260 million in revenue and 250 employees, it is largely a company of friends. But the ideal-based communication principles that drive Innocent's success are not just for small companies of friends. Let's now see how the same basic principles drove a sea change in communication at P&G, and how this in turn drove growth.

CONSUMER COMMUNICATION IMMERSION AT P&G

At Procter & Gamble in the 2000s, we took both the company as a whole and its individual businesses on an ideal-driven journey to achieve the quality of communication we just experienced at Innocent. We moved internally and externally from one-way, paternalistic, intrusive, rational communication to two-way, invited, rational and emotional—whole-brained—communication. We found new measures to track the trust, engagement, loyalty, and advocacy that this communication generated among employees, external partners, and consumers. Within the P&G portfolio, the further along on this journey our businesses traveled, the better their results became.

Immersive research with consumers is one way of learning about the implicit associations people have about a brand and making these data explicit to the leaders of a business so they can act on them. And immersive research both with consumers and with our retail customers, such as Walgreens and Carrefour, was crucial to new growth in such P&G businesses as Pampers, Olay, Bounty, Crest, and Iams pet food.

Iams had disappointing results as it entered Western Europe, and we set out to determine why. By engaging consumers in France and the United Kingdom in a deep one-on-one dialogue, we discovered that our marketing emphasis on enhancing pets' longevity was causing pet owners to think subconsciously about the end of their pets' lives. At the time the Iams advertising selling idea, or tagline, was "Good for life," which actually conjured up subconscious images of people's dear pets getting old and dying. Instead of making Iams stand for life, we were making it stand for death! We turned this around by repositioning Iams' marketing so that we were talking to consumers about offering the right nutrition for every life stage, from puppyhood and kittenhood on. And the brand's advertising selling line changed to "Life's better on Iams."

Agnès Sangan, who gave me so much help in bringing my Prague team together into a cohesive unit, guided the immersive work on Iams. In the last year of my tenure as GMO, I asked Agnès to apply her analytical and research skills to P&G as a whole. I also arranged with A. G. Lafley for Agnès to do immersive one-on-one interviews with him, his successor Bob McDonald, me, a large sample of A.G.'s senior management team, and key external partners. It was part of an effort to help us avoid complacency, now that we were growing strongly again, and take our commitment to the ideal of "touching lives, improving life" to a higher level. That meant moving to greater emphasis on our internal and external relationships, and improving lives through them, as our true reason for being and the source of our competitive advantage.

Even before this study materialized, A.G. was so intrigued with Agnès's research findings on our brands that he and I spent four hours discussing P&G with Agnès behind closed doors in Paris. We discussed what kind of company we wanted to be, and this ultimately meant what kind of relationship we wanted to have with consumers. In a lovely play on the company's initials, Agnès observed that P&G's greatest opportunities for continuing growth lay in our building a relationship of "pertinence and generosity" with consumers, and thus becoming more and more relevant to their lives. She also pinpointed how some of our strengths, including the brand-building framework that had powered our turnaround, could limit us if we didn't seek a higher purpose in all we did.

COMMUNICATION AND GROWTH

Two pivotal experiences at P&G showed me how improving the quality of our communication improved the quality of our relationships with employees and consumers, which led to growth.

When I took over the reins of P&G's business in the Czech Republic and Slovakia, I inherited a large portfolio of local communist-era brands acquired by my predecessor. Although one of the main charges from my bosses was to grow P&G's international brands in the local market, I recognized that local consumers, as well as our rank-and-file employees, who were of course also mainly Czech and Slovak, had strong emotional attachments to the local brands. However, the quality of these products fell far below P&G standards. The laundry detergent, for example, was mostly sand when we acquired the brand in the early 1990s. With Western brands from our competitors as well as our own portfolio entering the market, the local brands would have to be radically improved to survive. That would cost serious money in overhauling manufacturing processes and facilities and switching to new ingredients.

I decided that we would focus on a few of the local brands, and we began transferring technology from our dishwashing liquids Dawn and Fairy and our fabric care products such as Tide and Ariel. The P&G engineers overseeing these product changes wanted to make them all at once. But the dialogues we opened up with both our local employees and local consumers revealed that we should move more slowly and change the local brands in stages. Otherwise, consumers might reject them as frauds. In addition, making all the changes at once would force dramatic immediate price increases that the local market could not then accept.

One difficult wrinkle was that because the choice of consumer products was so limited during the communist era, Czech and Slovak consumers made each of these brands do double or triple duty and used them for more than the stated purpose on the label. The laundry detergent that was mostly sand? They used it for washing walls and floors as well as clothes. We had to make sure that the first few improved formulations of the detergent could continue to be used in all these ways.

We got an immediate financial payoff from these efforts, however. During my brief tenure in Prague and for some time afterward, the local brands represented more than half of the profitability of the business unit as a whole. But the larger and longer-term financial payoff came from how respecting the local brands improved our relationships with both local employees and local consumers. It contributed significantly to their accepting P&G as a company that was genuinely interested in improving their lives and took them and their opinions seriously. The result was that they gave us more trust and bonded more quickly and strongly with our international brands than they otherwise would have done. Consumers in the Czech Republic and Slovakia knew which brands came from P&G because, unlike in the United States, we advertised each brand as part of the P&G family.

Another important lesson for me in appreciating the emotional relationships people forge with businesses and brands took place a decade later, in the mid-2000s, after I assigned Portland-based advertising agency Wieden and Kennedy to work on Old Spice and a few other brands. Agency founder Dan Wieden and I had one of many conversations about how such bonds were formed and sustained. Dan mentioned that to his surprise, he found he really loved the P&G culture, because our people were so intent on improving our products to benefit consumers. But he felt we sometimes took that too far by focusing so much on improved product benefits in our marketing and advertising that we missed opportunities to develop consumers' relationships with our brands.

Dan and I had an ongoing discussion about the right balance between communication regarding the brand ideal and communication regarding what was new and improved in a brand's offerings. But we agreed about the direction P&G needed to go in; that was why I wanted to bring Wieden and Kennedy into P&G on the right brands. Wieden and Kennedy had never worked on P&G before I assigned them their first brands in 2005. Their campaigns for Nike exemplified a way of talking to consumers that subordinated product benefits to a brand's essence or higher purpose. Their eventual breakthrough work on Old Spice added impetus and urgency throughout the P&G portfolio to communication changes that we were already carrying forward on Pampers, Ariel, Febreze, Crest, Downy, and a number of our other brands, including Always feminine care products.

Always historically spoke to women in a one-way stream of communication about functional product benefits. Sparked by developments at Pampers in particular, the Always team in the early 2000s began to ask, what if Always' purpose, or ideal, could be about helping women embrace their womanhood in a positive way in all countries of the world? Leo Burnett, the Always advertising agency, fully embraced the new direction.

Guided by this ideal, the team identified a critical issue for girls in developing countries. In rural areas, lack of access to menstrual pads and tampons often forces girls to miss school days and contributes to their dropping out of school at high rates, a pattern with negative consequences for the girls themselves and their societies. In rural and urban areas of developing countries, traditional customs may also hamper the adoption of menstrual pads and tampons.

Together with Leo Burnett Worldwide, Always launched a "protecting futures" communications campaign internally and externally. It included a philanthropic element of contributing to the education of girls in developing countries as well as television commercials about how Always products helped girls avoid missing school days. With adjustments tailored to each country, but consistently portraying teenaged girls participating in nontraditional activities such as sports, this campaign expanded sales from South Africa to Pakistan. It also resonated powerfully with consumers of all income groups and demographics in North America and Europe. Not least of all, it stoked the pride and motivation of our employees around the world.

The strides we made in ideal- and relationship-centered communication as a company and in each of our businesses dramatically enhanced our innovation in reaching consumers when and where they were most receptive to our communications. We sold diapers over the Internet in South Korea when e-commerce was nascent. We reached new low-income moms in the Philippines via mobile phones before other companies had tried mobile marketing. We developed branded entertainment (a reapplication for a new time and place of P&G's producing the first television soap operas in the 1950s) such as the Head & Shoulders *Camino a la Fama* television talent show in Latin America. We offered Middle Eastern consumers a limited-edition Tide, for use during Ramadan, which contained a white musk fragrance traditionally associated with Ramadan observances. We pioneered efforts in customized direct-to-consumer cosmetics through Reflect.com, and we launched a start-up called Tremor to help P&G brands and other companies understand and scale word-of-mouth marketing.

None of the amazing innovative communications at P&G would have happened without innovation on what we called the "communications brief." The brief is a strategy document that inspires and guides communication choices for the people you seek to delight. It includes key quantitative information, such as business objectives and success criteria; insights about the brand's ideal and the people in your audience; and the action you want the communication to influence.

While creating a great brief seems like just good common sense, it is a major issue in business today. In mid-2011 John Harrobin, a vice president at Verizon Wireless, the second-largest advertiser in the United States, put his top 100 marketers on notice: their job performance would in part be measured by their excellence in creating briefs for its stable of communications agencies. Casey Jones, a former global vice president at Dell, has a consulting practice to help create excellent briefs. He dramatically sees the issue for companies in this way: "If you rated the industry on a scale from 1 to 10, with 1 being a horrifying piece of direction and 10 being optimal, I would say that companies are currently somewhere between a 2 and a 3."

Casey goes on to quantify the issue. "The amount of revenue dependent on the quality of these documents is in the billions of dollars. It sounds hyperbolic—until you've seen the quality of the briefs and realize that the work can't possibly drive ROI."

Another key takeaway from my experience and the Stengel 50 is the power in designing your organization—internally and externally with partners—for maximum creativity, speed, cost-effectiveness, and clarity in decision making. For the last two years of my tenure as P&G's global marketing officer, one of my highest priorities was tackling this large organizational issue at P&G. I hired the Monitor Group as a consultant to help me with this, as it was a huge global project.

The problem we were trying to solve was easy enough to state. How could we reorganize P&G's dozens of brand business teams and thousands (really) of communications agencies into a structure that simplified and accelerated decision making, produced advertising and other communications that drove faster growth, reduced time and cost, and resulted in teams that were happier and more inspired? The devil, as usual, was in the details.

After lots of external benchmarking, hundreds of interviews, dozens of meetings, and a few pilots, we began rolling out a radically new system for brand communications. We formalized the role within each major P&G brand of the brand franchise leader, who would be the brand's business artist, as we saw in the Pampers story in chapter 7. Previously, some brands had seven or eight decision makers located in the major regions and acting as brand franchise leaders. The new brand franchise leader role simplified decision making, and this person was accountable for brand ideal or purpose, communication strategy and plan, visual identity, innovation strategy, and all areas related to the brand ideal.

Once we clarified who within P&G called the shots on our major brands, we could then dramatically simplify our system with external partners. We reduced the number of agencies by more than 50 percent; we chose which capabilities each brand needed (e.g., in-store marketing, design, digital communications); we assigned one external leader for each agency team; and we compensated the teams exactly the same way instead of having several fee schemes. We compensated the external communications team on sales growth, and we depended on the leader to allocate the appropriate compensation to each agency team member.

Prior to this disruptive organizational innovation, each external agency partner reported to a different department within P&G, such as external relations, advertising, in-store marketing, design, and digital marketing. And they were all compensated differently. You can imagine the complexity and the blurred accountability for brand communications.

The new system clarified leadership and decision making, and resulted in better work, lower costs, and teams that were more inspired. P&G is still going strong behind this system, and continually learning how to make it even more effective.

Because so few companies think to innovate in how they design and deliver communications, I want to stress again that the same holistic communication approach served us equally well in our internal communications. In setting strategic business goals for the year, my marketing leadership team and I planned our internal as well as our external communications. Just as each of our businesses identified its most important consumers and prime prospects, we identified the influencers and prime prospects within marketing and other functions that we needed to become advocates for new initiatives. For example, when we were introducing a new methodology for measuring packaging impact and effectiveness, we identified key prospects within R&D, design, and customer business development to help launch the internal initiative effectively.

External publicity is an important and cost-effective way to send an internal message. It motivates people tremendously when they see positive media coverage about the business. At P&G we had a rolling campaign of communicating with key media, such as the *Wall Street Journal* and *Bloomberg Businessweek*, and academic and other thought leaders to generate stories, articles, and general buzz about the company as a whole and our brands. In 2005–6 we invited the *Financial Times* to shadow me for a few days to show how we approached ideals-inspired business. We invited selected business school professors to a "P&G Camp" in the summer to see what new innovations we were pursuing. I also thought carefully about the venues for my speaking engagements, all part of enhancing internal and external perceptions of P&G as a great company and a great place to work.

Over breakfast at the Broadway Deli in Santa Monica, Lee Clow, TBWA\Worldwide's global director, media arts, remarked to me that everything a business does is "media." As proof, he said the greatest ad of all time for his client Apple was not an ad, it was the Apple store. I'll try to explain what he means in the next chapter, on creating the ideal customer experience.

As we look at the customer experience, keep in mind Lee's observation that everything you do is "media." You must become an excellent communicator, because communication is the foundation of relationships, and great relationships drive business growth. And to state the obvious, this is more important than ever in a world of fast-response, always-on social media.

Here's what you can start doing Monday morning to set out on the path to become an ideals-based, growth-inspiring communicator inside and outside your company.

- **Treat communication as a critical driver of growth.** Ideal-driven communication is a top priority at Stengel 50 companies. It is not delegated; it is a leadership responsibility. Dan Germain at Innocent takes full responsibility for Innocent's internal and external communication.
- **Use a personal relationship metaphor in designing communication.** The same characteristics that make up a loving personal relationship—trust, honesty, love, respect, caring, warmth, humor—also make up a great business relationship. Innocent designs all its

communications for its "friends," and seeks to always genuinely deepen relationships with its employees, customers, and suppliers.

- **Measure your communications as you would measure a loving, loyal relationship.** We saw in the last chapter how Pampers changed the way it measured its communication, and then how its communications became far more effective in growing the brand.
- **Guide your communications partners through an inspirational, clear, and concise brief for every assignment.** This is one of the most powerful leadership actions you can take because this is where you make choices, give perspective, and set standards.
- **Design your communication system, internal and external, for maximum creativity, speed, and efficiency.** I demonstrated in my P&G story the potential for more effective ideals-inspired communication at a lower cost, with happier, faster teams. What's not to love?

Our next chapter discusses the fourth branch of the Ideal Tree, delivering a near-ideal experience. All the branches of the tree must work in harmony, but there is an especially close link between communicating your ideal and delivering an experience that makes the ideal a reality in your customers' lives.

9

Must-Do Number 4

Deliver a Near-Ideal Customer Experience

DELIVER
a near-ideal
customer experience

Back in 2001 when I was deciding whether to actively pursue the global marketing officer job at Procter & Gamble, one person I reached out to was Stuart Scheingarten. A management consultant who led leadership training sessions for P&G and was a troubleshooter on personnel issues, Stuart spoke with no holds barred. In his strong, nasal Brooklyn accent, he said the stuff that made people squirm, and he said it in the same way to everyone, no matter what their level in the company. When there was a problematic manager, P&G sent in Stuart to do an assessment. He interviewed the manager's family as well as his or her bosses, colleagues, and employees, and then he went back to that manager with brutally frank feedback, but also with concrete ways to change for the better. When Stuart unexpectedly died in his sleep in November 2005, the company held a memorial service for him at its global management meeting. Managers from all over the world spoke, with tears in their eyes, about the positive impact Stuart had had on their professional and personal lives.

Stuart and I got to know each other when I was a young brand manager, and he became a mentor and friend I could go to for advice on any subject. If Stuart was already on the scene, I didn't have to ask what he thought. He was sure to speak up and tell me.

I called Stuart for a lunch date, and he engaged me in a deep discussion of the GMO role and my potential fit for it. He also gave me the benefit of his unvarnished thoughts about P&G, which he knew intimately after twenty-five years of highly sensitive consulting. At the end of our talk, Stuart said, "You should go for it, Jim. But if you get the job, the worst mistake you can make is to fail to be bold. P&G has sometimes had harsh leadership over the years, but it is not used to bold leadership, and that's exactly what it needs right now. And you personally will need to be even bolder than you have ever been in any assignment at P&G."

Stuart's admonition to "be bold" not only ranks up there with the best and most timely career advice I've received, but it is especially apropos when it comes to delivering an experience that delivers on your brand ideal and delights customers. In fact, I think about it every time I walk into an Apple store.

Yes, I fully realize that you may have reached the saturation point when it comes to stories about just how fabulous Apple and its genius former CEO are. But consider this. Back at the turn of the millennium Apple was not the iconic success all the world reveres today. Ron Johnson, Apple's senior vice president of retail from 2000 to 2011, left his senior position at Target, a hot growth company, and moved his young family from Minneapolis to Silicon Valley in 2000 to join a company that was not doing all that well at the time. Moreover, selling computers in the retail environment seemed liked a fool's errand since conventional wisdom was that it was a doomed business. Dell was riding high. Consumers who bought from Dell did so directly, over the phone or through the Internet. Gateway was then in the process of shuttering its retail stores, and many analysts believed Apple was heading down the wrong road.

Let's cut to the chase and fast-forward to today. Apple is the most successful retailer in history, with an astonishing $50,000 in sales per square foot in their best stores (there is no close second) and roughly $13 billion in revenue in ten years.

What really happened here?

For the Apple stores to succeed, Johnson knew they had to express the Apple ideal of creative exploration and self-expression. That meant the stores could not focus simply on moving product but had to look beyond to changing lives by actively helping customers express their creativity. He envisioned the stores as places where consumers could test-drive Apple products and learn the "digital arts" of using those products, where they could join Apple retail employees and other consumers in a real-life, bricks-and-mortar, non-virtual community. He saw the stores as places that could best succeed—really, could only succeed—if they strove to inspire greatness in everyone who walked through the door.

Johnson's vision wasn't immediately understood by his new colleagues at Apple. That went right up to Steve Jobs, as I learned from Ron Johnson when we were both part of a program in San Francisco. But recall what I said about great business artists. They know their own strengths and weaknesses, and they empower and inspire others to lead in complementary ways. When Steve Jobs heard some of the ideas Ron Johnson and his team came up with, like the Genius Bar, he thought they were nuts. But he also recognized that this was not his expertise. He saw the fire in the eyes of Johnson and his team, and he backed them even when, late in the game, it meant postponing the opening date of the first stores and redoing them to correct problems.

Tens of millions of consumers and counting have now visited the Genius Bar, where Johnson says Apple employees "don't fix computers, they restore relationships," and have gone away happy. Millions more and counting have finished Apple Store classes and personal training sessions in the "digital arts" enlightened and inspired about what they can do with their personal technology. And everyone who has visited the stores has walked away knowing that there's nothing else like them in the world of consumer technology.

To accomplish this, Johnson set hiring criteria that, again, may seem counterintuitive for a retailer. He insisted on hiring people not for their sales instincts or skills as "closers" but for their life skills, their ability to relate to, say, both a grandmother and her fourteen-year-old geeky grandson. And when it came to measuring these employees' performance and compensating them, the quality of their interaction with customers was the number one metric. Likewise, the most important number that Johnson looked at for the stores as a whole was traffic, because if people are in the stores, then good things will happen.

Everything your business does comes together with the ideals-inspired experience you provide customers. It's not only your product or service but how people learn about it, buy it, use it, live with it, and share the quality of the experience with others.

The irony, though, is that you can't deliver a perfect brand experience. But you can deliver an ideal-for-now brand experience.

Does this sound contradictory, even a little crazy?

Well, we live in an imperfect world, where everyone—and every business—makes mistakes. Things break down, accidents happen, disasters strike. On top of that, even if the product or service performs as promised, a desirable brand experience is a moving target. The target moves unpredictably as time goes on and technology, lifestyles, and competitive offerings change.

But people understand these things and really don't expect perfection. Otherwise, we'd all be out of business and have no reason to get up in the morning.

What I've found is that the more you strive to improve people's lives and the more you demonstrate that in your products and services and all your interactions, the more customers and end consumers will reward you by becoming loyal advocates for your business. They'll welcome your efforts to bring your business's ideal to life. They'll give you the benefit of the doubt when you fall a little short, and quickly tell you what's wrong and offer their own passion, creativity, and support to help you fix it. They'll help you take a not-quite-right result and turn it into a win, as consumers in Method's "people against dirty" community did over the video of the mom in the shower.

The only thing they won't forgive is if you take them for granted and stop trying to improve their lives.

Remember the research in chapter 6 that showed people's ability to sense if the people behind a brand are bored and disengaged, simply by looking at the advertising, shelf presence, and packaging? If they pick that up from your ads and packaging, they're unlikely to sample the other elements of your brand experience. So long as they have alternatives, they'll turn to others for what they need and want.

THE IDEALS-INSPIRED BRAND EXPERIENCE AND INNOVATION

Brand experience and innovation go hand in hand. An imperfect world and a desirable brand experience that keeps changing—that combination creates a mandate for leaders to maintain a twin focus on execution and innovation.

Leaders who extend this mandate throughout their business send a great message to their people. All employees want to be part of a vibrant organization that is on the move. And it's a necessity on a par with anything in the compensation and benefits package for attracting the best talent, whether managerial or technical. As the sense of a higher purpose spread throughout P&G during the first decade of this century, it motivated everyone from IT and product supply to finance, marketing, and R&D.

The impact of P&G's renewed passion to provide a far better experience also had a profound positive effect on P&G's outside partners at communications and design agencies. At the start of the 2000s, the best creative talent from agencies were liable to jump ship if they were assigned to a P&G account. But during the 2000s, P&G brands became highly coveted accounts from a creative point of view, because of the inspired purpose and people behind each brand. The best talent clamored to work with P&G, as was the case with Wieden and Kennedy's highly talented creative team on Old Spice. I knew we had crossed a major threshold when founder Dan Wieden said to me in 2007 that some of his top creative people on Nike were asking if they could work on P&G projects. That blew me away—and shows the power of setting the goal of creating memorable, ideal-inspired experiences for consumers.

Making innovation the foundation for a better experience is a crucial senior leadership responsibility, starting of course with the ideal, the higher purpose a business aspires to serve. Only senior leaders in an organization can create the culture for innovation to thrive, and only senior leaders can direct attention, people, and resources to this effort and keep it forever improving.

HOW NETFLIX INNOVATES TO
DELIVER ITS EVOLVING IDEAL

Netflix is a brand I personally use and love. It is not a Stengel 50 brand, but it likely could be soon, even with its pricing and communication mishaps in late 2011. Since 1997, Netflix has provided a continually improving experience by keeping ahead of unpredictable moving targets such as changing technology and lifestyles. They provide a service that deftly combines innovation in its three forms: sustaining innovation (the daily work of continuous product or service improvement and upgrades), commercial innovation (creating demand through marketing without changing the product or service, i.e., finding new uses or occasions for uses), and disruptive innovation (inventing or reinventing a category that changes a business model).

Many people still perceive Netflix as a DVD rental and streaming subscription service. But it has quickly become much more than that. Thanks to a series of innovations in the experience it provides consumers, it is becoming a twenty-four-hour concierge for personalized entertainment. I believe that its brand ideal of personalized entertainment puts Netflix in the eliciting joy field, a strong position for what is otherwise a delivery service.

When Netflix launched as a DVD rental by mail service in 1997, its business model was itself a form of disruptive innovation: no more trips to Blockbuster (remember them?), no more late fees, far more choice in movies, and of course the recommendation service, à la Amazon. Still, many skeptics doubted that it could succeed.

Netflix went public in 2002, and by 2003 it had more than 1 million subscribers. It worked continuously to broaden its selection with new content licensing deals and to improve its delivery of DVDs by mail. Customers responded to this continuous innovation by telling everyone they knew that Netflix was wonderful, and the subscription base kept climbing steeply.

If it ain't broke, don't fix it, the saying goes. In 2007, however, despite naysayers who warned against it, Netflix started streaming high-quality content over the Internet. With this second disruptive innovation, this time to its own DVDs-by-mail system, growth exploded. As costs dropped with the delivery of more and more of its content via the much cheaper channel of the Internet, Netflix aggressively shifted resources into premium content licensing deals with the big media companies.

As the bottom fell out of DVD sales and customers demonstrated an increasing appetite for streamable content, that's when things got really interesting. The media companies began to say that Netflix, which they had initially greeted as found money, an attractive source of extra licensing revenue, was their worst enemy. Jeffrey Bewkes, CEO of Time Warner, took the lead on this in a series of media interviews and public statements at the close of 2010. Concerned about the impact of Netflix on both Time Warner's content production and content distribution businesses, Bewkes bluntly criticized the Starz movie channel, spun off from John Malone's Liberty Media empire, for licensing the right to stream its content, including Sony and Walt Disney movies, to Netflix too cheaply—$25 million a year—and letting Netflix show the content as soon as Starz itself had the right to do so.

According to Bewkes, "Why would anyone subscribe to Starz when they can basically get the whole thing for about nothing [from Netflix]?" This threatened the business model worked out between the media content providers and the cable television companies, said Bewkes, because "once you put [content] on Netflix, you really can't sell it anywhere else."

Lest anyone think that the CEO of mighty Time Warner feared upstart Netflix more than the behavior of his fellow media company heads, Bewkes predicted in 2010 that Netflix would soon be struggling, because at an average monthly subscription of "$8 to $10, it doesn't have the economics to support high-quality programming."

Rubbing it in, or trying to, Bewkes also said of Netflix's prospects, "It's a little bit like, is the Albanian army going to take over the world? I don't think so." Netflix would no longer be able to license desirable content so cheaply in the future,

Bewkes decreed: "This has been an era of experimentation, and I think it's coming to a close."

Well, maybe there's some cause for concern about the Albanian army. The whole world is in an era of experimentation that shows every sign of continuing to accelerate rather than slow down, much less end. At the end of 2011, Netflix had around 24 million subscribers in North America, within shouting distance of HBO's approximately 28 million subscribers in North America. More than two hundred devices for sale in the United States could stream Netflix. And the company boldly snapped up original programming rights to one of the most sought-after new television series, *House of Cards*, starring Kevin Spacey, for $100 million, and, replacing HBO, won the rights to stream content from DreamWorks Animation.

To Jeffrey Bewkes's credit as a business leader, he also did more than talk, overseeing the early 2011 release of an app for streaming all of Time Warner's standard and premium cable content to tablets and other mobile devices. It was an instant hit with Time Warner's customers. But other media content providers looked at Time Warner as a traitor in their midst and threatened to sue to stop it from streaming content to subscribers. The content producers said cable companies did not have the right to stream their content to customers as well as carry it to them by wire or satellite signal. Time Warner said this right fell under their present licenses.

As for Starz and Netflix, later in 2011 Starz imposed a three-month lag on Netflix's streaming of certain content and said it would not renew its deal with Netflix after it expired in February 2012. Meanwhile, Netflix pursued new content deals, raised its prices in July 2011, and announced, but later retracted, plans to create a separate DVD service brand called Qwikster.

Let's leave this story in midstream, if you'll excuse the pun, and notice how relentlessly Netflix elevated the role it plays in its customers' lives. Through sustaining innovation (even better recommendations and programming), commercial innovation (making the service available on multiple devices), and disruptive innovation, Netflix made it ever easier for subscribers to watch what they want, when and where they want. Their evolved ideal of being a concierge for 24/7 personalized entertainment inspired innovation to provide a better experience, one that, like it or not, the whole media industry has had to take seriously.

Big-time media companies, movie stars, the hottest films—it's easy to see how all this translates into a great customer experience.

But you don't have to be in a glamour profession to deliver an innovative customer experience that brings a great brand ideal to life. Like the Apple Store folks, you could be in supposedly boring retail. You could even be in the usually low-rent world of phone sales. In fact, the best customer experience in the world today—I give it the edge even over the Apple Store—happens over the phone at Zappos.

If you're like most people, you've probably had a less than optimal experience dealing with high-pressure, nail-the-sale-quickly tactics when you try to order something over the phone. Or you call about a problem with something you've already purchased over the phone or online, from a business that promises 100 percent satisfaction, only to get the runaround.

Zappos is the exception to the rule. It has transformed what is often a low-end career into something heroic through its lofty ideal of delivering not just a product but happiness through WOW service. It's an ideal that influences every touch point that employees, customers, and vendors have with the company. And it is the strongest example in the Stengel 50 of a brand lighting up the eliciting joy field.

MAKE IT PERSONAL

"Ta-da!" My October meeting at Zappos, the full-price online and telephone retailer of shoes, clothing, and an expanding lineup of other products, came to an abrupt halt as a parade of outrageously costumed employees with noisemakers marched through the office, out into the Las Vegas sunshine, and back again. This happy Halloween commotion was nothing, I soon learned, compared to the parade a few months earlier honoring a new record customer service phone call of over seven hours. It's the kind of event inspired by Zappos's quirkily phrased ten core values—such as number three, "Create fun and a little weirdness"—which, along with its astonishing sales growth, have brought it lots of often baffled attention from the media.

Zappos's people have remarkable clarity on why an ideal will increasingly be the difference maker in business. They understand that people want to interact with brands they can be friends with. And what works in personal relationships—trust, concern, honesty, warmth, transparency, openness, patience, humility, mutual growth—works in business relationships. We saw the power of a personal relationship metaphor in our deep dive at Innocent in chapter 8, and no one exemplifies this more than Zappos. The question Zappos asks itself is one every business should ask: how do we treat our customers so they become loyal, raving fans who wouldn't think of going elsewhere, no matter how much lower the price offered by the competition?

The Zappos experience flows from its higher purpose, its ideal. Its culture is its brand: customer service that "delivers WOW" by "delivering happiness," the phrase printed on every Zappos box. As Donavon Roberson, operations manager for Zappos Insights, the company's organizational consulting group, puts it, "We believe that if even for a moment we can take a person from where they are and make them happy by the service we offer, the product they can find with us, the overall experience they have with our company, then we've done something. We've invested in them, and we've added value to their life."

Putting this lofty ideal into action has earned Zappos extraordinary customer loyalty and advocacy, with 75 percent of its daily business coming from repeat customers. When Zappos does get new customers and asks them how they heard about the company, the number one response is that friends or family told them about it.

Zappos has achieved explosive growth through an emphasis on customer service that includes no-questions-asked returns, free shipping both ways—and lots of time on the phone with customers. Zappos earns extraordinary revenue per customer, with a loyal yet relatively small customer base as its biggest marketing asset. That small base means that it has plenty of room to grow. When employees tell others that they work at Zappos, the reaction is either "I love Zappos!" or "What's Zappos?" A big reason Amazon bought Zappos in July 2009 is that millions of people had not yet experienced Zappos—and when they do, they will become advocates. That meant lots of upside growth still ahead for Zappos, which Amazon could help accelerate through investment and expertise.

Zappos's core values, written on their walls throughout their home office, are:

1. Deliver WOW through service.
2. Embrace and drive change.
3. Create fun and a little weirdness.
4. Be adventurous, creative, and open-minded.
5. Pursue growth and learning.

6. Build open and honest relationships with communication.
7. Build a positive team and family spirit.
8. Do more with less.
9. Be passionate and determined.
10. Be humble.

Number three, "Create fun and a little weirdness," has probably received the most attention, and the most baffled commentary, from the media. I'll have more to say about that bafflement, a confusion of surface and substance, later in the chapter. For now let me just say that I think these ten values, albeit maybe with different wording, could successfully be embraced by any company in any industry, no matter how traditional or weird its internal culture might be.

These core values are the North Star or global positioning system for Zappos, the way it manages through its higher purpose of delivering happiness. To take one example, employees at the Zappos call center, known as the customer loyalty team, have no scripts, no requirements for handling calls within a limited and specified amount of time, and no sales quota. They are told to "make decisions based on the ten core values." Most people, says Donavon Roberson, get it. "They understand if they give too much away, the business goes under and they don't have a job. They get that we're about more than the bottom line, but that a healthy bottom line allows us to do a lot more."

The biggest challenge for most companies that seek to learn from Zappos is giving up entrenched habits and sidestepping the fear of losing control. "An environment like Zappos," says Roberson, "where every employee feels like they're the CEO, can feel dangerous if you approach it from the fear standpoint as, 'I'm going to lose control. It's my business. I want to run it my way. I know what's best.' If you approach it from that 'I' standpoint, there will be fear."

What needs to happen, Roberson says, is for leaders to flip it around and think, "'I've got the right people. I trust them to do the right thing. They know what we're about. Let's open this baby up and see what happens.' Look at it from that perspective, and be willing to take the risk." Many company leaders I meet talk about turning the hierarchy upside down, empowering employees, and adopting a service leadership mentality. Few really do it. Zappos is the best I've seen.

"You can figure out pretty quickly," says Aaron Magness, Zappos's head of brand marketing and business development, "if people are going a little too far. For example, our video and blogs team is always trying to do different fun things. But the team is predominantly younger guys. Sometimes we have to talk and I say, 'Hey, what you just put out there is funny. But is it funny for our customer, who is likely to be a fortysomething woman?'"

If people do color outside the lines of core values, the leadership team steps in. It's not a case of "I'm the manager, you're the employee. I'm right, you're wrong." It's "We love what you tried to do. We think the spirit behind it is right. We want to know why you think it fell within the core values, because we think it was outside the core values." Thanks to the whole company's commitment to the core values, leaders can talk with anyone in any part of the organization and have a hard discussion without its being political.

THE ZAPPOS BRAND EXPERIENCE AND THE CULTURE THAT CREATES IT

Zappos's people know that their culture and its ideal of delivering happiness are what really separate them from the competition. After all, consumers can buy the products they offer through many other online and retail store outlets. Zappos employees understand that the brand is not just the product, it's the overall experience the customer has, and thus how their interactions with customers reflect their ten core values and brand ideal.

Viewing a brand as the embodiment of a company's culture is a very fundamental insight that is at the heart of not just Zappos and other category-leading businesses in the Stengel 50, but those aspiring to lead their categories. When Tim Armstrong, the chairman and CEO of AOL, called me in late 2009 to ask me to join the board of directors of the company as it was spun out from Time Warner, he appealed to my belief in "brand as culture."

Tim worked at Google from 2000 to 2009, and he and I partnered on several initiatives across P&G and Google. Tim told me he wanted to repurpose AOL with a new brand ideal of bringing the most delightful, helpful, and intuitive consumer experiences to life on the Internet. He wanted my help in bringing AOL's employees to the point where they could embody that ideal in all their activities, because he had seen the power of that kind of employee alignment with brand ideals at both P&G and Google.

While the AOL story and ideal is still unfolding, the culture has become far more innovative and inventive. One example is the remarkable expansion of the Patch network of hyperlocal digital services, which have the potential to be the community news service for the twenty-first century.

Customers certainly agree that the Zappos brand is its culture. Although it is important that Zappos has a great selection of great products, that is not what customers want Zappos to talk most about. When Zappos started a product-driven ad campaign, customers responded, "That's not Zappos. That's not who you guys are." Zappos listened and shifted its marketing to be more about its culture and ten core values than its products.

When Zappos created a recent television ad campaign, the focus was on the best way to share the Zappos culture, letting people know that Zappos is built off customer service with great products to sell. One strong sign that consumers picked up on the culture they saw in the resulting ads, Aaron Magness says, "was the number of comments from people who said, 'I would like to work at Zappos.' That's huge. If someone sees your campaign and says that's a place they would like to work, I think you're pretty much top-of-mind for a purchase."

Likewise, in Zappos's use of blogs and other digital and social media it doesn't try to push products. It's all about the culture and customers getting to know Zappos and Zappos getting to know them. Zappos fans on Facebook would surely love to get discount coupons. But Zappos doesn't discount and it still has been able to grow a sizable Facebook fan base, with lots of interaction on their Facebook page, without ever sending discount coupons.

The higher you envision your ideal, the higher you can drive your performance. A higher purpose, as Zappos's leaders told me, is inherently more sustainable. Delivering happiness is a lofty but nebulous brand experience, which is the point. That helps keep it fresh. Zappos can't permanently define how to do it, because happiness is different for everyone.

Most of the Stengel 50 have extremely high ideals, and as we saw in chapter 2, they fall into one of five aspirational fields of fundamental human values. Zappos is, of course, in the eliciting joy field. Aiming high with your brand ideal is so fundamental to creating memorable customer experiences. It won't happen without the ideal as the starting point.

Joy and *delight* are not just buzzwords at Zappos. They genuinely describe the atmosphere I felt there, the attitude of everyone I met, and the behavior I observed.

Here again is Donavon Roberson: "When we're on the phone with customers, we're not trying to sell them a product. We're not trying to upsell them on anything. If they're on the phone and they're not sure about the product they called about, we'll move on. We feel that if we spend the time to build a relationship with you, a few things are going to happen. One, you'll trust us. Two, you'll tell other people about us. Three, eventually you'll buy. The customers that kind of flirt with us for a while and call us about different things but never really place an order, we feel that if we spend enough time with them, they will, because we've earned their trust and earned their business."

Earlier in the chapter, I shared what Ron Johnson looked for in Apple Store employees. He sought relationship builders, not salespeople. In his words, he wanted people skilled in "the art of relationships and empathy." When asked how he can tell people will be great relationship builders, Ron says he "looks into their eyes, as the eyes are the window to the soul."

While this all may sound rather Zen-like, a common thread through the Stengel 50 is a Zen-like passion for bringing their ideal to life through their customer relationships. This may come more naturally to service businesses such as Zappos, food retailer Wegmans, fashion apparel retailer Zara, and FedEx, but I even found it in unexpected categories, including packaged goods companies. We saw in chapter 7 how Pampers tripled its size through a relentless focus on strengthening relationships with moms.

Zappos understands you can never be complacent about the customer relationships that underlie its brand experiences. "Customers are a lot more vocal today," says Donavon Roberson. "You can't go to customers and say, 'This is who we are, this is what we're about, trust us,' without them putting it to the test. Customers definitely test our service. People call Zappos all the time just to see if what they've heard is accurate. And if it's not, they're not afraid to share it. Customers are not afraid to blog about a bad experience. They're not afraid to tweet about it. They're not afraid to post something on YouTube or Facebook about their experience. Customers are very vocal about the experiences they have."

This puts a premium on honesty and transparency in the Zappos brand experience, as the same factors do for all brands. If you allow customers to look behind the curtain and they still like the person they see, it really works in your favor.

HAVE THE RIGHT MIX OF INNOVATION TO AMPLIFY YOUR IDEAL

No matter what their main job is going to be, everyone at Zappos goes through call center training and spends time answering phones in the call center when joining the company. During the Christmas holidays, Zappos's peak season, everyone puts in another ten hours on the phones. All of this phone time, says chief technology officer Arun Rajan, "helps you connect the dots in terms of what the technology really needs to do to service the customer."

The training and time on the phone are eye-opening experiences. Many of the ideas that the Zappos technology people have for making their system stronger or easier to use come from their own stints in the call center. When they talk about technology features, the conversation starts with how it's going to impact the customer. Zappos wants people who are thinking not about the perfect solution from a technology aspect but about what's going to be the best solution for the customer.

Zappos had problems with off-the-shelf technology packages and now builds mission-critical technology on its own or with trusted partners. Many if not most companies try to make everything as self-service as possible on their websites, and then cut back on their call centers. It's a whole lot more expensive to deal with customers on the phone. While Zappos keeps evolving its website to give customers more self-service features and functionality, it also deliberately sets up extra cues on its website to encourage customers to phone the call center. And no matter how high call volume rises, it answers all calls in under twenty seconds, drafting employees from other areas— already trained for the purpose—at peak call times. Zappos has learned that once customers call in, speak with a Zappos employee, and feel what it's like to be a Zappos customer, they're highly likely to become customers for life.

Building, running, and controlling their own technology systems is a competitive advantage for Zappos, says Arun Rajan. "It's easy for a retailer to say, 'I'll drop in so-and-so's retail software or website platform, and I'll be good.' But we've learned that's not the right answer for us because we can't service our customers and our partners the way we want to that way."

Because of its continuing sustaining innovation in its technology, Zappos has been able to achieve continuing innovation in its brand experience, steadily adding new categories of products to its retail offerings. Arun explains, "The systems that we build internally have to support our customer service ideal, and they have to scale with our business. That's a hard combination for any retailer. That's Amazon's advantage, and that's certainly Zappos's advantage. We are able to create things like a catalog that's product-agnostic. We have been a retail shoe company. But we can now sell any category of product. We can be a retailer for anything, and we can make those transformations with the underlying technology that we have."

Zappos's technology prowess also made possible one of the most significant innovations in its brand experience: its 2003 decision to end drop shipping, a system in which goods remain in the possession of the manufacturer or a wholesaler until a sale is made. Instead, Zappos now owns and has physical possession of every item of inventory and can track its exact location and history. That visibility extends all the way through the call center. So when a customer has a question about shoes she's received, the customer service person can see that they were purchased a year ago, returned, and then purchased a second time and also returned. The Zappos employee handling the call can then zero in on what the problem is and how to resolve it.

No longer drop shipping meant that Zappos could make the customer not just someone who buys stuff, but part of the supply chain. That's a difference maker for Zappos since it elevates the importance of every one of the people in the supply chain to be part of the brand experience.

Once when Arun Rajan was on the call center phones he spoke with a customer who couldn't print out his return label. The customer said, "I've never had this problem over the eight years I've been shopping with you." Arun tried to solve the problem but couldn't do so during the time the customer had available to speak on the phone right then. The customer said, "I love you guys so much. I want this to work. Call me anytime, and I'll help you test it."

"For the next couple of days," says Arun, "we spent several hours on the phone together, like friends. We worked together to solve his problem, and got it fixed for him and, as it turns out, for other customers as well. The fact that he took so much time out of his life and spent it with a company that's just a place to buy stuff is what's so amazing. That's the endearing relationship we have with our customers." And perhaps the most interesting part of the story is that the customer had no inkling that he was being helped by Zappos's chief technical officer. "He thought I was a full-time customer service agent," says Arun.

Elevating everyone in the Zappos supply chain applies to vendors and employees as well as customers. Zappos expects vendors to have the same culture fit as employees. "Would I hire them to be on our team? That's the question I ask," says Aaron Magness. "There are a lot of amazing companies out there that you could work with. But if they don't get what we're really trying to accomplish here, it's not going to work."

Donavon Roberson adds, "The vendor relationship is very important to us; they're an extension of our team. I met a vendor when he arrived to take a tour with us, and asked if I could help carry his bags inside. He did a double take. He said he'd been selling shoes for seventeen years, always carrying five or six bags of samples with him, and this was the first time anyone offered to help him. That puzzles me. Vendors are folks we want to build long-term relationships with. They want us to buy their product. We want them to work with us on pricing and other important issues. Beyond that, we want to deliver WOW to them and treat them like human beings."

This includes giving vendors access to the information about their products in Zappos's systems. Arun Rajan added, "Our vendors probably have access to more information than any other company would be comfortable sharing with their vendors. They have access to almost everything their buyer at Zappos has access to. Which means it's now a level playing field. Most companies say, 'We're gonna keep that information advantage and negotiate a better deal from the vendor.' We try to come to a deal that makes sense for both parties. We don't try to squeeze our vendors, we don't try to squeeze our partners. We're transparent with them about what the situation is and work out the best solution for the relationship." It's a philosophy that extends to technology service vendors, not only product vendors.

Zappos understands that their business model lives or dies with the enthusiasm and commitment of their people. They have a very low employee turnover rate, and the reason they do is that, like Method, they spend so much time making sure they hire the right people. Then they "make sure they know that we appreciate them, that we love them, that we need them here as part of the Zappos family," says Donavon Roberson.

Aaron Magness elaborates, "Every person we hire goes through a long process. That's tough, because you often need people right away. But you have to remind yourself that if you don't get the right person in place, maybe this one doesn't matter, but when they are in a hiring position, they're not going to choose the right person. But if you have the right people, everything happens naturally."

Added Donavon, "Younger employees are also looking for businesses that respect them and that have a higher purpose or vision beyond just the bottom line. Businesses that they really can belong to and be a part of something great."

When I was GMO at P&G, I asked Terry Leahy, then the CEO of the U.K. retailer Tesco, what P&G could learn from Tesco. Tesco at the time was one of P&G's largest and fastest-growing retail customers. Terry shocked me, and the other P&G leaders who were with me, with a profoundly simple answer. He said, "Treat your employees the way you want your customers treated." I think Terry would be very comfortable in the Zappos culture.

THE FIVE KEY TAKEAWAYS ON
HOW TO DELIVER AN IDEAL EXPERIENCE

Zappos is a well-publicized, highly admired, high-growth company. Thousands of people visit their headquarters every year. Still, people struggle with how to apply what works in the Zappos culture to improve their businesses. Many see the parades, noisemakers, and overall weirdness in the Zappos culture, and struggle to find the underlying principles to reapply in their business.

It's that third core value, "Create fun and a little weirdness," that baffles some outsiders, just as Method's "Keep it weird" does. But every business needs to create an environment for its people that enables them to be themselves, have fun, and learn and grow as people. That's what "Keep it weird" and "Create fun and a little weirdness" really mean.

Here's how Donavon Roberson handles questions from companies, mostly larger ones, on what they can learn and reapply from the Zappos experience. "To larger companies that say, 'We can't do what Zappos does,' we say, 'You're right. But what can you do? How can you have a higher purpose?' If you go into a men's hair salon and ask them, 'What is your job?' they might say, 'Our job is to cut hair.' Okay, but what if they saw their job as taking clients out of their lives for a few moments, providing them a place of escape, giving them an amazing experience, and then sending them on their way feeling like brand-new people? Then the service they provide is cutting hair, but their job is actually adding value to people's lives."

Donavon's excellent advice leads to a number of major takeaways from the stories we have explored in this chapter on delivering a near-ideal experience.

Start with the Ideal. A great brand experience, and the innovation that feeds it, must begin with the ideal, the higher purpose the business wants to serve. This is how Pampers moved from an overriding emphasis on dryness to innovation in the experience of helping with baby development. It is why Zappos gives their employees freedom to innovate within their WOW service ideal. It is why the P&G brand Old Spice stopped concentrating solely on deodorant efficacy and envisioned a new role helping boys become confident men. It is how Netflix moved from being a DVD rental by mail service to becoming a twenty-four-hour concierge for people's personalized entertainment.

Make Innovation Personal. You will not deliver a delightful brand experience without getting personal. You must have more than the clinical research that so many companies rely on, including surveys, quantitative data, and the thousands of PowerPoint presentations bouncing back and forth within companies. You must experientially understand customers and their lives.

We started the chapter with the phenomenal story of how Apple Stores found success and growth through a focus on building customer relationships to deliver a wonderful brand experience. We have learned from many of the Stengel 50 brands that what works in your personal relationships also works to improve and innovate in your brand experience. It is a simple and profound truth: what works in life's relationships also works in creating amazing brand experiences. People will love your experience, and reward you through their brand loyalty.

Collaborate Widely. The third key takeaway is to think more broadly about innovating in your brand experience by collaborating with more than just the usual suspects. Too often businesses define innovation too narrowly and silo it, usually in R&D. We learned from Zappos how they think about their suppliers and vendors, and how important they are in delivering a brand experience. And we learned from Netflix that their brand experience has been richly enhanced by their growing collaboration with content creators.

Have a Portfolio of Innovations. Fourth, have the right mix of innovation in improving your brand experience. Your journey to improve it is never over, and you must always have a robust portfolio of forward-looking innovations. We learned from Netflix how they have grown through a portfolio of sustaining, commercial, and disruptive innovation. Many great companies have done this implicitly, but I have found that it is very helpful to make your portfolio of upcoming innovation explicit.

You should always strive to have a rich portfolio of innovation and not rely overly on one particular type of innovation. At P&G, we asked every category to provide us with a forward-looking future outlook on their portfolio mix. In fact, we even had targets for each type of innovation: about 60 percent sustaining innovation, 20 percent commercial innovation, and 20 percent disruptive innovation.

Establish a Process for Innovation. My fifth and last takeaway on delivering a near-ideal experience is that you must establish a repeatable, teachable process for innovation that enhances your brand experience. Many of the companies in the Stengel 50 have structured processes for innovation, while certainly allowing for serendipity. A clear innovation process gives an organization a common language, common criteria for go/no-go decisions on initiatives, and a way for everyone to see and adjust the innovation portfolio.

So far we have explored four of the five branches of the Ideal Tree, the must-dos for leveraging a brand ideal.

We learned from Jack Daniel's, Pizza Hut, and Discovery how to discover a brand ideal in one of five areas of fundamental human values.

My P&G experience in the cosmetics industry, in the Czech Republic and Slovakia, and on Pampers provided examples of how to build your culture around your brand ideal.

The U.K. brand Innocent is a stellar case study on how to communicate your brand ideal to engage employees and customers.

In this chapter, Netflix and Zappos teach us how to deliver a near-ideal customer experience and how continuing growth depends on doing so consistently.

There's one more branch to the Ideal Tree: evaluate your progress and people against your ideal. If you do not evaluate your progress and people against your ideal, none of what you do in the other branches will be sustainable. In the next chapter, we'll see what that involves.

Must-Do Number 5

Evaluate Your Progress and People Against Your Ideal

EVALUATE
your progress and people
against your ideal

We saw early on, when we looked at the results of a Millward Brown Optimor study of the market capitalization of the S&P 500 (see page 1), that brand has become the biggest single asset in business and the decisive factor you must leverage for present and future growth. The study found that in 1980, brand value contributed little if anything to the market capitalization of the S&P 500. Since then, however, brand value has risen to become the single biggest asset category in the market capitalization of the S&P 500 in B2B and B2C sectors alike.

Brand value now represents more than 30 percent of the total market capitalization of the S&P 500. But that's only half the story. Brand equity is more and more important to today's fastest-growing businesses.

Consider these examples, spanning only the 2000s, from the Stengel 50, businesses that are growing at a rate three times or more than that of their competition:

Brand Contribution* of Selected Stengel 50 Brands
2001–2010

	Brand Contribution 2001	Brand Contribution 2010
Accenture	19%	47%
FedEx	17%	55%
IBM	34%	44%
Samsung	12%	42%
Starbucks	26%	57%

Source: Millward Brown Optimor.

The trend is unmistakable. To me, it is an open-and-shut case. If you're not measuring and managing against a brand ideal, you're consigning your business to the middle of the pack or the side of the road.

This is where the rubber meets the road. Everything discussed so far—from discovering the ideal to delivering a near-ideal experience—can reach fruition only if a business evaluates its progress and people against its brand ideal.

Brand value is already your key driver of business value. But is it driving growth or decline? Is it attracting new customers and building great relationships with them while strengthening the bond with existing customers? Or is it losing its attraction for both existing and new customers? Is the health of your brand inspiring employees and partners, or is its hollowness disillusioning them?

Lord Kelvin, the nineteenth-century British mathematician, physicist, and engineer, had it right when he first coined the

*Brand contribution, a metric derived from customer perception and behavior data, helps determine the percentage of a brand's revenue attributable to the emotional bond between brand and customer.

oft-quoted phrase "If you cannot measure it, you cannot improve it." If you are not measuring all you do against your brand ideal, you simply cannot expect to achieve the growth you want.

Based on my experiences at P&G, the companies I've worked with as a consultant, and the Stengel 50, I want to offer you four principles for measuring a brand ideal to drive sustained growth:

1. Measure your progress against your ideal with the customers and stakeholders most important to your future.
2. Define your key performance indicators in terms of your ideal.
3. Measure your people against your ideal by making contributing to the ideal part of every employee's work plan.
4. Measure and reward time spent with customers and end consumers.

1. MEASURE YOUR PROGRESS AGAINST YOUR IDEAL WITH THE CUSTOMERS AND STAKEHOLDERS MOST IMPORTANT TO YOUR FUTURE.

Dell is a very data-driven company. It is one of the pioneers in lean manufacturing and direct selling, so measurement is in their organizational DNA. But over the years, their systems have been set up to measure financial and transactional information, not their brand ideal or brand health.

The gap at Dell between what was being measured and what needed to be measured is in part what led, shortly after I left P&G in 2008, to my beginning to work with Dell and their now former chief marketing officer, Erin Mulligan Nelson. Erin, who coincidentally had worked at P&G on Pampers in the early

1990s, had just returned home to Austin from Ireland, where she'd had responsibility for Dell's marketing in Europe, the Middle East, and Africa. My brief was to help Erin get started quickly and to help shape the strategies and plans to accelerate Dell's growth through better marketing.

With the help of Allison Dew, head of Dell's global insights group, Erin set out to establish measures on their emerging brand ideal and brand health. Today, Dell is measuring their brand health through a quarterly brand health index whose key elements include employee engagement with the ideal, corporate reputation, and progress on customer recommendations. Believe me, with these data, the conversation is changing within Dell. It is not that Dell has stopped measuring financial and transactional results. But now that information has a much richer context in terms of business customer and consumer purchasing decisions and ownership experiences.

Crucially, this work has helped reframe Dell's ideal. More than any other company in its industry, Dell is the one that democratized access to information technology. That was Michael Dell's signature achievement in founding and leading Dell. Since he returned to the CEO's chair after a period serving only as chairman, he has been leading a realignment of Dell around an evolved version of the ideal of democratizing access to IT: delivering technology solutions that enable people everywhere to thrive, to do more.

Dell still has many opportunities to improve, as every company does. But it is gaining momentum, especially in business-to-business services. And my conversations with Michael Dell and current chief marketing officer Karen Quintos are getting easier, because we know where we stand with customers on the brand—consideration to buy Dell is up significantly—and our knowledge of what drives that is far deeper.

■　　■　　■

Dell's journey to measure its brand health and brand ideal mirrors my experience at P&G. Nothing is more symbolic than changing what a company evaluates; it goes to the core values of the company and its leadership. It shapes strategy making and governs who advances within the company.

I remember vividly the day in early 2002 when A. G. Lafley stopped by my desk and talked about taking a huge step forward in how P&G evaluated its businesses. "Jim," A.G. said as he paced in front of my desk, "we need to put the same emphasis on our key measures of brand health as on our financial measures. And we need to do this transparently and publicly, so if we have an issue with a brand's health, the entire management team can chip in to help."

We had just begun to have regular quarterly top management meetings in person at locations around the world. These meetings involved about thirty-five of us at the time, all the business unit presidents and the corporate officers. It may be a shock to you, but this kind of regular meeting of our senior leaders was new. Previously we met only once a year in early November as part of a much larger annual management meeting. A.G. believed, and he was right, that we could not build a collaborative global company without building stronger relationships among the leadership.

Part of the flow or rhythm of those quarterly meetings was to look at all the key measures of our businesses by brand and category. That eventually included a new measure on the health of our brands, which essentially measured our progress against our brand ideals and the variables that drove the ideal. We had lots of data on a variety of aspects of brand health, such as the effectiveness of the advertising, but we did not have one integrated, holistic measure that could be compared across our brands. We needed to create that.

I had already been having lots of discussions with Kim

Dedeker, P&G's talented vice president for consumer and market knowledge, and her team about innovation in brand measurement among consumers. Working with several external partners, Kim and her team eventually created P&G's integrated, holistic consumer measure of brand health, which we rather prosaically named the Combined Benefit Index or CBI. This gave P&G what we needed, a strong measure that guided our leadership to focus on the right things to grow our businesses in the short and long terms.

The important point is ensuring that you have some kind of measure that is correlated with brand health and growth, and that your leaders hold themselves and the organization accountable to it. To design and build such a measure, you must identify where your business creates, or in future can create, the most value for customers and consumers. Then ask yourself how you can track this in quantitative and qualitative terms.

At P&G, we did not stop with one quantitative measure, CBI. The CBI anchored everything, but we developed an entire Brand Building Scorecard to be sure every brand was measuring the right inputs to the CBI. The inputs were things such as trial and loyalty among important consumer segments, the shopping experience, pricing, and communication effectiveness.

When you have designed and built a useful brand health measure and scorecard, look for ways to apply that measure throughout the business. At P&G, once we had developed the CBI and related scorecard, we kept looking for ways we could use them to drive growth behaviors. It was great to have this measure and to project it to the entire management team quarterly for all the important brands. It helped us analyze issues, generate solutions and ideas, and share best practices on our strongest brands. But the CBI showed its ultimate worth, as I'll explain below, when we built it into the annual evaluations of our general managers and marketing directors.

2. Define your key performance indicators in terms of your ideal.

This is where you get the necessary depth and detail for measuring your progress against your ideal. As I've just described, the Combined Benefit Index (CBI) and Brand Building Scorecard at P&G gave us concrete key performance indicators (KPIs) that reflected our progress in realizing our overarching ideal behind each brand, and of calibrating this in all of our businesses. Every business needs to align its KPIs with its brand ideal in this granular way, especially in times of trouble.

In late 2010, Toyota reached out to me after a very difficult year in which multiple recalls threatened their business and shook their confidence. They wanted to take the opportunity the crisis presented to evaluate how they manage their brand globally, and also how they work as a team globally. They wanted to elevate their brand ideal and consider different ways of working to accomplish this.

For insights on their brand ideal, we studied their history, interviewing users and non-users; we tapped into employees, communications agencies, and dealers; we sought advice from Gen X and Gen Y drivers; and we ensured that our direction was building upon new CEO Akio Toyoda's vision for the company.

The essence of the Toyota brand ideal is to bring two seemingly contradictory ideas together, delivering both excitement and unparalleled reliability.

Toyota is a brand I have long admired. My first car out of college was a Toyota Starlet, and I have been a loyal Toyota customer since. I have studied the company and the "Toyota

Way" (their values, beliefs, and principles) throughout my career, and I traveled to see them and their agencies for benchmarking several times when I was GMO at P&G. When they called to ask me to help them, I jumped at the chance.

To kick off our working relationship, many of the leaders of Toyota's global marketing organization gathered for a three-day meeting at the UCLA Anderson Graduate School of Management, where I teach.

Part of the agenda was—no surprise—how Toyota evaluated progress for improving brand health, and whether or not they held their people accountable for that. I was not sure what I would find, especially after a year when many in the organization were totally consumed by the recalls. Would this be like P&G in the late 1990s, when the only thing that seemed to matter was this month's sales?

What I found was actually quite astonishing. It reassured me that this company would bounce back very fast from the business crisis of 2010, and also from the devastating impact on Toyota and all of Japan from the March 2011 earthquake and tsunami.

Despite the tumultuous year, every leader from every region was focused on complete customer satisfaction, dealer trust, and employee engagement to drive the Toyota brand ideal. Of course some of these measures dipped during the recalls, but it made Toyota's people even more determined to keep measuring and keep working to improve.

As David Buttner, senior executive director for sales and marketing at Toyota Australia, put it regarding measurement, "We ask three questions. Are our dealers engaged? Are our employees engaged? We can have all the goals and aspirations in the world, but none of them will be fulfilled unless our people feel good about themselves and the company they work in. The last and most important question is customer satisfaction. Are we giving customers what they want, whether it be in terms of product, the face-to-face experience at the dealership, or the after-sales ownership experience? If we can be exemplary in answering these questions, then we can create passionate advocates for the brand and customers for life."

When I talked individually with the other marketing and sales leaders at the meeting, their answers were uncannily similar. This is even more amazing when you consider that Toyota manages the marketing and sales of their brand in a very decentralized fashion. But I kept hearing common themes: engage employees so they are happy and understand what drives Toyota brand health, build great relationships with dealers so they can deliver the brand ideal through their people, and show passion and respect for the customer at all touch points as the top priority. When I asked Vince Socco, senior vice president of Toyota Motor Asia Pacific, about measurement, I loved how he talked about the heavy industry car and truck business being a "people" business.

Vince told me, "There's a very serious dedication to people at Toyota. First of all the customers—there's a sincere desire to ensure that the vehicles we build, the service we provide, every touch point, that we are able to deliver the best that we can as a company to each and every customer. [Funny how these echo the words of that nineteenth-century American business artist Jack Daniel: "Every day we make it (the whiskey), we'll make it the best we can."] It applies to the whole organization as well, the respect for employees and our partners, our suppliers and dealers. Toyota really is a family, and for me that's what it's all about. Of course we're in the automotive business, but this is also very much a people business."

Toyota is not on the Stengel 50 list, but would have been if the study ended with 2009 results. Their results in 2010 bumped them down. My strong feeling is they will jump back up in the second decade of the twenty-first century, with one big reason being their focus on KPIs in the context of their brand ideal. Toyota is taking a global approach, looking at standardizing and simplifying its hundreds of KPIs across the world. This will enable better comparison for benchmarking best practices, but more important, it will get everyone around the world measuring their progress against their heritage- and consumer-inspired ideal.

Visa is a terrific success model for developing brand ideal-aligned KPIs. I invited Antonio Lucio, Visa's global chief marketing, strategy, and corporate development officer, to the Toyota meeting at UCLA Anderson to share his learning on leading the Visa brand globally, in a way that was centered on their ideal, and how they are measuring progress against their ideal.

Antonio is a seasoned and inspirational leader. After stints at P&G and then Pepsi, he joined Visa in 2008, on the eve of its going public, as its first global marketing and strategy officer. Antonio has had a major impact at Visa across many areas, and none of it would have been possible without unifying his corporate marketing team—and Visa marketing around the world—through a global brand ideal framework much like the Ideal Tree. Until it went public in 2008, Visa really operated as seven autonomous regional entities, and Antonio faced a huge challenge in creating one team with one dream.

Visa is a misunderstood company. Most people think it issues credit and debit cards, but the banks that sell you the cards are the ones that issue them. Visa is actually a high-tech payments processing company. Its global network, known as VisaNet, is a massive technology platform that processes more than 70 billion transactions a year for the banks and for the merchants that accept your Visa card as payment.

Visa is one of the Stengel 50 businesses leading the way in linking evaluation and measurement to a brand ideal. Visa's ideal is to provide the freedom to people to follow their passions by providing better money for better living. Visa deeply believes that when people and organizations move from cash and check to Visa electronic payments, their lives improve due to the convenience, efficiency, security, and freedom Visa enables.

This ideal is basically unchanged since 1975, when what was then BankAmericard was rebranded as Visa. Dee Hock, a former Bank of America employee and Visa's first CEO, led this move, and he articulated the Visa brand ideal with great vision and clarity almost forty years ago.

In the late 1960s, Hock presaged the potential of Visa by asking, "What would be an ideal organization to create the world's premier system for the exchange of value? What if money became fully electronic? It would become nothing but electrons and photons that move around this world at the speed of light at minuscule cost." This would make it possible to create "the universal currency of life," a digital currency that would provide "better money for better living, more reliable, convenient, and secure than cash and check."

At the center of the global brand ideal work that Antonio Lucio led for Visa is the Dee Hock–inspired brand ideal of "providing better money for better living," one ideal for everyone in the world to work against. To make it relevant and actionable, Antonio and his global team designed one set of measures to ensure progress against the ideal. These measures include the building blocks of their ideal: rational product attributes, such as Visa's being the most trusted, secure, and reliable electronic payment card, and emotional attributes, such as its providing empowerment, freedom, and control.

Everything in the new brand ideal framework hits these

four building blocks of the Visa brand ideal: reliability, security, convenience, and empowerment. When delivered with excellence by Visa employees, these building blocks bring the ideal to life and are reflected in the satisfaction scores of both banks and consumers, the two external groups that are most important to Visa's future.

That brings us to measurement principle number 3.

3. MEASURE YOUR PEOPLE AGAINST YOUR IDEAL BY MAKING CONTRIBUTING TO THE IDEAL PART OF EVERY EMPLOYEE'S WORK PLAN.

Imagine the power of every person in your business having a measurable plan to bring the brand ideal to life in their area of responsibility. It's what Zappos does in its amazing, innovative culture, by linking work plans to its happiness ideal.

I love how Discovery thinks about making the ideal part of the day-in and day-out actions of every employee. They have identified "growth traits," as they call them, that they see as essential to fulfilling their brand ideal of satisfying curiosity: clear thinking, innovation, customer focus, expertise, diversity, accountability, and people development. They know that they cannot bring their brand ideal to life unless they measure and reward these things, and employees are expected to incorporate a growth trait of their choosing into their work plan every year.

Adria Alpert Romm, Discovery's senior executive vice president for human resources, gave me a vivid example. "Let's take diversity behind and in front of the camera," Adria said. "We know if we have diverse faces on air, if we have storytelling that is about diverse people and cultures, then we are going to be fulfilling our ideal and attracting more people to our brand."

There are situations in which advancing the brand ideal means respecting the past and changing very little, and this must also be in the work plan. Hermès, the French luxury goods purveyor and a Stengel 50 brand, prides itself on staying true to its ideal of celebrating timeless luxury craftsmanship. They value continuity of people, and living this ideal is in every role in the company.

Jack Daniel's is another example where continuity with tradition is explicit in the work plans of employees. In the words of brand historian Nelson Eddy, "The Jack Daniel's brand is larger than any one brand manager, it stands above them. People who work on Jack Daniel's know it is about the brand and its timeless ideal, not about any individual making a name for themselves."

In building their brand ideal into employees' work plans, Visa is about as good as it gets. Delivering their ideal of "freedom through better money for better living" comes up spontaneously in every conversation with people at Visa. More important, every leader understands how critical it is to link progress against the ideal to employees' work plans.

Bill Sheedy, Visa's group president for the Americas and a nineteen-year Visa employee, describes Visa employees' connection with the ideal this way: "There has been such a strong and clear vision from the beginning about building something bigger and more powerful around the electronification of commerce. The vision was about eradicating cash and checks, and making the interactions between buyers and sellers more efficient. It's not curing cancer, but the vision has always been compelling. Every quarter, every year, we were able to see specific ways that every employee connected personally with the vision, that we were slowly but clearly achieving the larger objectives around creating a digital currency that fulfilled our ideal of better money for better living."

If Visa can link their ideal to employees' work plans, anyone can. Visa has one of the more complicated business ecosystems; it is both a B2B enterprise and a B2C brand. A typical credit card or debit card transaction involves four parties: the bank that issues the card, the cardholder, a merchant that accepts the card as payment, and an acquiring bank that handles the merchant's card transaction. Visa must provide services to all these entities, across more than 200 countries in 160 currencies—a mind-boggling business challenge.

Here's what Elizabeth Buse, Visa group president for Asia-Pacific, Central Europe, the Middle East, and Africa, told me about evaluating Visa managers: "You have to perform, the business results have to be there. But what you do is only half of the evaluation; the other half is how you do it. We manage the what and the how equally. Because if you have the what and you don't have the how, then the what will dry up over time."

Imagine that: 50 percent of Visa managers' evaluation rests on how they treat people, build the culture, get things done, and bring Visa's brand ideal of "better money for better living" to life. In my experience, it is rare to weight half of managers' performance on how they get the job done, rather than putting the majority of emphasis—very nearly all the emphasis in most companies—on business results.

One way Visa measures how executives are getting their business results, and not just what those results are, is by tying a portion of their compensation to an employee engagement score. If a manager's people collectively have a low employee engagement score, the manager will see that reflected, negatively, in compensation and bonus.

Here again is Visa's Elizabeth Buse, describing the power and adaptability of the building blocks to guide employees' behavior: "Reliability, convenience, security, and empowerment mean different things for the banks, merchants, and consumers. And they mean different things in different parts of the world. Reliability in a developing African country where electricity is unreliable means a very different thing from reliability in a developed country. Convenience means something different in Japan, where everyone was using their phone for Internet access before that was even possible in the United States. Because what the Visa brand really stands for is increasing this set of high-level benefits across the payments system, we can be very flexible in how we deliver them, yet always evaluate our employees' efforts consistently against the same standard."

Ellen Richey, Visa's global chief enterprise risk officer, analyzed the impact of employee engagement with the ideal in terms of pride—being proud to work for Visa—as a virtuous circle. "The brand's higher purpose, the work we do to secure the whole electronics payment system as well as VisaNet, comes back around as a huge driver of employee engagement."

Visa's approach to performance reviews resonates in harmony with everything my senior management colleagues and I experienced at P&G in the 2000s.

It had always been part of the P&G way to evaluate its people against their business results, their results in developing people, and their progress in growing market shares and brand equity. But in the chaos of the late 1990s and the beginning of the 2000s, we lost our focus on this triumvirate. Trying to turn the company around, we became excessively focused on the short term, and we simply got sloppy. We were rewarding people for their short-term business results without the proper balance of how they achieved their results, as Visa's Elizabeth Buse eloquently describes above.

I heard this loud and clear from our marketing people soon after I started as global marketing officer in August 2001. During my first 100 days, traveling and talking to P&G marketing people and current and retired P&G senior leaders, it became clear that we had to return to measuring the complete leader, not just the short-term operator. Everyone agreed on that. The question was how to do it.

I first strengthened the human resources capability on my marketing leadership team. I brought in a full-time HR director, Renée Dunn, reporting to me. Renée had experience in line positions in P&G marketing before moving into HR and was perfect for the role. Renée was an HR business partner, a confidante, and a steward for the organizational health of the marketing function, even when unpopular decisions had to be made.

Renée connected into my global marketing leadership team, and she tapped in to the P&G global HR network to form her own team of HR leaders to help us redesign the evaluation and measurement system. We began by listening to marketing employees via detailed engagement surveys. This led to creating global standards for career pathing and talent management systems, including standardizing the templates for performance reviews and also the templates for everyone's work plans. Sounds simple, but it is not. We had destandardized over the years, and everyone liked they way they did things. So we listened, evaluated the input, and then locked on one design.

Our design was a bit back-to-the-future for P&G. We had three basic sections: business results, brand health results, and organization development results. Every manager in the marketing organization received an annual rating in each area, as well as a composite rating. These ratings then guided career development, promotions, and compensation. The big change was that people could not move forward within P&G without proven results in all three areas.

There was plenty of pushback when we instituted these performance measures. People were very upset that the rules of the advancement game had been changed on them. "How can you hold up my promotion for something you've just started measuring me on?"—that was a typical complaint. But we held our ground. When people accepted the new measures, they began to have a much more positive impact on P&G's results— and their own careers.

How people advance is the strongest message a leader can send, and A. G. Lafley sent a similar message to the general managers across the world. With our global human resources officer, Dick Antoine, A.G. redesigned how general managers would be evaluated and ranked. Short-term business results were not adequate anymore; all general managers had to show capability results in building their organization's strength, as well as delivering the business. They also had to demonstrate they were furthering their business unit's competitive advantage through their strategy, innovation pipeline, and, yes, the health of the brand as measured by the CBI. And every year, all the general managers saw how they did and where they ranked among their peers.

We linked executive compensation to CBI, and again we held our ground to enforce that link. Two presidents of large business units who could not get the health of their brands to improve moved on from P&G.

I am absolutely convinced these changes drove the sustained growth of P&G, where for more than six years we over-delivered our quarterly sales and earnings goals.

And as we reviewed at the beginning of the chapter, when we looked at the Stengel 50 in terms of brand contribution to shareholder value, if your people aren't focusing on brand health in the twenty-first century, your business is going to suffer.

4. Measure and reward time spent with customers and end consumers.

This is a subset of the principle we've just been discussing, but it is important enough to deserve separate attention. If you and your people aren't close to customers and end consumers, and don't understand their fundamental values, you will not be able to execute on your ideal. In some organizations, it may seem unnecessary to emphasize time spent with customers, because most of the organization's people spend time with customers every day. But even retail shopping floor personnel can easily get sidetracked doing everything but directly helping customers.

In my early days as P&G's GMO, I looked at how much time our marketing people actually spent with end consumers or retail customers. Based on roles and assignments, I expected to see a range of 20 to 50 percent. It was shocking to find that it was under 5 percent. Here was the company that aspired to be the most consumer-centric in the world, and its marketing people were spending more time in line at Starbucks than they were with consumers.

We changed that with several symbolic steps. One of the best ideas came from Jorge Uribe and Jorge Luis Diaz, respectively the president of P&G Latin America and its vice president for marketing. They declared that every new hire to P&G must spend his first month living with low-income consumers, working at a small neighborhood grocery store, or bodega, or shopping with consumers at both modern retail establishments as well as neighborhood shops.

P&G recruited at the finest schools in Latin America, so our new employees were generally from relatively wealthy backgrounds. Putting them in a low-income environment, among people with very limited financial resources, was for many a life-changing experience. They got the message loud and clear: the people they met over that month were P&G's most important consumers, the backbone of P&G's Latin America business. P&G's future depended on our brands attracting these people, and our people needed to have an empathy for and understanding of them, or they did not belong at P&G.

Uribe and Diaz did not stop with new hires. They also began to measure time with consumers and customers for all employees in marketing, and putting this into work plans. They believed that P&G could not build a culture on brand ideals without empathy for those who were most important to P&G's future. It's no coincidence that Latin America has been one of P&G's strongest high-growth markets.

Throughout P&G as a whole in the 2000s, we ensured that everyone knew that consumer immersions and retailer visits were considered core work, and we visibly rewarded them for it. Start doing the same sort of thing in your business by asking who outside the business is most important to its future, and then taking concrete steps to ensure that your people are reaching out to them, interacting with them, and developing a deeper understanding of their fundamental values.

Whether you are largely a B2B enterprise like Visa or a B2C enterprise like Jack Daniel's, these four principles for evaluation and measurement systems work. In fact, they are essential to drive growth. And if you do not complete the Ideal Tree with focus and discipline on evaluation and measurement, all other work will be for naught.

One final point. Never let your measurement system, whether of individual or operational performance, become a static end in itself. Continually correlate it with your ideal, and change the measurement system's components as necessary to keep pace with customer need and behavior. Regularly ask yourself if there is a better way to track how you are generating differential value compared to competition.

For example, we've already seen how neuroscience measures are offering deeper insight into how ideals shape people's behavior. We saw in chapter 2 how Millward Brown's neuroscience team identified the influence of brand ideals on consumers' responses to selected businesses in the Stengel 50 and some of their competition, and this area of knowledge will only get deeper and better. Researchers at the MIT Media Lab, working with a company called Affectiva to commercialize the findings, are uncovering how facial expressions and skin responses relay both positive and negative reactions to brand products, messages, and experiences.

The more accurately you can measure your progress and people against your ideal, the more vividly you can bring that ideal to life, and the more positive distance you can put between yourself and your competition.

We have now gone all the way through the five branches of the Ideal Tree. You will grow faster as you apply these principles. The data from the Stengel 50 suggest you can even triple the growth rate of the competition in your category. You must execute against the Ideal Tree with great conviction, energy, passion, and perseverance.

There's only one catch: as you execute, you must never be complacent on your core reason for being, your brand ideal. I'll share powerful examples of avoiding complacency and finding ways to evolve your ideal for new growth in the next chapter.

Keep It Going

Evolve Your Ideal to Renew Competitive Advantage

Both Method and Innocent are highly successful companies, growing rapidly, attracting exceptional talent, and setting new benchmarks in their categories. Still, their leaders are restless.

I saw this restlessness firsthand when Method co-founder Eric Ryan asked me to join him for a drink at the end of the day with the Method leadership team and Dan Germain, Innocent's director of communication, who was also there. When we all sat down together at an outdoor patio bar in Chinatown in San Francisco, Eric wanted to probe whether Method's ideal of inspiring a revolution in healthy household care was strong enough and inspirational enough. Dan shared how Innocent constantly challenges itself to ask if it is bringing the business's ideal of "making it easy for people to do themselves good" to life as effectively as possible.

After much discussion and a few drinks, we decided the Method ideal is terrific as it is. It inspires employees and attracts top talent. It continues to fuel growth. The challenge is to execute brilliantly against it across the Ideal Tree, especially in new categories like laundry.

And now and then to do what we were doing that evening: ask if the ideal or the approach to serving it needed any change to remain fresh and vital. A little restlessness is always good.

In my work with companies such as Intel, Toyota, and Luxottica (whose brands include LensCrafters, Oakley, and Ray-Ban), several factors prompt a decision to evolve the brand ideal. For Intel, consumer habits are shifting away from laptops and toward smart phones and tablet devices. For Toyota, the new vision of CEO Akio Toyoda must be reflected in the ideal. And for LensCrafters, their long-standing promise of one-hour service is just not adequate to delight consumers in the complicated and emotional purchase decisions in eye care and eyewear.

The point is simple. Be restless and curious about whether your ideal is still relevant and growth-inspiring. Does it need to evolve? Should you redefine it in response to changes in technology, customer behavior, the competition? Is your approach to fulfilling the ideal still appropriate?

It is no small undertaking to evolve an ideal, and it must be done with careful thinking, planning, and execution. To illustrate that, I want to share how Motorola Solutions and HP, a Stengel 50 business, have recently grappled with the need to evolve their brand ideals. As we'll see, Motorola and HP both had relatively urgent cause to evolve their ideals, and their experiences offer rich perspective on the process.

Motorola Solutions came into existence in January 2011, when parent Motorola, founded in 1928, separated into two independent public companies. The part of Motorola focused on consumer technology became Motorola Mobility, with $12 billion in revenue and 19,000 employees. Just eight months later, in August 2011, Motorola Mobility announced it would be acquired by Google in one of the largest tech mergers ever. The Motorola business focused on serving government, public safety, and business enterprises became Motorola Solutions, with $8 billion in revenue and 25,000 employees.

Both Motorola Mobility and Motorola Solutions faced the challenge of defining a new identity as independent companies. Both had morale problems, always an indication of the need for a business to work on its ideal.

I joined the Motorola board of directors in 2005. On the consumer side, morale problems were the result of wild swings in financial results, as the superthin, fashion-before-technology Razr phone went from must-have item to has-been status. This turbulence had an impact on the enterprise side. During the extended downs in Motorola's consumer cell phone sales, the enterprise organization, which consistently generated healthy revenues, kept the whole company going. Yet the consumer business got most of the media attention, and because of its troubled state also occupied most of the board's attention during these years.

As a split into separate companies approached, the consumer business again got most of the media attention because of its very successful partnership with Google and Verizon to develop the Android smart phone market. The Motorola Droid was in a different league from the Razr. Far more than simply a fashionable object, the Droid was quickly becoming the center of an ecosystem of other technology products and services.

Early in 2009 Eduardo Conrado, senior vice president for marketing in the enterprise organization, enlisted my help in defining a higher purpose that would inspire everyone and position the business for growth. Eduardo had been kicking around ideas with BBDO, Motorola's U.S. ad agency, for a marketing campaign to launch as a separate company, but realized that it needed to be "bigger than that. We need to launch everyone's mind-set about who we are and what we stand for."

Motorola Solutions had a well-known, if slightly battered, brand name that it would share with Motorola Mobility. There were pluses and minuses there. Even more serious a problem was that Motorola Solutions was starting life as an independent public company in the shadow of a failed attempt at evolving the brand ideal. Pre-split, Motorola articulated an ideal of "enhancing life through seamless mobility," but never got very far with it.

Greg Brown, then co-CEO of Motorola and soon to be CEO of Motorola Solutions, felt strongly that the enterprise organization had "fallen in love with innovation for innovation's sake." He told his leadership team, "The business needs a fire lit, a sense of urgency in terms of accountability and purpose."

Greg put his finger on an issue that a great brand ideal can help you solve. Way too often businesses get caught up in innovation for innovation's sake, or a preoccupation with functional benefits versus focus on the entire consumer experience. Remember the Pampers move from a benefit of superior dryness to an ideal of baby development? Greg knew his evolved ideal needed to be based on delivering an amazing customer experience, which in turn would drive growth.

Motorola's enterprise organization felt that its contributions to financial results and its product and service innovations were not fully appreciated. Beneath that was the more serious issue Greg diagnosed: the misplaced focus on innovation for innovation's sake. Motorola's design and development engineers, the lifeblood of both the consumer and the enterprise organizations, felt whipsawed by the cell phone business's ill-fated decision to put form over function and push the Razr's thinness, missing out on the whole first wave of the software-driven smart phone market. In reaction to that and the relative lack of attention to their own work, the enterprise organization had turned inward and become fixated on technological product benefits, not on what those technology features meant in people's lives. Also, because the business was financially healthy, there was no burning platform, generating a certain amount of complacency.

Greg was right that the business needed a fire lit. It was very similar to what happened at P&G in 2005 and 2006, after we'd turned the financial results around. To avoid complacency we needed to elevate the entire organization's sense of purpose, as I described earlier, just as Greg Brown and his senior management team now needed to do.

Eduardo Conrado did external benchmarking of ideals-inspired organizations, learning from companies such as Southwest Airlines, Zappos, and IBM. And he assigned a team to do a series of internal interviews, asking people, "Paycheck aside, why do you get up in the morning? If your part of Motorola disappeared tomorrow, what would happen? What would the world lose?" As I mentioned, I asked a similar set of questions at Pizza Hut in 2009, as their leadership team faced the challenge of evolving their brand ideal.

It took a while for Motorola Solutions' people to get past comments like "If we disappeared, our competitors would just take up the business." But over the course of the interviews, Eduardo told me, "people began defining the organization's purpose as more than 'We make enterprises and organizations more productive,' which is generically true of us and all our competitors. Bit by bit more interesting thoughts about individual end users in the contexts of their jobs and their organizations started to emerge."

These thoughts concerned moments in the lives of enterprise and government customers when a cascading impact of glitches occurred unpredictably in mission-critical and business-critical events. The results ran the gamut from inconvenient and costly to lethal, from food spoiling in transit to delays in handling life-threatening emergencies and breakdowns in disaster response. The stories revealed a deep pride in Motorola's heritage of serving government and enterprise needs, from law enforcement to supply chain management. They also revealed a deep hunger for the enterprise organization to succeed as an independent company.

Motorola made its first two-way radios for police departments in the 1930s. Its innovations in the 2000s include software-definable radio networks for public safety and transportation systems, as well as the most sophisticated radio frequency identification networks for inventory control. The enterprise organization had much to be proud of, and much to offer.

The core insight distilled from the interviews was that the enterprise organization was really all about the higher purpose of helping people be their best in the moments that matter. It was about helping police officers and firefighters and EMTs and health care, retail, and operations people in all kinds of settings to do these absolutely essential jobs. But people in the organization didn't see this clearly.

The evolved ideal has roots in Motorola's rich legacy of providing mission-critical technology. But this legacy had become obscured as the consumer side of the business drove the public image of Motorola.

To bring the evolved ideal into sharp focus for everyone in the organization, in early fall 2010 Motorola Solutions created eight posters about the enterprise organization's products and services being used in "moments that matter." The posters, based on real customer cases, brought together the left-brain, rational benefits of these products and services with their right-brain, emotional benefits. For example, one poster showed a public street festival with the twenty-four-hour dateline *15:26, Notting Hill, London, UK*. The copy read, *Right now, our communications systems are reuniting father and daughter. He is frantic. He's lost sight of his 6-year-old daughter in the carnival crowd. Thanks to the police constable's Motorola MTH800 radio and the Airwave network, every police officer within a 2-mile radius is instantly alerted and the family is reunited within a few minutes. The party continues with no harm done.*

The eight "Moments Captured" posters provided all the proof that the enterprise organization's senior management needed to know that they had their evolved brand ideal: Motorola Solutions would devote itself to "helping people be their best in moments that matter." Shelly Carlin, who had recently become head of HR for all of Motorola and eventually stayed on to lead HR at Motorola Solutions, saw how "helping people be their best in moments that matter" could become the center of everything in HR, from recruitment and training to retention, career development, and performance management.

The important lesson here is that Motorola Solutions took the words off the page and dramatized their ideal in context through the posters. The reason the posters hit a nerve—not just with HR and marketing but through the organization—is because they made what Motorola Solutions' people do every day both heroic and believable. They evoked pride. They confirmed identity. They brought the evolved ideal to life in ways that resonated with all employees.

I always suggest the companies I work with do a video of their ideal for this purpose. Posters are fine as well, but video better captures the real emotional resonance and authenticity of an ideal. I will never forget when we first showed a video we made to capture and evoke P&G's higher purpose of "touching lives, improving life." Many in the organization thought these words sounded generic, not very exciting.

However, when we brought it to life via a video, with images and music, and showed it at our November management meeting, "touching lives, improving life" moved even the most hardened P&G leader. Many had tears in their eyes. We subsequently used that video thousands of times—with recruits, new hires, to start important meetings, with shareholders, customers, and analysts.

The Motorola posters were to Motorola as the P&G video was to P&G. They enthused the entire organization, and no one was more enthusiastic than CEO Greg Brown. With the posters, data, and other collateral, Greg, Eduardo, and Shelly easily got the board's strong endorsement for rallying everyone in the enterprise organization to support the ideal of "helping people be their best in the moments that matter."

Eduardo presented the evolution of the enterprise organization's higher purpose to the board of directors around the same time that the consumer organization was getting traction with the Droid phone. I knew then that we had made the right call as a board to separate the two parts of the company and turn them loose to compete on their own.

Greg Brown naturally wanted to activate the evolved purpose throughout the organization as quickly as possible. It's possible to move too fast in these situations, however, and sometimes slowing down early on helps you accelerate to a higher speed later. I love how Intel's CEO Paul Otellini says it: "You often must go slow in order to go fast." What he means is that the proper planning must be done or the organization will not be fully engaged and prepared to execute the ideal.

The deliberate pace Motorola Solutions followed was most helpful in enabling the enterprise business to develop the tone and voice in which it could best communicate its higher ideal and best engage in dialogue with all its stakeholders. This was difficult for an engineering-dominated organization whose first conscious responses to any situation were usually rational rather than emotional. But as we've seen in looking at what neuroscience has to teach us about the business value of ideals, emotion and instinct play a decisive role in all human decision making, often while remaining completely subconscious, no matter how purely rational people think they are.

The eight posters, by combining the rational and the emotional aspects of moments that matter, became a template for teaching the organization how to communicate more effectively. They showed how to tell stories that blend the rational and emotional benefits that Motorola Solutions provides to organizations and individuals into an organic whole—how, in effect, to express all the depth and complexity of the evolved ideal simply, clearly, imaginatively, and compellingly.

After Eduardo Conrado explained the new higher-purpose strategy to the enterprise organization's top global leaders, poster-making workshops took place in a selection of the organization's twenty-seven major installations around the world. The poster-making workshops produced 150 additional posters of moments that matter, all gleaned from the stories of Motorola Solutions people at all levels, in all lines of business. In fact, the group of employees that became most engaged in telling their stories via these posters was the engineering staff. Clearly this technically minded group longed to get past the bits and bytes of their work and tell bigger stories of the human impact they were making in people's lives every day.

The workshops also provided opportunities to identify 600 "brand ambassadors" from among the enterprise business's country managers and its global marketing, communications, and HR staff. The brand ambassadors became internal "brand ideal experts," and they coached and trained others throughout the organization on the meaning of the evolved ideal. They ensured every employee understood the ideal and their individual role in bringing it to life.

Crucially, Eduardo pointed out, "the ambassador group also included representatives from BBDO and Siegel & Gale, our lead agencies in the U.S., and all our other agencies around the world. We wanted to localize the new higher-purpose framework as fast as possible, and the agencies' participation was key to making sure they understood the higher purpose and the brand voice, so that all the new material we were going to create fit the framework."

As a test of the higher-purpose strategy, Eduardo Conrado and Shelly Carlin rebranded the enterprise organization's executive floor with a number of the posters produced in the global workshops. The impact was almost immediate.

The superintendent of Chicago's public schools had a meeting with Greg Brown right after the posters went up on the walls. Earlier in his career the school's chief was a police officer and then had a senior-level job in Chicago's public transportation system. So he was very familiar with Motorola products and services. When Greg walked him out after their meeting, he remarked that "the posters are visceral. They resonate." It was a typical response from people visiting the executive floor.

The success of this test set the stage for the next development. Over the course of one weekend, all twenty-seven major installations around the world were redecorated with moments-that-matter posters featuring customers in their own regions. When employees walked in Monday morning and saw these images, it was the prelude to a global town hall meeting and celebration that opened with remarks by Greg Brown.

The posters were put up in October 2010, right around the time that the trapped Chilean miners were being rescued. An English employee said, "I bet our products are being used." And they were.

Shelly Carlin told me, "Greg sent out a global email, not to brag, but to say, 'This is why we're here.' Motorola's role in the rescue of the Chilean miners was a quintessential moment that mattered, and the poster bringing that story to life captured the hearts of employees. The response to that news throughout the organization told Eduardo and me the higher purpose is real. And it told me this is how we will drive employee engagement."

The emotional impact of the posters and the global town hall meeting might have fizzled out if the higher-purpose effort had not also included a new set of values and performance criteria for people in every sort of role—individual contributors, managers, and senior leaders. The new criteria highlighted specific desired behaviors in the areas of personal conduct, customer-focused strategy, business results, and people development. Basically, Motorola Solutions rebooted its performance criteria to reflect its evolved ideal (we saw in the previous chapter how critical that is to success). The 600 brand ambassadors took these criteria into the field. Eduardo said, "The brand ambassadors had the lead in developing local plans and running with implementation. They took the framework around the world and gave us global coordination with local ownership."

Everyone at Motorola Solutions can see themselves and their work in terms of moments that matter. It is impossible to overstate how important that is. In Eduardo's words, "It fires up the engineering community because of how it celebrates technological innovation and shows its impact in people's lives. The higher ideal has become a litmus test for senior management in strategy discussions. When you connect the rational and the emotional, it makes salespeople's lives easier. Sales leaders now kick off everything with the purpose, and how it inspires them on a personal as well as a professional level. The head of sales in Australia says, 'It makes us unique.' Motorola Solutions' channel partners have the same reaction. Even financial analysts have responded positively. And customers love it.

At a business meeting in the Bahamas, the head of the police force came up to me and said, 'Your products work. But you also talk to me through the heart.'"

The best thing about the evolved Motorola ideal is that it is open-ended. It can keep extending to industry verticals and customer segments, so that Motorola can touch more people in the moments that matter most to them, and accelerate its growth in so doing. Although it is too early to judge victory, Motorola Solutions, after about a year as an independent company, is off to a fast start.

EVOLVING THE HEWLETT-PACKARD IDEAL

More than forty-five acquisitions during Mark Hurd's tenure as CEO from 2005 to 2010 played an important role in making Hewlett-Packard—or HP, as it has always been known for short—the world's largest technology company in 2011, with $126 billion in revenue. The biggest acquisition was the $13.9 billion purchase of EDS in 2008. And despite a tumultuous 2011, with the announcement of new CEO Meg Whitman and major strategy questions, HP did a great job of building their brand value over the last ten years, as we reviewed in chapter 1.

The acquisitions of the 2000s transformed HP from mainly a hardware business to a hardware, software, and services company with the IT industry's broadest product portfolio and more than half of revenue coming from enterprise software and services. In the wake of this expansion, HP faced the daunting challenge of successfully integrating such a broad product portfolio and such a large number of acquired companies.

One senior executive at HP explained the challenge to me in powerful words: "Under founders Bill Hewlett and Dave Packard, people internalized the HP values and culture so deeply that they became the connective tissue that made HP what it was. Everybody knew that HP was about making great technology that made a contribution to society. But that connective tissue was weakened through the tremendous growth by acquisition. And it was not being strengthened because it was no longer in the dialogue and the explicit values of the leadership. That this was missing was really a problem for HP people."

The problem became apparent at a meeting this executive, along with three other people from HP, had with the CEO of a customer. One of these three other people told the CEO, "I'm from what used to be Compaq." The second one said, "I'm from what used to be EDS." And the third one said, "I'm legacy HP." The CEO looked at them and said, "Well, I thought you had one company." It was a lightbulb moment for this HP executive.

Moments like this showed HP's senior leaders the importance of bringing all the pieces of the company together under a "pan-HP brand." Without better alignment, without giving all employees a shared reason to exist, they were not going to be able to fulfill the potential of all the recent acquisitions. Even Mark Hurd, well known as a pragmatic operator, saw this quickly and clearly. Employees told me that he became an advocate, even a zealot, for the "B-word," his shorthand for HP the brand. Hurd saw the power in building one HP brand globally, and he also recognized this had to begin with one aspirational, evolved ideal. With her background at P&G and eBay, Meg Whitman will likely also be a strong proponent of building one HP brand.

To grow and thrive, HP had to evolve its ideal as well as its product portfolio. On paper the broad portfolio of hardware, software, and services that came together in the 2000s made good strategic sense, but in the short term things were far from seamless for employees or customers. Half of HP's

320,000 employees in 2011 had joined the company since 2006 through its many acquisitions.

Kelly Hampton, HP's global director of brand strategy, tells me, "HP as a whole is highly decentralized. It's actually 320,000 people in their own canoes, and we have to get those canoes going in the same direction. Each of the three main business groups—imaging and printing, computing, and enterprise services—is organized differently. So it is difficult for employees to understand our extended portfolio."

Three hundred and twenty thousand people going in different directions? Kelly may be exaggerating, but not by much. To its credit, even with the rapid pace of acquisitions, HP managed to keep growing its image with consumers and its revenues; 2011 brought more change, with the August announcement to explore alternatives for its personal systems group, which sells PCs. With all this change, there clearly is an overriding need to evolve the HP ideal to encompass the shifting, diverse brand portfolio and give the company a coherent identity in the minds of both customers and employees.

With regard to customers, Kelly says, "Consumers and many small and medium business customers knew us primarily for our printers. Enterprise customers understood only the particular slice of what they did with us; they didn't know the breadth of our enterprise offers. We really needed to connect the dots for all three audiences: consumer, small and medium business, and large enterprise."

As we've seen throughout this book, the ideal has to gain traction internally with employees before it can gain traction externally with customers. HP understood that but lacked a framework like the Ideal Tree to guide them. Glenna Patton, vice president for brand strategy and experience design, says, "Even as the majority of our acquired companies came to be branded HP, there was no process or framework for integrating people into one HP culture and integrating the businesses into one HP brand strategy. Meanwhile, the awareness of us on the part of customers was narrowly rooted in printers, and in the enterprise space in servers. The gap between what the customers would consider buying and the total HP business proposition was massive."

In 2009 Kelly Hampton and Glenna Patton, together with their teams in the marketing organization, made the business case to senior management for unifying the product portfolio under a "pan-HP brand," as Kelly puts it. This required redefining *brand* in a company that had long equated it narrowly with advertising and had recently decentralized responsibility for advertising, along with the budgets, to the different business groups.

In a series of internal workshops with people from every function and business group within HP, including both long-termers and acquired-company participants, Glenna and Kelly and their teams sought, in Glenna's words, "to get under the skin of 'Who are we? What do we stand for? Why are we all here? What is an inspiring position for HP?' That led to such a greater understanding of our people, our culture, and the higher purpose that is authentic to HP."

They discovered two critical insights. First, the "HP Way," the principles of founders Bill Hewlett and Dave Packard, still guided legacy HP's behavior, and it exerted a magnetic pull on acquired companies and new employees. Deepak Sainanee, HP's director of corporate marketing research and enterprise customer insights, attests to this when he tells me about joining the company in the early 2000s, after stints in start-ups, consulting, and academia. Deepak says, "What is unique about HP is our DNA from Bill and Dave. A lot of people say it's gone, that was old HP and now there's a new HP. I have a different perspective. The values and attitudes are very much here. I could sense it when I arrived. It is a mixture of innocence and resilience that all entrepreneurs and all entrepreneurial organizations need."

The second initial finding was the absolute consistency of how HP people, "legacy" and acquired, wanted to evolve their ideal. It was like the aha moment at Motorola Solutions, when people realized that they should be about helping people in the moments that really matter. For HP, as for Motorola Solutions, the evolved ideal had origins in its heritage, but it set the future direction for all the diverse businesses of HP.

The basic concept behind their evolved ideal is advancing human progress. Describing the aha moments that happened across the company in the many workshops, Kelly Hampton says, "Identifying HP with human progress is real. The fact that multiple groups, made up of old and new HP people, independently came back with that tells you something about the focus of the organization and the tightness of the culture, even though we are highly decentralized administratively. 'Human progress' beautifully captures our higher-order reason for being. It's not fluff. People here really believe in that. They come to work every day to discover and develop and deliver things that are for the greater good. That's how we do business every day."

HP wasted no time in putting the evolved ideal into action. In 2010 its executive committee made an impressive ten-year commitment to the corporate ideal and brand strategy of "human progress."

HP is in the midst of a multiyear process with its evolved ideal, but it is already achieving early results, even with all the turmoil at the top. Glenna Patton sums it up beautifully: "The journey to 'human progress,' defining the higher-order reason for being that we stand for, knowing that it is grounded in our past but has a vision toward the future—the most overwhelming case for that is how it influences the emotions and behavior of our people. It's already led to industrial design work where different hardware products were revisited, extraneous elements were rethought, and sustainable new materials were brought into play."

Motorola Solutions and HP are works in progress, as really all businesses are. They are great cases for evolving an ideal, and they will be fascinating to continue to watch over the years as they hopefully unify their organizations and execute their plans in line with their ideals. To conclude, let me share a few parting thoughts on accelerating this movement to a more ideals-inspired approach to business.

Conclusion

Start Big or Start Small, But Start Now

When I moved to Cincinnati in 1983 at the start of my career with Procter & Gamble, one of the first people I met was Jerry Kathman of design firm LPK. Jerry always seemed to be at P&G carrying a portfolio of design options for one of our brands. He was all about the client back then. And he hasn't changed.

Now one of the world's leading brand design agencies, and the largest to be employee-owned, LPK has expanded from its base in Cincinnati to include offices in London, Geneva, Frankfurt, Singapore, and Guangzhou. In the 2000s LPK was frequently P&G's design agency of choice as we sought to capture and evoke higher ideals in P&G's many businesses. When Pampers found a truly global focus in the ideal of partnering with moms in their babies' development, Jerry and his colleagues worked with us to evolve and unify Pampers' visual identity and packaging design in markets around the world.

When I decided to leave P&G in the fall of 2008, I called Jerry, now LPK's CEO, to tap in to his creative mind about my plans to write this book, teach, and consult. He quickly offered LPK as an incubator for my fledgling enterprise. He made available work space among his dynamic design and strategy teams, administrative and technical support, and talented designers who helped express the Jim Stengel Company's brand ideal and craft how it is communicated through my logo, stationery, and digital presence. Since then, LPK has helped me with trends analysis and visualization of complex material for my consulting clients and my students at UCLA Anderson School of Management. In turn, I have mentored some of their young leaders and collaborated with them on a few client projects.

As I developed the ideas and research for this book, I regularly shared my progress with Jerry and the rest of LPK's senior management team. In addition to great feedback based on their experience with businesses such as Hershey's, Kellogg's, Expedia, and U.S. Bank, to name only a few, they astonished me by asking me to lead a workshop to help them on their own brand ideal. LPK was growing rapidly. But Jerry and his colleagues believed they could better accelerate and sustain their success if they could articulate the implicit ideal that had always been the firm's essential reason for being and activate it across the organization.

We began the workshop with the recognition that an effective ideal needs to balance inspiration with true actionability. The ensuing discussions and brainstorming crystallized LPK's core beliefs. Jerry told me, "The workshop brought into focus our belief that there is boundless creativity in all of us, that design's inherent focus on how things work in people's lives is what enables design to help businesses perform better, that nothing of consequence happens without the courage to fail, and that as creative people we have a responsibility to sense and contribute to the unfolding future."

From these beliefs flowed a set of core values—freedom, honesty and trust, curiosity, collaboration, accountability, excellence—as fuel to propel their ideal. With newfound clarity, Jerry and his colleagues now saw LPK's ideal as *bestowing the creativity, vision, and courage that brands need to be extraordinary.* And on that basis, they challenged themselves to achieve a bold vision. They have vowed that, within the next decade, LPK will become globally renowned as a creative authority people turn to when they want to make a powerful and positive difference with their brands. It is an ideal centered in the overlap of two of the five fields of fundamental human values: inspiring exploration and impacting society.

To stop there would only have been to sketch a pretty picture that soon faded. To make its ideal a reality, LPK has set to work reengineering its creativity (the methods its teams use, their organizational culture, and even their physical surroundings), its vision on behalf of itself and clients (how it senses and analyzes developing trends), and its courage to be passionately honest with itself and clients (its ability to provide perspective, deliver sound strategy, and, by increasing its power of persuasion, reveal the reward in the risks that growth requires).

Whether your business is in the Fortune 500 or a new venture, whether you are in senior management or beginning your career, getting started on an inspiring ideal is the foundation for changing the narrative of business. That narrative centers on growth and profit, to be sure, but as we've seen in this book, the real path to sustained growth and profit lies in improving the quality of people's lives.

The reasons why the narrative of business must change are right in front of us every day. Frenetic business cycles and a winner-take-all mentality have turned "value" into no more than a ticker symbol that must be chased quarterly and that can virtually disappear overnight. We are also living in an increasingly transparent world where elaborate shell games of boosting image cannot obscure or cancel out bad behavior. Most telling of all for any business serious about its future, we have a generation of young people who are three times more likely to work for a company that does something they care about.

A movement is building, a profound shift to shared growth and prosperity based on ideals of improving people's lives. The

Stengel 50 show the extraordinary achievements in growth and profit of this nascent movement. But the best is yet to come.

LPK has joined this movement. It has planted its own Ideal Tree and begun growing it throughout the organization and its interactions with clients.

Will you be part of the movement? Will you plant your own Ideal Tree in your business and career?

Go to www.facebook.com/jimstengelideals and give me your pledge. What is your ideal and how are you going to bring it to life?

I'll be reporting via social media on the Ideal Projects, as I'm calling them, at LPK, the Stengel 50, and elsewhere, including those you share with me. These Ideal Projects can give our world a new kind of intellectual property on which to build a better future for business.

Together, we can change the narrative of business.

Start big or start small, but start now.

It's time.

APPENDIX

The Stengel 50

The Stengel 50 and Their Brand Ideals

Brand	Ideals Statement*
Accenture	Accenture exists to help people accelerate ideas to achieve their dreams.
Airtel	Airtel exists to enable people in India and southern Asia to enjoy and benefit from local, regional, national, and global conversations.
Amazon.com	Amazon.com exists to enable freedom of choice, exploration, and discovery.
Apple	Apple exists to empower creative exploration and self-expression.
Aquarel	Aquarel exists to provide healthy hydration to people and their communities.
BlackBerry	BlackBerry exists to connect people with one another and the content that is most important in their lives, anywhere, anytime.
Calvin Klein	Calvin Klein exists to define modern luxury.
Chipotle	Chipotle exists to empower people to positively impact food culture.
Coca-Cola	Coca-Cola exists to inspire moments of happiness.
Diesel	Diesel exists to inspire imagination and endless possibilities in style.

*These ideals statements are from my and my team's research and judgment. While we evaluated individual company information, these statements were not generated by the companies themselves.

APPENDIX

Brand	Ideals Statement
Discovery Communications	Discovery Communications exists to satisfy people's curiosity about their world and the universe.
Dove	Dove exists to celebrate every woman's unique beauty.
Emirates	Emirates exists to connect people with the world through a new lens of perception.
FedEx	FedEx exists to deliver peace of mind to everyday interactions.
Google	Google exists to immediately satisfy every curiosity.
Heineken	Heineken exists to help men be worldly—resourceful, confident, open-minded, cosmopolitan.
Hennessy	Hennessy exists to savor satisfaction in life's accomplishments.
Hermès	Hermès exists to celebrate timeless luxury craftsmanship.
HP	HP exists to foster the human capacity to innovate, progress.
Hugo Boss	Hugo Boss exists to evoke confidence through European sensibility.
IBM	IBM exists to help build a smarter planet.
Innocent	Innocent exists to make it easy for people to do themselves good.
Jack Daniel's	Jack Daniel's exists to celebrate and evoke pride in personal authenticity, independence, and integrity.
Johnnie Walker	Johnnie Walker exists to celebrate journeys of progress and success.
Lindt	Lindt exists to provide joy through small luxuries.

L'Occitane	L'Occitane exists to share natural and cultural traditions.
Louis Vuitton	Louis Vuitton exists to luxuriously accentuate the journey of life.
MasterCard	MasterCard exists to make the world of commerce simpler and more flexible.
Mercedes-Benz	Mercedes-Benz exists to epitomize a life of achievement.
Method	Method exists to be a catalyst in a happy, healthy home revolution.
Moët & Chandon	Moët & Chandon exists to transform occasions into celebrations.
Natura	Natura exists to promote well-being and strengthen relationships.
Pampers	Pampers exists to help mothers care for their babies' and toddlers' healthy, happy development.
Petrobras	Petrobras exists to support the sustainable development of Brazil and every country it operates in.
Rakuten Ichiba	Rakuten Ichiba exists to help the business-consumer partnership flourish.
Red Bull	Red Bull exists to energize the world.
Royal Canin	Royal Canin exists to support people's lifelong, loving relationships with their pets.
Samsung	Samsung exists to inspire imagination and enrich lives in a world of limitless possibilities.
Sedmoy Kontinent	Sedmoy Kontinent exists to improve Russian society by elevating the retail experience beyond what was thought possible.
Sensodyne	Sensodyne exists to nourish life's happiest asset, a bright smile.

Brand	Ideals Statement
Seventh Generation	Seventh Generation exists to help human needs and the needs of the planet be one and the same.
Snow Beer	Snow Beer exists to celebrate everyday moments of success.
Starbucks	Starbucks exists to create connections for self-discovery and inspiration.
Stonyfield Farm	Stonyfield Farm exists to inspire all of us to enhance the health of people and the planet through organically produced food.
Tsingtao	Tsingtao exists to infuse the joy of life with the passion of Chinese brewing.
Vente-Privee.com	Vente-Privee.com exists to celebrate exhilarating shopping experiences.
Visa	Visa exists to provide the freedom to people to follow their passions by providing better money for better living.
Wegmans	Wegmans exists to transform and heighten people's interactions with food and drink.
Zappos	Zappos exists to deliver happiness through "wow" service.
Zara	Zara exists to democratize fashion trends.

A Note on Sources

Nearly all of this book is based on primary research for the Stengel Study of Business Growth or on my own business experiences.

For more information on Millward Brown's BrandZ and Link databases, discussed at length in chapter 2, see www.millwardbrown.com.

The *Advertising Age* story "Does P&G Still Matter?," mentioned on page 22, was written by Jack Neff and published September 25, 2000.

For an account of how consumers turned away from some companies' "green" cleaning products but not others, as discussed on page 46, see "As Consumers Cut Spending, 'Green' Products Lose Allure," by Stephanie Clifford and Andrew Martin, *New York Times,* April 21, 2011.

For a representative account of BP's reputation problems after a series of environmental and safety crises, as mentioned on pages 49 and 202, see "BP: 'An Accident Waiting to Happen,' " by Peter Elkind and David Whitford with Doris Burke, *Fortune,* January 24, 2011.

For Apple design chief Jonathan Ive's views on form and function, mentioned on page 82, see "Design According to Ive," by Leander Kahney, *Wired,* June 25, 2003.

For the new attention being paid to communications briefs, mentioned on pages 224–28, see "Marketers, Quit Blaming Your Agency—It's Your Brief at Fault," by Rupal Parekh, *Advertising Age,* May 23, 2011.

For Time Warner CEO Jeffrey Bewkes's comments on, and competitive response to, Netflix, discussed on pages 234–38, see

A Note on Sources

"Time Warner Views Netflix as a Fading Star," by Tim Arango, *New York Times,* December 12, 2010; for the ensuing moves of both Starz and Netflix, see "Starz to End Streaming Deal with Netflix," by Brian Stelter, *New York Times,* September 1, 2011; "Latest Move Gets Netflix More Wrath," by Jenna Wortham and Brian Stelter, *New York Times,* September 19, 2011; and "Netflix Secures Streaming Deal with DreamWorks," by Brooks Barnes and Brian Stelter, *New York Times,* September 25, 2011.

ACKNOWLEDGMENTS

This book has been the largest collaboration of my life. I wanted the process of this book to be a "movement," to provide a forum and catalyst for people who want to improve business, both the results and the way to achieve results.

It has indeed been a movement, or journey, with thousands involved. Here are some of my inspirations, my collaborators, and the people who have had a profound effect on my life, thereby influencing the ideas in this book.

My wife, Kathleen, whose advice on matters of business and life is always uncannily perceptive and wise, and who has had an impact on me and the ideas in this book more than she will ever realize. I treasure her love, compassion, intelligence, honesty, and humor every day.

Our children, Claire and Trevor, who have cheerfully moved around the world during my peripatetic P&G career, and who have been a source of joy and pride for more than two decades. They have also been participants in this journey, from Claire joining me for the Cannes Lions Festival of Creativity to spot trends and ideas to Trevor helping in the initial stages of research for this book.

My mom and dad, who were married for fifty-five years (my dad passed away in 2006), who provided a home full of love, support, encouragement, and trust for me and my five brothers and sisters, and who simply always loved me and believed in me.

My brothers, Larry, Bob (more about Bob later), and John, my sisters, Mary Beth and Kathy, and the cohort of boys I grew up with from preschool through high school—Mark Diehl, Chuck Erisman, Roche Fitzgerald, Tom Geiger, Steve

303

Hinnenkamp, Tom Simpson—who all remain dear to me and whose shared experiences helped shape who I am and what I value.

My mentors in business and leadership over the last thirty years: Barb Bridendolph, a classmate from Penn State's Smeal College of Business and an executive coach who helped launch my current venture in consulting, teaching, and writing, who taught me to follow my passions and the rest will follow; Beth Kaplan, who was my general manager on two pivotal early assignments at P&G, Crisco and Noxell, and who taught me how to ask the right questions; Mark Ketchum, who was the president of baby care at P&G and my boss during the Pampers years, the most significant brand assignment of my career, who taught me to be courageous when you know you are right; A. G. Lafley, the chairman and CEO of P&G while I was the global marketing officer, who taught me the power of simplicity, high standards, and focus; Maurice Lévy, chairman and CEO of Publicis Groupe, who always had thoughtful, meaningful counsel on any issue, and who taught me to always take the high ground; Roger Martin, dean of the Rotman School of Management at the University of Toronto, who taught me about strategy throughout my career, and who encouraged me to begin this "second" career of consulting, teaching, and writing; Bob McDonald, current chairman and CEO of P&G, who was an early believer in elevating the purpose, or higher ideals, behind brands, and who taught me the power of purpose across a business model; John Pepper, former chairman and CEO, P&G, and current nonexecutive chairman of the Walt Disney Company, who taught me the impact of genuinely caring about people, and the power of inspiration in its most pure form; Agnès Sangan, a marketing director for P&G, who taught me the boundless possibilities when we truly understand people and their unarticulated needs, wants, dreams, and desires; Stuart Scheingarten, a leadership consultant for P&G who passed away in 2005, who taught me about the positive energy unleashed when you get the people part of business really clicking; Herbert Schmitz, my boss in my first P&G general manager role in Prague, who taught me that the first—and always urgent—priority is growing shipments faster than competition, and the way to do that is always treating your people with honesty, high expectations, and compassion; John Smale, the chairman and CEO of P&G when I joined the company, who taught me that winning in business is always about delighting the consumer and that takes constant, meaningful innovation; Sir Martin Sorrell, the CEO of WPP, who taught me that great client/agency relationships start with defining and then solving the biggest challenges on a business; Roy Spence, co-founder of GSD&M, who taught me that business success always begins and ends with inspiring people around purpose and ideals; Bob Wehling, my predecessor as P&G's global marketing officer, who taught me the power of showing confidence in someone, as he did with me in actively supporting me as his successor; Dan Wieden, co-founder of Wieden and Kennedy, who taught me the difference creativity can make in a business and culture; and John Wren, president and CEO of Omnicom Group Inc., who taught me that finding and developing talent is always the most important priority for a leader.

The teams at Millward Brown (Eileen Campbell, Mackenzie Murphy, Gordon Pincott, and Heather Stern), Millward Brown Neuroscience Practice (Barbara O'Connell, Graham Page, and Sarah Walker), and Millward Brown Optimor (Chelsea Brown, Karen Dwek, Benoit Garbe, Grace Gu, Anastasia Kourovskaia, Dan Lewen, Thalia Madrazo, Christiana Pearson, Mario Simon, Eric Tsytsylin, and Oscar Yuan) that I partnered with on the research for this book. My relationship with them goes back to my time at P&G, and this book simply would not be possible without them. They have been 24/7 colleagues for the past three years, helping not only in designing the right research for the questions I was asking but also in collaborating in the framework and the deep-dive cases that are at the heart of this book. They believe deeply in the ideas in this book, and have put them to work in their own business.

Beyond the teams at Millward Brown, there were a number of people who were simply indispensable in this book's journey. Without them, this book would not have evolved to what it is today. They all believe in the ideas and want to see them flourish. I thank Chris Allen of the University of Cincinnati, who debated this book's ideas with me and provided invaluable counsel on the manuscript; Matt Carcieri, who was a source of inspiration for many of these ideas while we worked together at P&G; Laurie Coots, of TBWA\Worldwide, who gave me the encouragement to start this and then helped enormously in every step of the way, from the initial concept to the final manuscript; Nick Corser, a student at Vanderbilt University, and Alyssa Dunn, a student at Bucknell University, who helped with refining and substantiating the data in this book; Leah Frank-Finney and Grey Hall of LPK, who helped in the visualization of the Ideal Tree that is the framework of this book; Betty Gabbard, my talented and committed business manager, who ran the complex book project with insight, care, discipline, and charm; James Haskett, a consultant and former P&G brand franchise leader, who provided insightful input on the manuscript; Hilary Hinzmann, my writer/collaborator, who put his heart and soul into this because he believes in the potential impact of these ideas; Cassie Hughes and Danny Kraus of Grow Marketing, who jumped in early to help with the development, marketing, and publicity of the book; Greg Icenhower and Ed Rider of P&G, who provided insightful input on the manuscript; Peter Kaufman, who strengthened the ideas in the book; John Mahaney, my editor at Crown Business, who always had time for me, a first-time book author, and who always asked the right questions, always put the reader first, and simply brought thoughtful insights to the structure and language of the book; Tina Constable, Tara Gilbride, and Meredith McGinnis of Crown, who provided great commercial advice and support, and collaborated so well with my team to bring *Grow* to market; Richard Pine, my agent at Inkwell Management, who took my meeting, got this all started, and provided counsel on the content every step of the way; Leonora Polonsky, a brand strategy consultant and former colleague at P&G, whose thinking helped shape the Ideal Tree framework in *Grow*; Sue Whitehouse, my executive assistant, who somehow helped manage my time and schedule to devote time and energy to the book; and Jane Wildman, a former Pampers brand franchise leader, who collaborated with me on the Pampers story in chapter 7.

The Stengel 50 businesses provided the stories, the inspiration, and the validation of this book's central hypothesis—that brands driven by a higher ideal grow faster and longer than their competition. I want to thank all of these businesses, some of which I visited (more below on that), and some of which I studied and admired through interviews and secondary research. The inspired businesses in the Stengel Study of Business Growth are Accenture, Airtel, Amazon.com, Apple, Aquarel, BlackBerry, Calvin Klein, Chipotle, Coca-Cola, Diesel, Discovery Communications, Dove, Emirates, FedEx, Google, Heineken, Hennessy, Hermès, HP, Hugo Boss, IBM, Innocent, Jack Daniel's, Johnnie Walker, Lindt, L'Occitane, Louis Vuitton, MasterCard, Mercedes-Benz, Method, Moët & Chandon, Natura, Pampers, Petrobras, Rakuten Ichiba, Red

Bull, Royal Canin, Samsung, Sedmoy Kontinent, Sensodyne, Seventh Generation, Snow Beer, Starbucks, Stonyfield Farm, Tsingtao, Vente-Privee, Visa, Wegmans, Zappos, and Zara.

Several of the Stengel 50 opened their doors to me and my team. Some businesses not in the Stengel 50 also opened their doors to us, as I felt they were other businesses that were great examples of brands and people on their journey to be a high-growth, ideal-inspired business. Without exception, these businesses and people were generous in their openness, candor, insights, and time. They were also great fun to visit! So I wish to give a very special thanks to these companies and people: Discovery Communications (Joe Abruzzese, Clark Bunting, Jocelyn Egan, John Hendricks, Peter Liguori, Ian Parmitter, Adria Alpert Romm, and David Zaslav); HP (Caroline Barlerin, Kelly Hampton, Engelina Jaspers, Greg Johnson, Anna Mancini, Glenna Patton, and Deepak Sainanee); IBM (John Kennedy); Innocent (Dan Germain); Brown-Forman/Jack Daniel's (Nelson Eddy and Kris Sirchio); Lindt (Ernst Tanner); Method (Drew Fraser, Andrea Freedman, Michele Hall, Josh Handy, Matthew Loyd, Eric Ryan, and George Shumny); Motorola Solutions (Greg Brown, Shelly Carlin, and Eduardo Conrado); Toyota (Luiz Carlos Andrade Jr., David Buttner, William Fay, Guillaume Gerondeau, Hiroshi Kono, Nihar Patel, and Vince Socco); Visa (Elizabeth Buse, Albert Coscia, Antonio Lucio, Jim McCarthy, Doug Michelman, Ellen Richey, and Bill Sheedy); Yum! Brands/Pizza Hut (Chris Fuller and Brian Niccol); and Zappos (Brent Cromley, Drew Kovacs, Aaron Magness, Arun Rajan, Donavon Roberson, Rob Siefker, and Maura Sullivan).

I began teaching as an adjunct professor at the UCLA Anderson School of Management in January 2010, when the ideas in this book were just beginning to gel. I want to thank the students in the classes I taught with Professor Sanjay Sood; these bright students have researched and tested these ideas for validity, and their discussions in class have made this book stronger.

I want to give special thanks to Dean Judy Olian and Professor Sanjay Sood at the UCLA Anderson School of Management for their support and advice, and to the UCLA Anderson MBA student team—Jessica Kellett (who was also a summer intern for me), Juan Pablo Villegas-Karpf, Eliot Wadsworth, and Michal Zeituni—who completed a major applied management research project on the top 50 businesses in the Stengel Study. The student team helped give birth to the five fields of fundamental human values, one of the central findings of the Stengel Study. I also want to thank Kevin Raymond, a UCLA Anderson recent graduate, who built on the work of this team to pursue deeper research on many Stengel 50 businesses, and who helped refine the brand ideal statements of each of the Stengel 50.

If it is not already obvious, I love involving students in my consulting and major projects like this book. It is a win/win. I try to do it as much as I can. With the help of Professor Chris Allen at the University of Cincinnati, I involved five University of Cincinnati MBA students—Chris Banner, Mick Hondlik, Mike Neugent, Jessica Shankland, and Jim Wolff—early in my journey of this book hypothesis. I thank them for their enthusiasm, their clarity of recommendations (many which I followed), and their continued interest in the ideas within *Grow*.

In early 2009, when I began this project, I reached out to a variety of business thought leaders for their thoughts and feelings about brand ideals and the possibility of a new framework for business. They were kind enough to share their ideas, many of which germinated in different parts of this book. Many, many thanks to Scott Bedbury, founder of Brandstream and author of *A New Brand World*; Lee Clow, global director of Media Arts, TBWA\Worldwide; Laura Desmond of Starcom MediaVest

Group; Liz Dolan of Fox International Channels; Susan Fournier of Boston University; Susan Gianinno of Publicis Worldwide; Seth Godin, bestselling author; Steve Goldbach of Monitor; Robert Greenberg of R/GA; Tamara Ingram of Grey Group; Jerry Kathman of LPK; Kevin Keller of Dartmouth College; Tom Kelley of IDEO; Hamish McLennan, formerly at Y&R; Adam Morgan, founder of eatbigfish; Miles Nadal, founder of MDC Partners; Brian Perkins of Johnson & Johnson; Mark Pocharski of Monitor; Suzanne Powers of Crispin Porter + Bogusky; Stephen Quinn of Walmart; Mark Hans Richer of Harley-Davidson; and Marian Salzman of Euro RSCG Worldwide.

I had the tremendous good fortune of working for nearly three decades with some of the most remarkable and creative communication and design agencies in the world. Their potential to help businesses change the game in their industries is too often underestimated. I learned so much from them throughout my career, and I want to express my gratitude to my friends at the greatest brand-building agencies in the world, who believe in the ideas in this book: BBDO Worldwide, Beacon Communications, Burrell Communications, Carol H. Williams Advertising, Dentsu, DeVries Public Relations, Grey, Grow Marketing, GSD&M, IDEO, IMC2, Kaplan Thaler Group, Leo Burnett Worldwide, LPK, Marina Maher Communications, Possible Worldwide, Publicis Worldwide, R/GA, Saatchi & Saatchi, Starcom MediaVest Group, TBWA\Worldwide, and Wieden+Kennedy.

I began these acknowledgments with thanking my family, beginning with my wife, Kathleen. I would like to close with acknowledging my younger brother Bob, who died at the age of fifty-one when I was nearing the end of this project. I dedicated the book to him, and I was able to tell him that before he died.

Bob was the most remarkable human being. His life was a model of love, kindness, caring for others, humor, achievement, and happiness. He was a family doctor for all the right reasons, and he never, ever lost sight of what was important in life and relationships. He was a loving husband, an inspirational father of three children, a devoted son, a brother who was also a unique friend. And he remained curious and involved throughout a long illness, learning new skills and expanding his interests.

Bob's life was certainly a model for me, and it seems to me to be a model for all of us in our daily work and lives.

When I was promoted to P&G's highest marketing job in August 2001, I was on top of the world. Two weeks later, my brother Bob called me to tell me he had leukemia. I committed myself at that time to approach that role, and to approach my life, with him in mind.

Bob's life was one of higher ideals, higher standards, without ever expecting anything in return. He was 100 percent committed to his patients, friends, and his family, simply because it was how he approached life. These were his values and beliefs.

Bob left this world prematurely, but he left it a far better place. I don't think it is too far a stretch to end the acknowledgments to this book with a challenge for all of us in business, inspired by the life my brother led. Let's embrace the principles in this book and make the world a better place through what we do every day. Because it is the right thing to do. Because you will be happier. Because you will be more successful. Because the people you serve will appreciate it and reward you.

My thanks to my brother Bob for helping me see this so clearly.

INDEX

INDEX

Index

INDEX